Framing the Victim

SOCIAL PROBLEMS AND SOCIAL ISSUES

An Aldine de Gruyter Series of Texts and Monographs

SERIES EDITOR

Joel Best, *University of Delaware*

Framing the Victim

Domestic Violence, Media, and Social Problems

NANCY BERNS

Aldine de Gruyter
New York

About the Author

Nancy Berns
Assistant professor of sociology, Drake University, Des Moines, Iowa.

ALDINE DE GRUYTER
A division of Walter de Gruyter, Inc.
200 Saw Mill River Road
Hawthorne, New York 10532

This publication is printed on acid free paper ∞

Library of Congress Cataloging-in-Publication Data
Berns, Nancy.
 Framing the victim : domestic violence, media, and social problems / Nancy Berns.— 1st ed.
  p. cm. — (Social problems and social issues)
 Includes bibliographical references.
 ISBN 0-202-30740-9 (cloth : alk. paper) — ISBN 0-202-30741-7 (pbk. : alk. paper)
1. Social problems—United States. 2. Social problems in mass media—United States. 3. Family violence—United States. I. Title. II. Series.
 HN59.2.B468 2004
 361.1′0973—dc22

2004001465

Manufactured in the United States of America

10 9 8 7 6 5 4 3 2 1

To my husband, David, our daughter, Lydia Grace,
and in memory of our son, Zachariah

Contents

Preface

Whether you are drawn to this book because of an interest in media, social problems, or domestic violence, I hope reading it will help you better understand the impact media stories have on our perceptions of social problems. Readers should find this book useful for understanding not only domestic violence but also the larger picture of how politics and processes shape how we understand and respond to social problems. This book critiques the stories that emerge when social problems are shaped by media guidelines that promote entertainment, empowerment, drama, inspiration, and politics. I investigate this process through an in-depth look at domestic violence.

The importance of this process of shaping and understanding social problems is vividly apparent each time I sit down with abuse victims. I have spent many hours listening to stories of abuse, intimidation, assault, humiliation, rape, and other tragic experiences. The pain I have felt for the people who have shared their stories with me is merely a glimpse of the pain that they themselves have endured. As I talk with people who are in abusive relationships or listen to the parents of sons and daughters who are being abused, I do what I can to offer them help, comfort, and guidance. However, on another level, I want to help victims by exploring the problems that occur when we describe domestic violence as a *victim's problem*. In writing this book, I aspire not only to expose the problems with how we talk about domestic violence, but also to offer hope for change.

It was only with the support and encouragement of many people that I was able to write this book. I want especially to thank the following individuals for helping me along the way.

I thank the women I encountered at battered women shelters, as well as the students, friends, and acquaintances who have all shared their stories of abuse. Your courage and your pain continue to fuel my passion for studying domestic violence and teaching others about the violence that too many people face every day. I thank those individuals who gave their time and shared their personal lives during the interviews for this research. Also, I thank my students, who have heard many of the ideas in this book, have asked important questions, and have provided inspiration for me to continue teaching about how we understand social problems.

I am grateful to my parents, David and Sharon Berns, who have been active supporters of my career and family. I appreciate the love of my sister, Kathy Conway, and my brothers, Brian and Keith Berns, and their families. I am also thankful for my parents-in-law, Don and Nancy Schweingruber, for their encouragement and interest in my research and life. I am indebted to Tom and Deb Niehof and our friends at Trinity Christian Reformed Church for their sustained care, encouragement, and prayers that upheld my family through some difficult times during the years that spanned the research and writing of this book.

Many people helped me craft this book. I thank each of them for the time and interest they devoted to this research. I am especially grateful to Phyllis Baker, Joel Best, Kathe Lowney, Deb Niehof, David Schweingruber, and Frank Schweingruber, who each read an entire draft of this book and provided great ideas for revisions as well as doses of encouragement to keep me going. I also thank those who helped me by reading drafts of chapters, giving critical feedback, and assisting in other ways. They include Norm Denzin, Ann Herda-Rapp, Dave Hopping, Emily Ignacio, Elizabeth Jenner, Kirk Johnson, Leslie King, Cheris Kramarae, John Lie, Jackie Litt, Donileen Loseke, Bill Martin, Clark McPhail, Madonna Harrington Meyer, Anastasia Niehof, Kristin Niehof, Hal Pepinsky, Judith Pintar, Laurie Scheuble, Joseph Schneider, and Stefan Timmermans.

I also appreciate the many people who shared their questions and comments about this work during presentations at Drake University and meetings of the Midwest Sociological Society, the Society for the Study of Social Problems, and the American Sociological Association.

Parts of Chapter 4 appeared in "'My Problem and How I Solved It': Domestic Violence in Women's Magazines," *Sociological Quarterly* (1999) 40:85–108. A different version of Chapter 6 was published as "Degendering the Problem and Gendering the Blame: Political Discourse on Women's Violence," *Gender & Society* (2001) 15:262–81.

The editor of this series, Joel Best, has been a wonderful source of inspiration and guidance. I appreciate Joel for encouraging me to write this book and for advancing our knowledge about social problems through his own research.

Finally, I am forever indebted to my husband, David, for his unconditional love and support. Thank you for spending countless hours discussing my research, reading numerous drafts, lovingly poring over every page, and sharing my struggles. Your unwavering encouragement eased a difficult journey. I dedicate this book to you, our daughter, Lydia, and in memory of our son, Zachariah.

1

Zooming In (and Out) on Social Problems

A recent *Oprah* episode titled "What Should We Do When Families Turn Violent?" focused on the role victims have in abusive relationships. In the introduction to the show, the host, Oprah Winfrey, explained:

> For years, I have done shows on battered women and domestic violence, and for decades, it has been believed that family violence was a social problem with one solution: Men who are violent should be punished, and the women they hurt are victims and helpless and should leave. But now there are new voices that are challenging how we look at and how we treat violence in the family. It is not as simple as we had thought. They say the truth is that most battered women choose and even want to stay with their abusers. And these women don't want their abusers to go to trial, and most of all, they want to keep their families together. Some experts also say—and this is very controversial—that we are underestimating the role that women play in an abusive relationship. (*Oprah Winfrey Show* 2003)

Oprah asked unidentified victims of abuse how they contributed to the abuse:

> Oprah: But this is a question I'm really trying to get to, and be as honest as you can about it and not worry about what the rest of the world is going to think, 'cause this is the core of the question: What have I done to contribute to this situation? Do you feel that you were a part of the sick dance?
>
> Unidentified Woman 8: Oh, yeah. You know, you allow them to do things just one more time. I'm sure just being there, I guess you have to be.
>
> Unidentified Woman 9: I was the choreographer half the time. (ibid.)

As I listened to Oprah say "We've only played the women as victims and never asked them to ask themselves: What is your role in this?" I

1

wondered how many thousands of viewers she was instigating to ask this same question. How many people will now turn to victims and say, "What are you doing to cause this problem?" And why do we not have shows that suggest that people ask what role abusers have in family violence?

* * *

One Sunday I heard a pastor give a sermon that included the following story.

> A mother of four children met a man through the internet. They had been living together over a month when the mother's boyfriend beat to death her 4-year-old boy, David. The boyfriend beat David with a homemade paddle after the child wet his pants. The boy was beaten so severely that a CAT scan could not identify his swollen brain. According to the local paper, even the police spokesman said that he would not comment more on the case because he could no longer be impartial after viewing the hospital photos of the boy. He said, "My capability to be objective was destroyed the moment I saw the hospital photos of this child's injuries. All any of us can do now is offer our most earnest prayers for the jurors who will have to listen to the details of how little David died."[1]

After describing the horrific details of the story, the pastor said that one question came to mind for him. I waited, thinking it would be something about how violent our society has become. Instead he asked, "What was that mother thinking having that man around her children?

* * *

"Underhand is the way to throw a skillet, experts say"(Melendez 2003). Thus began a newspaper article that celebrated a small town's skillet-throwing contest. Teams compete to score the most points by knocking a "basketball head" off the stuffed dummies that stand several yards away. Replete with humor and celebration, the article makes no mention that "brandishing an iron skillet" is a reference to domestic violence. I wonder if abuse victims who have been the target of skillets would find this contest amusing. Why do we not read articles about the cultural jokes, attitudes, and rituals that foster domestic violence?

* * *

These stories are examples of how we talk about domestic violence and how we do *not* talk about it. Domestic violence has become a social problem *about the victims*. Most media stories focus on the victim. The victim is celebrated for having the courage to leave the abusive relationship or, conversely, blamed for staying and letting the abuse continue. He or she is accused of provoking the abuse and held responsible for ending the abuse. The victim is told to take back his or her power and refuse to tolerate the abuse anymore. Though not every story covers all these themes, together they represent the dominant portrayal of domestic violence in popular media. This focus may help build support for programs that help victims of domestic violence. However, it does little to develop public understanding of the social context of violence and may impede social change that could prevent violence.

Along the way, the violence and the abusers have gotten lost. Domestic violence is not depicted as a social problem about the abusers. So we do not talk much about the abusers. And domestic violence has not emerged as a problem about the social and cultural context that tolerates and fosters this violence, so we do not talk about those issues either. Of course there are activists, advocates, professionals, and other individuals who focus on the abusers and on the social context of violence. However, the information these people can provide us has not seriously influenced the general public's understanding of domestic violence and our society's typical public policy response to the problem.

This book examines how social problems are used in the media and understood by the public. I analyze how the media transform social problems and shape them into stories that will best sell magazines, newspapers, television shows, and movies. These stories then play an important role in how the public understands social problems, which in turn influences public policy. I analyze this process in-depth by closely investigating one issue, domestic violence. I have chosen this problem for several reasons. First, it is a relatively "new" social problem. This may be surprising to hear since people in families have been violent toward one another as long as there have been families (remember Cain and Abel?). However, this has not always been considered a social problem. In many times and places it was expected that some people in families were allowed to use violence on other people. The public "discovery" of domestic violence did not really happen until the 1970s. This late public discovery has allowed me to examine a large proportion of the media representations of this problem. Second, domestic violence is a good example of how a social problem may have more than one possible perspective or *frame*. All of the issues, information, and situations related to domestic violence, or any other social problem, constitute a vast landscape. However, often one or more frames are dominant in the media while others are ignored. This is crucial, since most people use the media to help them understand social problems. And finally, I have spent many years on my own journey of trying to understand domestic violence and trying to teach others that it is much more complicated than our focus on the victim would suggest.

MY JOURNEY

In 1990, as a sophomore in college, I took a class called Deviance. For one of the assignments, I had to write a report on some type of deviant behavior. I chose the topic of battered women. Earlier I had found a book called *Terrifying Love*, which was about battered women who kill their batterers (Walker 1989). I was fascinated by this topic and thought that it fit the description of deviant behavior. After all, why would anyone stay in an abusive situation? Fortunately, I had never been in an abusive relationship, nor was I aware of anyone else who was a victim of abuse. I had seen movies about battered women and read stories about them, but I did not know anyone involved. I could not imagine why the victims would stay for so long that they would end up killing their partners. I had long been interested in criminal behavior, but I was particularly fascinated by this idea of "terrifying love." By reading the book I learned more about why women stay in abusive relationships. However, I still could not understand why women would remain in those relationships, and so I proceeded to write about battered women for my Deviance paper.

Even after the class was over, I continued to wonder about these victims of domestic violence. Two years after reading *Terrifying Love* I did an internship at a nearby battered women's shelter. During my time there I went through a training and orientation program where I learned more about what victims go through, what services are available for them, and why it is so difficult to leave an abusive situation. One of my main responsibilities was handling incoming calls on the crisis line.

One of the calls I received haunts me to this day. The phone rang and when I answered it, a woman's shaky voice was on the other end. She said her husband had been beating her and that she was trying to get help. She told me that if she quickly hung up the phone it would be because he came into the room. Not long after that, the phone went dead. I was not able to find out who she was, where she was calling from, or what happened to her. I still wonder what happened. Did she ever get help? Did the abuse ever stop?

Another night the phone rang and I found myself talking to a mother whose daughter was in an abusive relationship. I had been told during training that until the victim is ready to get some help, there is little if anything the family can do to help. The victim has to decide to leave. I did not know what to tell this mother. I did not have any advice for her. What could she do? It seemed that we all had to wait for the victim to realize that she needed help.

I entered a graduate studies program in sociology about a year after these phone calls and many others like them. I continued to be intrigued by battered women and decided to pursue that topic in my studies. For the next several years, I volunteered in another domestic violence shelter and also immersed myself in the vast amount of research that had been collected on the topic. Through my study I learned how individual behavior, including abuse, is influenced by and situated within our larger social structure and culture. For example, I began to see how strict ideas about what it meant to be a man or a woman might affect how people see their roles in a relationship. I read about theories that connected violence in the family to our violent culture. I learned to see beyond the victim and started to recognize the effects of social factors, such as public attitudes that tolerate violence in the family, media images that glorify violence against women, and a criminal justice system that treats domestic violence as a private matter. I started examining how domestic violence is connected to factors such as the economic system, gender discrimination in the workforce, inadequate childcare, and low-income housing.

Several years after I first wrote about battered women for my college Deviance class, I read Donileen Loseke and Spencer Cahill's article, "The Social Construction of Deviance: Experts on Battered Women" (1984). In their article, Loseke and Cahill argue that not only is it misleading to say that women are deviant for staying in abusive relationships, but also that focusing on battered women places the blame and responsibility on the victims and not on the abusers. I was beginning to see how limited my own picture of domestic violence had been. I was using a telescopic lens for viewing domestic violence and I had zoomed in on the victims. What I needed, and was gradually gaining, was a wide-angle lens that allowed me to not just zoom in on the victim, but also to zoom out and see more of the problem. I was excited about the knowledge I was gaining about domestic violence and I no longer saw it as an issue just about "battered women." Sure, they were still an important part of the problem, but I was able to see so much more of this issue.

Today, instead of focusing on why victims stay, I can also ask: Why do people use violence in relationships? Why do we so often accept violence as a normal part of relationships? Is domestic violence influenced by our larger culture of violence? Why is it so hard for us to believe that the charming, respectable person we know in public may be abusing his or her family in private? How and why does our culture teach men that dominance, aggression, control, power, and showing no emotion but anger are positive things? And how might this picture of masculinity be connected to violence in the home? How is women's violence different from men's violence? Are we teaching our children nonviolent conflict resolution strategies?

It is not that I have forgotten about victims. Not only do I still think about those phone calls from years ago, but I continue to sit with victims and listen to their stories. Every semester I have students share with me stories of their own experiences with rape or abuse, and occasionally a student will tell me that she is currently in an abusive relationship. And, unfortunately, I still talk to parents who are hurting because their son or daughter is in an abusive relationship. I do not sit down with these individuals and say "You know, we talk about victims too much in this culture, so let's spend time discussing how the culture or structure is helping to foster your abuse." I recognize that this is a time when victims and their families need to hear information on what they can do about their situation. They need to know what resources are available to them and how they can protect themselves, how they can get the legal system involved if they want to, or how they can leave the abusive relationship. This is very much an important part of focusing on the victims, and I am very thankful there are shelters and other services available for victims. Many people have been helped because our society started talking about victims of domestic violence. The problem lies not in the existence of this perspective, but in the dominance of the victim-focus as the overarching way of understanding domestic violence as a social problem.

This book results from trying to understand not only why I focused on victims for so long, but also why the general public, still today, continues to highlight victims as the main characters in its understanding of domestic violence. It attempts to answer questions that arose during my own journey: Why are people not asking about why individuals abuse others? Why do they not ask how abusers continue to get away with their behavior? Why are so few people talking about violence itself or social and cultural factors that foster it? Why are most media stories about victims? Why are we framing the victim for this problem?

SOCIAL PROBLEMS RESEARCH

In this book I argue that we hold victims responsible for the problem of domestic violence, particularly female victims. The title of this book, *Framing the Victim*, expresses this argument with two meanings of the word "frame." Victims are framed because dominant perspectives (or frames) focus on them. They are also framed because they are falsely blamed for a crime committed by someone else. I use the word "frame" to talk about how the public, media, activists, politicians, and anyone else portray social problems. The term "frame" has been adopted from Goffman (1974) by social problems researchers to describe how people identify, interpret, understand, and label their experiences. Frames provide a way for people to make sense of what they experience. Sociologists have used frame analysis techniques to identify the contesting interpretive frames found for issues like nuclear power, crime, fear, and child sexual abuse.[2]

We might think of this type of framing as similar to the framing a photographer does when deciding the composition of a shot. The photographer tells a particular story about a scenic landscape by focusing on, say, a single blooming flower. A lot of information will be left outside that frame. Another photographer (or the same one on another shot) may instead take pictures of a herd of deer, or a mountain range on the horizon, or the sky. Each composition involves making a decision to focus on some things while leaving other things out.

While a landscape may be very complicated, a social problem is even more complicated. We can use the example of juvenile delinquency to see this complexity. Social scientists, politicians, and other experts have suggested many causes of juvenile delinquency: parenting, neighborhoods, friends, genes, media, and so on. There have also been many suggested solutions, including harsh punishment, various types of counseling, social programs to alleviate poverty, and better schools. On top of this, millions of people have had some contact with the juvenile justice system, and millions more would have if they had been caught; each has a unique story. So there are literally millions of stories to tell. Any reporter, script writer, or television producer is going to have to frame his or her story, telling only a tiny part of the whole landscape of juvenile delinquency. They might, for instance, focus on "superpredators" who cannot be rehabilitated, or a new antigang program, or a particular type of crime, like school shootings.[3] Furthermore, each of these topics must be approached in a limited way, such as that schools are getting more dangerous or that the answer to youth crime is more involvement by the clergy. Each will have just a few examples of particular individuals to illustrate these stories.

Now, even though there may be many ways to explain juvenile delinquency or any other social problem, most people are usually only exposed to a small number of these frames. As I will discuss more in Chapter 3, most people use the media to learn about social problems. Significantly, research on media frames suggests that usually a small number of frames (or maybe just one) are dominant, while others are completely ignored. As I will explain in this book, media choose to frame social problems in ways that complement their own needs for seeking a large audience or for pleasing a particular niche market.

Media differ in their target audience, which influences how they frame stories. I illustrate these differences by examining stories in both mass entertainment media and the political media. Particularly in the mass media,

producers are more often in the business of using social problems to enter-
tain their viewers rather than to educate them. Political media frame social
problems to fit the political interests of their targeted audience. Whether the
focus is on entertainment or politics, social problems are shaped in ways
that will help sell the magazines, television shows, movies, or newspapers.

An example of narrow framing is illustrated by the research on media
portrayals of rape. Social science research indicates that most rapes are
"acquaintance rapes," where the victim knows the perpetrator. However,
most media stories about rape focus on the "stereotypical stranger rapes"
or "gang rapes."[4] Susan Caringella-MacDonald (1998) argues that coverage of acquaintance rape would require addressing male power and
everyday sexism. Instead, media focus on rapists who are "sick." Numerous other studies illustrate how media representations distort images of
social issues such as crime and violence.[5]

This leads to an important idea: How a problem is framed suggests a
solution to the problem. By identifying what the problem is about and
what its causes are, a frame at least implies, if not stated outright, what
should be done to solve it (Best 1995). For the example of rape, if the
underlying cause of rape is everyday sexism, then solutions will be quite
complicated since they would involve reevaluating how different institutions—schools, families, workplaces—operate. If the cause of rape is a few
"sick" men, than rape becomes a law enforcement and medical problem.
The solution is to identify and round up these deviant men. Unfortunately,
the framing of a social problem that becomes most popular is not necessarily the one that leads to the best solutions.

Social problems are characterized through this process of framing that
locates a cause and recommends a solution (ibid.). Each frame or perspective suggests factors that produce social problems and implies how we can
solve them. Although there are often competing perspectives on the same
problem, one particular perspective often gains dominance—thus silenc-
ing alternative perspectives (Foucault 1979). Several studies of the construction of social problems have demonstrated this claim. Foucault argues
that the way we talk about criminology creates a particular category of the
criminal and leads to a narrow view of judgment and punishment (ibid.).
Cicourel illustrates how the media and researchers framed children from
"broken homes" as more likely to be delinquent than children from two-
parent homes (Cicourel 1968). This dominant frame impacted the attitudes
and actions of police and probation officers in that they were quicker to
arrest children from broken homes. In her analysis Loseke demonstrates
that "wife abuse" and "battered women" are socially constructed categories that produce the need for a particular solution—the battered woman
shelter (Loseke 1992).

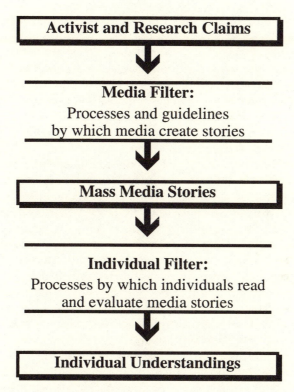

Figure 1. Tracing social problems frames.

So how do these frames take shape in the first place? Who is behind that camera that zooms in on the social problem landscape? There is a large body of research on how social problems are constructed; I have given a few examples already. Many of these researchers use the tools of a perspective called *social constructionism* to study how particular perspectives on social problems are created, how they are disseminated, and how they influence public debate, through the media and other methods. Social constructionism assumes that what people believe and think about social problems has been constructed through claims-making (Spector and Kitsuse 1987). Claims-making refers to the activities of individuals, groups, or organizations that attempt to persuade others that a certain condition should be viewed as a social problem.[6]

In Figure 1, I illustrate how social problems travel from the early frames of activists and researchers, through the media, and finally to the public.

The media and individuals have filter systems that transform the stories that originated with the activists. For the media, this filtering system includes mission statements, editorial guidelines, advertising concerns, audience expectations, and economic interests. These factors influence which stories about social problems are told and how they are shaped. The individual filter refers to the process people use to choose and evaluate media stories. For evaluating social problems, individuals filter stories through their own experiences, other sources of information, and general opinions about types of media.

Most social problems researchers begin their analysis with the primary activists who are influential in establishing early portrayals of a problem. Often these early activists are a part of a larger social movement—at least those activists who are very successful in getting their frames out through the mass media to the public. For domestic violence, as I will explain in Chapter 8, the most influential activists for shaping the problem were a part of the battered women movement. After analyzing the activists, researchers often explore how those activists' portrayals are disseminated through the media and to the public. Most research focuses on the work that the major claims-makers, including the activists and the media, have to do to persuade their audience (often the general public) to accept their particular frames of the social problems.

Rather than starting in this book with the activists, I begin with the public. It is true that the activists in the battered women movement jump-started the public discovery of domestic violence, but I am reversing the investigation of the claims-making process and following the trail backwards. Part of the reason I do this is because of my own journey in understanding domestic violence. The questions I have about how we understand social problems led me to start with the public rather than the activists.

Another important reason to start with the public is because the public understandings of a social problem influence decision-making at many levels. Lawyers, judges, police officers, clergy, friends and family of abusers and victims, legislators, journalists, doctors, nurses, teachers, voters, and jurors are a few of the people who help make decisions and influence action (or inaction). There may be a vast array of theories and perspectives on domestic violence in research and among activists. However, if those perspectives do not make it to the public, then they have little influence on how the public responds to the social problem. This is important. Investigating how we talk about social problems, or seeing what frames we use, is not simply an academic exercise. Examining how we talk about social problems is important because it influences what we do about those problems—and what we fail to do.

In Figure 2, I illustrate the pathway that this book uses to trace the social problem frames for domestic violence. What do individuals think about domestic violence? What sources do they use to understand social problems, and how do they evaluate those sources? Because a primary source is the media, and not activists, the investigative trail leads next to how the media frame the problem. How and why do media shape social problems? Those who produce media images and stories shape the stories to fit their own needs. They interpret and transform social problems in a way that helps to sell magazines or television shows. Or they frame issues to support particular missions and political orientations. The media also need a source for information, which is where the activists come in. Activists provide stories and information for the media.[7] What frames do activists use to describe the problem and how do these frames impact the media stories? At the end of this trail, I address the question of what implications this process has on how we respond to social problems. And finally, I suggest how we can reframe the way we think about social problems. Following is a chapter summary to further outline the questions investigated in this book.

INDIVIDUAL UNDERSTANDINGS AND FILTER

Chapters 2 and 3 explore the public understanding of domestic violence, the significant role the media play in shaping attitudes about social problems, and the filter system used to evaluate the media. In Chapter 2, I first paint a broad picture of the vast landscape of domestic violence. Then I explain that the public's view of this landscape is actually quite narrow. To illustrate how the public thinks about domestic violence, I draw from several data sources, including large national public opinion survey research and in-depth interviews with individuals. Even though most people say domestic violence is not right, there are still situations that people believe are "private" and there are some circumstances that people believe justify the abuse. Furthermore, they hold the victim personally responsible for solving the problem and, at times, for causing the abuse. People do not have as much to say about the abuser. When people do talk about the abuser, they focus primarily on alcohol use and childhood abuse, factors that do not hold the abuser personally responsible. The general public uses an individual and psychological frame for understanding the problem and does not expand this to include the structural and cultural context.

In Chapter 3, I illustrate how people use the media as a primary source for understanding domestic violence, how they evaluate the media, and how firsthand experience with abuse affects both the critique of the media

Chapter 2	What do individuals think about domestic violence?

Chapter 3	What sources do individuals use to understand social problems? How do they evaluate those sources?

Chapter 4	What frame do women's magazines use to portray domestic violence?

Chapter 5	How do editorial guidelines of mass media, such as women's magazines, shape their stories about social problems?

Chapter 6	What frame do men's magazines and conservative political magazines use to portray domestic violence? How do the politics and missions of these magazines shape their stories?

Chapter 7	What frame do liberal political magazines use to portray domestic violence? How do the politics and missions of these magazines shape their stories?

Chapter 8	How and why do activists frame domestic violence and how do these frames affect media stories? What implications do the frames of domestic violence have on societal responses and policy?

Chapter 9	How can we reframe the way we think about violence?

Figure 2.   Outline of questions investigated in this book.

and the understanding of the problem. People's experience with domestic violence affects their ability to critique media messages. Those who only have media-based experience lack the ability to critique the media messages or the content and instead evaluate the media based on media formats and hierarchies of credibility. However, even though people claim to use systems for evaluating sources of information, they continue to use information from forgotten sources. Often media-based experience from forgotten sources turns into "common knowledge." Without prior experiences with abuse other than media sources, individuals are more likely to accept and use common media explanations.

MASS MEDIA STORIES

Since most people use the media to understand social problems, it is important to analyze media stories. I analyze several different genres of magazines in order to describe the different frames used and also the accompanying missions and guidelines of the respective magazines that help shape those frames. Though I apply arguments to other media, I focus in depth on magazines to better illustrate the editorial process that shapes the articles and how this process differs across genres. Using magazines also helps to capture the changes in time. I analyze articles on domestic violence from 1970 to 2002. This time period covers the battered women movement and the "public discovery" of domestic violence in the 1970s.

Chapter 4 illustrates the *victim empowerment frame,* which is found in magazines, television talk shows, movies, and everyday conversations. I use women's magazines to illustrate the dominance of this perspective. The victim empowerment perspective tells the story of domestic violence as a private problem. And not only is it portrayed as a private problem, but most often it is the *victim's* problem—and she has the responsibility for solving it. It focuses on the victims' experiences while ignoring not only the role of the abuser but also that of society. The victims in these stories are treated sympathetically. "Experts" encourage women who are abused, telling them that the answers to their problems lie within them. They use slogans like "take control of your life," "refuse to be a victim," and "you have the power to end abuse." This frame is sympathetic and wants to empower the victims. However, the victim continues to be held responsible for solving the problem. The audience can be expected to come away concerned about the problem of domestic violence but hopeful that victims will be able to change their own situations.

Chapter 5 examines how and why the mass media use social problems and discusses the processes and guidelines that shape the stories. Those who produce media stories transform social problems to fit their own needs, including increasing ratings. Chapter 5 also discusses changes in journalism over the past few decades that impact the coverage of social problems, including the use of news as entertainment. This chapter specifically focuses on how editors of women's magazines, as well as other entertainment media, shape stories on social problems to be inspiring, uplifting, and emotional. I draw from in-depth interviews with editors from *Ladies' Home Journal, McCall's, Seventeen, Essence,* and *Good Housekeeping.* Then I discuss how commercialism, the focus on entertainment, and the loss of investigative research have impacted journalistic reporting and the media coverage of social problems. To illustrate this shift in journalism, I draw from other studies on media production and from my research on advice books written primarily for freelance writers spanning the 1940s to the late 1990s.

In Chapter 6, I discuss men's magazines *Penthouse* and *Playboy* along with the political magazines *The New Republic, National Review,* and *Reason.* These magazines use what I call the *antifeminist frame,* which is not really focused on the problem of domestic violence. Instead, it claims that the real problem is the battered women movement itself. The antifeminist frame tells a different story of domestic violence and yet also holds victims responsible—at least women victims. Furthermore, this frame emphasizes the responsibility of female abusers and battered women activists. I discuss how the political orientation and publishing missions of these magazines shape how they portray domestic violence. In particular I draw from in-depth interviews with editors at *The New Republic* and *Penthouse* to illustrate this process. Finally I discuss the concerns and implications the antifeminist frame has for how we understand and respond to domestic violence.

The *social justice frame,* the topic of Chapter 7, focuses not on the individual level of responsibility but rather the social and political contexts. Major themes include distorted images of male violence, too much focus on women's responsibility, "joking attitudes" toward domestic violence, welfare programs, and race. I analyze articles from *The Nation, The Progressive,* and *Penthouse* in this chapter. Drawing from interviews with editors at these three magazines, I explain how they shape their stories to support their political viewpoints. Finally, I address concerns and implications this frame has for how we understand and respond to domestic violence.

THE BATTERED WOMEN MOVEMENT AND IMPLICATIONS OF FRAMING THE VICTIM

Chapter 8 explains the emergence of domestic violence as a social problem through the work of the battered women movement and describes the consequences the dominant focus on victims has for public policy. The public "discovery" of domestic violence did not start as a portrayal of abusers as criminals who needed to be held accountable, but rather of battered women as victims who needed help to end their abuse. Because of the political and cultural context of the time, domestic violence emerged as a victim's problem. Furthermore, the translation of the activists' claims in the media has increasingly targeted the victim as the main character and the individual held most responsible for the problem. Though the original activists wanted to address social and cultural factors that contributed to the problem, most media translate their claims in ways that strip this context out of the stories. I discuss how the advocates' use of victimization differs from the popular use of victimization found in entertainment media.

Also in Chapter 8 I explain the implications that "framing the victim" has on public policy. This overemphasis on the victim helps abusers escape responsibility and public scrutiny and leads to victim-based solutions. Instead of focusing on preventing abuse before it starts or punishing the abuser after it happens, media stories primarily focus on the victims' needs and problems. Using a victim frame does little to address potential structural or cultural causes or solutions of domestic violence, which are crucial for any progress towards preventing violence.

IN SEARCH OF A *NEW* SOCIAL PROBLEM ABOUT VIOLENCE

In the concluding chapter I offer recommendations on how to construct a social problem that focuses less on the victim and more on the abuser and the cultural and social context within which the violence is learned and tolerated. Already there are advocates, programs, research, and the occasional media story that focus on these angles. However, I argue that we need to move those ideas into the mainstream media stories and the public understanding of domestic violence. Chapter 9 also describes the need for a cultural change in how we think about social problems. This change should include expanding our sources of information, challenging the entertainment and individualistic focus of social problems, and raising standards for how media cover these issues.

One of my students who was taking my domestic violence class said that at the beginning of the semester he wondered how we could ever spend the whole class talking about just domestic violence. How complicated could it be? He said he found out that there was so much more to the problem than he ever realized. I hope that this book helps others realize how complicated social problems are and that media stories do not give us the whole picture. May this book aid you in your own journey of understanding social problems and becoming more aware of the processes and motivations that lead the media, and other claims-makers, to create stories that shape our images of and responses to social problems.

NOTES

1. In reporting details from the pastor's story, I used two articles from the *Des Moines Register*: "Boy, 4, Dies from Alleged Beating" (2002) and "Boyfriend Gets Life for Murder of Child" (2003).

2. There are numerous studies that use frame analysis. Some examples of this research include Gamson and Modigliani's (1989) study on nuclear power, Sasson's (1995) research on how people talk about crime, Altheide's (2002) study on fear, and Beckett's (1996) study on child sexual abuse.

3. "Superpredators" is a term that John DiIulio used in the late 1990s to warn of a new generation of juvenile delinquents that would soon threaten the nation. This perception of juveniles as superpredators has been discredited by other scholars, but the image certainly can still be found in popular media. See Kappeler, Blumberg, and Potter (2000) for more information on the myth of juveniles as superpredators.

4. For more examples of media coverage of violence against women see Caringella-MacDonald (1998), Meyers (1997), and Soothill and Walby (1991).

5. For examples of research that shows media distortions of crime and violence see Beckett and Sasson (2000), Best (1999), Brownstein (2000), Ferrell and Websdale (1999), Fishman and Cavender (1998), Jenkins (1994), Potter and Kappeler (1996).

6. For an excellent introductory text on social constructionist perspective on social problems see Loseke's *Thinking about Social Problems* (2003).

7. See Best (1999) for more information on how the media depend on activists for stories and information and also how the activists rely on the media to get their claims publicized. Best describes this process as part of an "iron quadrangle" of the institutionalization of social problems.

2

The Landscape of Domestic Violence and the Public's Narrow Picture

Near the end of the semester in my course on gender and violence, the class was discussing how to prevent violence and abuse in intimate relationships. One of my students, Kristin, brought with her a piece of pink paper that she had found in her coed residence hall mailbox.[1] Written on the paper were tips on how to prevent becoming a victim of rape. Those tips included advice such as not going to parties alone, being aware of your surroundings, and not leaving drinks unattended for fear of the date rape drug being used. She noticed that only about half of the mailboxes had these pink pieces of paper. When looking more closely at the mailboxes, it appeared that only the women received these flyers. She asked the desk attendant if any of the men had received the same pink sheets of paper. No, they had not. In class, Kristin said that she probably would not have thought twice about this situation except that we had been talking all semester about how we hold the victim or potential victims responsible for ending and preventing abuse. She raised the point that by excluding men from the distribution of these flyers, it was not only assumed that men could not be victims, but also that men were not responsible for whether or not women on campus were raped. No flyers were given to students that said friends should not let friends make jokes about violence, abuse, or rape. No flyers told students that it was wrong to assault other people, or that people should help create an atmosphere where the attitudes and behaviors that fostered rape are eliminated.

Another student in the class, Jen, gave more information about those pink flyers. The women's studies group on campus, of which Jen was president, had prepared and distributed these flyers in order to raise awareness about sexual assault on campus. Though she understood Kristin's points, she said that their group felt that it would be useless to attempt changing a potential abuser's behavior or the overall attitude on campus about violence against women. Jen felt that any progress toward preventing assaults was going to be up to the potential victim. Jen was not the only student in the classroom who felt that the victim had to be the one to prevent abuse.

It seems that this view has not changed very much over time. Sheri, a fifty-year-old woman, told me what she had been taught over thirty years ago about preventing assaults:

> It was also brought up that it is the girl's responsibility to make sure things don't go too far. You go out on a date, and you park, and you're necking— this dealt more with what they call date rape, they used to call it going too far—it was your responsibility—not the guy's—to stop. You had to stop because guys couldn't help themselves. Guys just can't control themselves.

Holding the victim responsible for preventing abuse is also a common way that people talk about domestic violence. Sheri said that her mother told her, "If a man hits you once, he'll hit you again. If a man hits you once, it's his fault. And if he hits you twice, it's your fault." Ann, who is only twenty years old, also received this advice from her mother: "I remember as I was getting older she would say, 'Always be careful about the boys you date.' She said, if a man was to ever hit you once, to just get out because he's never going to change."

Women are more likely than men to talk about a woman's responsibility to prevent sexual assaults or to leave an abusive relationship. One of the reasons women may talk about this more than men is because abuse is often seen as a "woman's issue" and thus it is a "woman's responsibility" to stop it or prevent it. As Jen told my class, it is because women are so concerned about protecting themselves that they are not going to wait for men to stop the abuse.

It is not that my students, Sheri, or Ann think that women are the only ones involved in these social problems. They all are concerned about abuse and want to protect themselves and others. Even though people understand at one level that the problem is much larger than just the victim's behavior, they still have a hard time imagining prevention that actually targets people other than the victim. As I have discovered from listening to my students and from interviewing individuals for my research, people do not have many references for understanding why abusers abuse, and they do not understand what social and cultural factors tolerate and foster violence. The problem of domestic violence and the responsibility for ending it continue to be viewed as the victim's responsibility.

There are two parts to this chapter. First, I illustrate the complexity of the landscape of domestic violence. This outline of the problem is not intended to be an exhaustive list of all issues related to domestic violence, but it should help to widen the picture of domestic violence. I do not attempt to explain the problem of domestic violence but rather aim to outline how complex and multifaceted the problem is. This landscape should serve as a reference for better understanding how individual opinions and media images are often narrow in their depictions of the problem.

After painting a picture of the landscape, I begin tracing the roots of social problem frames for domestic violence. My investigation of how domestic violence is framed as a social problem begins with the public, as illustrated in Figure 1 (Chapter 1). I start by looking at how the public understands domestic violence and then investigate what sources the public uses to form those opinions. In this chapter, I describe the narrow frame that the general public uses to make sense of domestic violence. To illustrate how the public thinks about domestic violence, I draw from several data sources, including large national public opinion survey research and in-depth interviews with individuals. Then in Chapter 3, I continue analyzing public opinion by investigating how the media are the main sources of information that most people use to construct their understanding of social problems. This is why it is so important—and the main focus of the book—to analyze the media transformation of social problems that are shaped by guidelines that promote entertainment, victim empowerment, drama, and politics.

THE LANDSCAPE OF DOMESTIC VIOLENCE

In Chapter 1, I compared the concept of framing to a photographer choosing a particular snapshot from an expansive scenic landscape. Domestic violence also has a vast landscape. The general public's picture of domestic violence only focuses on part of that landscape. To give a better idea of how much is left out of the public understanding, I will briefly outline the social problem landscape of domestic violence.

There are multiple levels of any social problem's landscape. I define these different levels as cultural/structural, institutional, and individual. I should point out that by grouping particular aspects of a social problem into these categories, I am already imposing my framing on how one might understand the issues. It is impossible for anyone to explain social problems without using some kind of frame. I am not suggesting in this book that we can bypass frames, but rather that it is important to be able to identify frames and understand the effects and implications they have on our images of and responses to social problems. I use the organizational structure of multiple levels for two reasons. First, I can offer a panoramic view of domestic violence that can then be used to better understand the public's narrow picture. Second, throughout the book I refer to cultural/structural, institutional, and individual levels of domestic violence. A brief portrait of those levels here will give these later references more context. Before exploring those levels, I discuss sources and terms used to describe this landscape.

How do we "see" any social problem landscape? Where do I get my information in the first place in order to try and pass on what the larger landscape contains? Our sources of information often include people directly involved, such as victims and abusers, researchers studying the problem, and advocates or professionals whose work involves the problem. Though not all of these sources agree on what the problem "looks like," they offer windows from which we try to see the scope of the problem. The following is an attempt to draw together some of these different windows in order to paint the bigger landscape.

For this book I have decided to use "domestic violence" because it is the most common term used in the media and by individuals. However, the labels and scope of the problem become varied and complex. Other terms used by people have included domestic dispute, family violence, conjugal violence, spouse abuse, partner abuse, marital aggression, battered women, battered men, abused women, wife abuse, husband abuse, and wife beating.[2] Other types of abuse include sibling abuse, parent abuse, elderly abuse, and, of course, child abuse. It is important to remember that though I use the term domestic *violence,* not all abusive tactics are "physical" or "violent" in nature. The behaviors that fall under this social problem include physical, sexual, verbal, emotional, and/or psychological abuse. Types of physical abuse might include choking, pushing someone down the stairs, twisting or breaking arms, burning someone with cigarettes or scalding liquids, stabbing, punching, kicking, dragging someone across the room, shoving one into the wall, or throwing objects at a person. Examples of sexual abuse could include forced sex, forced prostitution, and unwanted touching of any kind. Strategies of emotional, verbal, and psychological abuse include verbal assaults, threats, isolation from friends and family, control of finances, forced drug use, threats to kill children and other family members, killing of family pets, beatings and forced sex in front of children, locking the victim in a room, public humiliation, insults, psychological games to make the victim feel insane, control over every decision, telling the victim no one else loves or ever will love him or her, and blaming the victim for the abuse. The landscape of domestic violence includes abusive strategies that, though often very oppressive and controlling, do not always fit what many people normally think of as "violent."

Cultural and Structural Level

The cultural and structural levels of the landscape include such issues as family structure, gender role socialization, social attitudes, media, sports culture, unemployment, poverty, and sex discrimination.[3] Cultural and structural factors can be either part of the problem or part of the solution. Many of these issues can be part of the problem because they help to foster an environment that may encourage, or at least tolerate, violence. If these issues are part of the problem, then solutions would include changing the sexist character of family and society, reducing violence in the media, and reducing unemployment and poverty.

There are numerous studies that use a social learning perspective to explain how people learn to use violence. These theories are often developed to explain men's violence. For example, through the media, peers, and other sources, boys may learn that violent behavior and the objectification and degradation of women are normal.[4] In addition, a cultural violence theory proposes that in some subcultures there is a significant theme of violence in the values, attitudes, and norms that make up the socialization process and the relationships of individuals (Anderson 1999, Wolfgang and Ferracuti 1982). This perspective assumes that violence is learned and reflects the larger social acceptance of violence as appropriate behavior. And, as mentioned above, many people do learn that violence in the family is an acceptable means for resolving conflict. Through cultural images, including television, movies, sports, and fairy tales, individuals may learn that cultural rules often legitimate or require violence. In response, there are programs designed to teach batterers different ways of interacting with their partners and to teach them how to respect women.[5]

Sex role socialization and male dominance in society may also contribute to violence in the family. For example, men grow up in a culture that emphasizes male dominance over women. The battering of women may be a normalized outcome of the male socialization process, in which domination over women is expected and taught.[6] Gender socialization might also play a role in domestic violence because women are not taught how to defend themselves physically to the same degree as men are. Women are often taught less assertiveness than men and are encouraged to be passive and self-denying. Issues of gender and power at the cultural and structural level are also factors related to domestic violence and other forms of violence against women.[7]

Institutional Level

The institutional level of the landscape includes many people and agencies involved with intervention and prevention. The efforts (or lack of effort) to intervene can contribute both positively and negatively to the problem. There are the many agencies, organizations, and institutions whose work in some way connects to social problems, including law enforcement, counselors, social workers, clergy, the court system, schools, and the medical institution. Various people who might have a role in this process include police, clergy, battered women advocates, psychologists, lawyers, judges, family, friends, journalists, legislators, doctors, nurses, jurors, or neighbors. But what does this intervention mean for the victims and abusers? Sometimes intervention helps the victim seek safety, legal protection, or medical help. Other times intervention may escalate the danger because of the messages people send the victim and abuser. Police who come to the door after being called but do nothing may be sending the message that the violence is acceptable. Clergy may tell an abused wife that she should learn to please her husband. Often the effectiveness of intervention depends on the training of those individuals. Police, lawyers, judges, clergy, counselors, doctors, and nurses need to be trained to be more aware of domestic violence and to intervene in more effective ways.

Additional issues that complicate the landscape involve laws and policies that affect the problem. Are there enough laws against violence in the family and intimate relationships? Are these laws effective? Legal innovations designed to address domestic violence include orders of protection, mandatory arrest, no-drop prosecution policies that allow states to prosecute without the victim being involved, and increased punishment for batterers.[8] Yet many people think that batterers do not get enough punishment through the courts. Would tougher sentencing deter abusers? Are crimes of family violence taken less seriously? Others argue that domestic violence is an issue of state responsibility and that failure on the part of the state to protect victims of family violence violates international human rights laws. They claim that domestic violence has not been analyzed as a human rights issue because it is most often viewed as a private issue.[9]

Individual Level

At the individual level of the landscape are the victims and abusers. No one victim or abuser has the same story or the same social context within which the violence is occurring. First, I discuss victims. I use the label "victim" to refer to the person who is portrayed or identified as being battered or abused. People are often considered "victims" when they meet the following conditions: (1) they have suffered a loss unfairly or undeservedly; (2) the loss has an identifiable cause; and (3) the legal or moral context of the loss entitles the sufferers of the loss to social concern (Bayley 1991). Not all battered women and men consider themselves "victims"; many of them prefer the term "survivor." These conditions described above that are used to define a victim are socially constructed and subject to interpretation, which I discuss more in Chapter 8. Part of the politics of framing a social problem includes who is labeled as a victim. Even for those who do get this label, there are many differences that distinguish the victims' experiences and situations.

The characteristics and circumstances of domestic violence victims vary greatly. Some victims are unemployed and live in poorer neighborhoods while others work as lawyers, doctors, or politicia... up with abusive parents but others did not. Victim... sexual orientation, class, race, religion, and nation... tims and men are victims. Children are victims of... only when they are the primary targets but also ... abuse in the home. Some victims of abuse have go... relationship but others remain. Some victims are ... their abusers. Some victims have children, but not all of them do.

Abusers are also part of the landscape. Most of the diverse characteristics described for victims apply to abusers also. Both men and women use abusive strategies in relationships. Abusers also vary by age, sexual orientation, class, race, religion, and nationality. Some abusers use physical violence but not all do. Explanations for why individuals abuse are also complex. As I discuss later in this chapter, most people attribute blame to childhood abuse and alcohol use, but these explanations are far too simplistic and often do not apply at all. Some batterers were abused as children, but many others were not. Furthermore, many people who are abused as children never grow up to be abusive. So even though childhood abuse, or even witnessing parents fighting, may be an important contributing factor, it is not the easy answer.[11] Alcohol and drug use are also complicated issues. Though research shows that alcohol and drug use may be present in many incidents of family violence, most experts do not think that the drug use is the causal explanation for abuse.[12]

This is just a brief glimpse at how complicated the problem of domestic violence is. This overview does not cover every story about domestic violence. I still have not captured all the different faces of the victims and abusers. There are millions of stories that are not yet reflected in this picture. There are many other cultural and structural issues that relate to domestic violence that I have not included. I do hope, though, that this quick look at the landscape will help in seeing how much is left out of the general public opinion, which is described next. Though domestic violence could be understood in the broader, more complex level of cultural and structural issues, the dominant frame of the problem remains at the narrowest level—the individuals.

PUBLIC OPINION ON DOMESTIC VIOLENCE

This section presents four main points regarding public opinion in the United States about domestic violence. First, even though most people say domestic violence is not right, there are still situations that people believe ✓ are "private" and some circumstances that they say justify the abuse. Second, the public holds the victim personally responsible for solving the problem (and sometimes for causing the abuse). Third, when people do talk about the abuser, they focus primarily on alcohol use and childhood abuse, factors that obscure the abuser's personal responsibility. And fourth, the general public uses an individual and psychological frame for understanding the problem and does not expand this to include a structural and cultural context. Before elaborating on these four points, I briefly describe the data used to assess the public understanding of domestic violence.

Many of the studies that explore public attitudes about domestic violence rely on survey research. I draw upon several of these survey studies to provide a picture of what the public thinks about domestic violence. Most of these survey studies define domestic violence as men's violence against women and focus primarily on physical violence.[13] This research gives us a start in seeing how the public views domestic violence, at least as defined as men's violence against women. More research is needed to better assess what the public thinks about other types of abuse.

One of the largest survey studies on public opinion regarding domestic violence was conducted from 1992 to 1996 by the Family Violence Prevention Fund. Part of the goal of this survey was to follow public knowledge and attitudes about domestic violence over time and to see if a massive media education campaign made any difference. Early data from this study helped launch the *There's No Excuse for Domestic Violence* advertising campaign, which started in the summer of 1994. One of the main themes in the ads was that domestic violence is everybody's business and that there is no excuse for it. In one of the ads viewers see a couple in their bed listening to the sounds of neighbors fighting and a woman screaming. The couple exchanges looks and then turns off the light rather than calling the police. The screen goes black and the message appears saying "It *is* your business."

The Family Violence Prevention Fund research conducted multiple surveys over several years so it was able to track changes over time. During this period, the O. J. Simpson case occurred and caused a huge increase in media coverage of domestic violence. The O. J. Simpson case was a high-profile domestic violence story. O. J. Simpson, a beloved sports commentator and former football star, was charged with the murder of his ex-wife, Nicole Brown Simpson, and a friend of hers, Ronald Goldman. The murders happened on June 12, 1994. During the coverage of the trial, the media highlighted Simpson's previous acts of domestic violence. Simpson was charged, tried, and acquitted. The media covered the trial and related events in more in-depth coverage than perhaps any previous case. This study found that over 70 percent of respondents said they learned about domestic violence from the media coverage of the O. J. Simpson trial. Most of them said they learned that domestic violence is a serious problem, that women who are physically abused are more likely than other women to be killed by their husbands, and that people need to find out more about how to handle domestic violence (Klein, Campbell, Soler, and Ghez 1997:160). The increase in media coverage due to the O. J. Simpson trial along with the *There's No Excuse for Domestic Violence* ad campaign seems to have influenced the public awareness of domestic violence. I will discuss this research along with smaller survey studies on public opinions about domestic violence.

Though survey research is designed to investigate the opinions of large numbers of people, it is less useful for discovering how people developed those opinions. To learn more about this, I conducted a small, qualitative study of how individuals understand domestic violence and what sources they draw upon to develop their opinions. I conducted in-depth interviews with twenty people (eleven women and nine men).[14] Four of the twenty people (three women and one man) had firsthand experience with domestic violence, i.e., they had been victims. Three others (one woman and two men) had been abused as children (but not as adults). People with firsthand experience also had a lot of secondhand experience through friends and professionals, such as domestic violence advocates. Thirteen people had no firsthand experience with domestic violence. I draw from these interviews here to show what these people think about domestic violence and in the next chapter to illustrate how they use the media to construct those opinions. My qualitative analysis illustrates the process that people go through in developing their opinions. However, because it is a small sample, I do not generalize to the larger public from that research. The interviews, which support the public opinion findings, are used to give examples and a richer context of the trends found in the larger surveys.

Domestic Violence Is a Problem But . . .

People have not always thought that domestic violence is wrong (Dobash and Dobash 1979; Straus 1976). In the past two decades there has been a gradual increase in the percentage of people who think domestic violence should be considered a social problem (Frieze and Browne 1989). Today, most people responding to public opinion surveys agree that domestic violence is a problem and should be taken seriously. However, the details of their answers show lingering acceptance and justification for violence in certain situations. When confronted with specific scenarios and asked more detailed questions, a majority of respondents in several studies indicated that some domestic violence may be needed or justified, depending on the situation (Klein et al. 1997).

Most people still tolerate some abusive behavior by men against their female partners, considering it a private matter. Many people think that unless physical injury is evident, abusive behaviors—including verbal, emotional, and psychological abuse—do not warrant official intervention. Disputes between couples that involve verbal violence are viewed as private affairs that are best resolved with counseling and improved communication skills (Klein et al. 1997:148).

People also tolerate a measure of physical violence in relationships. Part of the reason that people think domestic violence is sometimes acceptable, justified, or not entirely wrong is that they feel the victim is responsible for the situation. Though people say that domestic violence is unacceptable, they continue to agree that "slapping a wife around" may be necessary when the wife is described as flirting, having an affair, or nagging the husband (Hilton 1993). A national survey found that "the vast majority of Americans hold covert attitudes that condone battering and help create an environment in which inaction is the norm rather than the exception" (Klein 1997:89). Overall, the public does not believe that stress or drunkenness is an excuse for abusing a woman. However, there is a common belief, particularly among men, that some wives provoke their husbands into abusing them. One in two men agree that some wives provoke abuse, while one in three women believe this claim (Rhode Island Violence Prevention Program 1997; Klein et al. 1997). In my in-depth interviews, however, people did not argue that some wives provoke abuse. It could be that this attitude shows up in the survey research because respondents feel more anonymous and willing to express those feelings. Instead, individuals in my study focused on trying to explain why victims stay in abusive relationships.

Research shows differences in how men and women think about domestic violence: Men are more likely than women to believe that victims provoke abuse. Women are more likely than men to think that domestic violence is a common occurrence and are more concerned about the increase in family violence (Klein et al. 1997; Locke and Richman 1999). Men are more likely than women to accept rationalizations for domestic violence and to believe that the media exaggerate the problem of domestic violence. And women are more likely than men to advocate arresting physically abusive men, while men are more likely than women to think the police should just talk to the abuser in the home rather than making an arrest (Klein et al. 1997).

The Victim

Even though there continue to be attitudes that blame victims for provoking abuse in some situations, public opinion research indicates that the general public has shifted in the way it talks about victims (ibid.). There is more sympathy and understanding for victims today than there was just fifteen years ago, when studies showed more explicit victim-blaming attitudes. Even studies conducted as recently as the early 1990s show that many people had a tendency to blame victims of abuse. Two of these studies asked potential jurors about their understanding of battered women. Potential jurors thought that battered women are masochistic and stay with their partners because they enjoy the violence or that battered women could leave if that is what they really wanted (Hilton 1993; Schuller and Vidmar 1992; Dodge and Greene 1991). Though these beliefs still exist, they appear to be showing up less frequently in public opinion surveys. Instead, more people are able to explain why it may be hard for a victim to leave the abusive relationship. However, the victim is still being held responsible for the problem even if there is a greater understanding of what the victim goes through. Even when people have more "understanding" about why it is hard to leave, victims are still expected to take responsibility for leaving.

Those individuals in my study who had no firsthand experience with abuse talked a lot about the victims, describing their typical characteristics and reasons why they have trouble leaving abusive relationships. Their descriptions of the problem were more clear-cut, formal, and typified than those who had firsthand experience with abuse, which I discuss in the next chapter. The typical characteristics and reasons nonvictims gave for why victims stay include financial problems, love, guilt, threats, low self-esteem, and no social support. These ideas are the foundation for the narrative that they use to make sense of domestic violence.

Sheri was typical in that she could give several reasons why women stay in abusive relationships, including children, financial difficulties, and low self-esteem:

> I think a lot of women stay with men who abuse them because of their kids. You know, they say that there are women who have very poor self-images and they stay with these men because they think they deserve it or for financial reasons and it's like most of the times he's pretty good and if he gets wacky a couple times a year it's not that bad.

Individuals with no firsthand experience with abuse had images and certain profiles in mind when they thought about victims of domestic violence. The characteristics most often attributed to victims were low self-esteem, passiveness, and weakness. Carol had a very definite image of victims and even called some people "natural-born victims." She said that some people have no self-esteem nor any confidence in themselves:

> [Victims are] people that don't have very high self-esteem. They don't have any confidence in themselves whether or not it's imagined or someone has told them this over and over as they were growing up. Some people are not

strong personalities. Some people are willing to let people tell them what to do. They can't make up their mind. I suppose it goes back to no self-confidence or no self-esteem because they don't think they can make good decisions.

Kathy referred to victims as being weak and not able to control situations. She said that she saw "the victim as kind of being a weak person. Not aggressive enough to take control of the matter."

Curtis described a "typical victim" as having low self-esteem. He thought that the woman does not usually want to press charges because she hopes the abuser will change, that he did not mean to do it, and he still loves her. Brian thought that victims stay because they want to make the relationship work. He said that was a hard thing for those on the outside to understand:

> I would think the victim hangs on longer than those of us on the outside looking in on the relationship can understand. We can't understand why they stay in that relationship as long as they do. The victims are people who want to make a relationship work. They really care for the other person and that's why they put up with it as long as they do.

Lori's explanation combined both low self-esteem and fear of more abuse. She thought through what process makes the victim think she cannot do anything:

> It may also be reasons like low self-esteem and not feeling like they could survive without their husbands. I guess with the husband on a day-to-day basis saying negative things to her—saying "You can't do this and you can't do that"—a woman just starts to have a low self-esteem and starts to think that she can't do anything at all.

There has been an interesting shift in the public understanding of domestic violence. People are less likely to think that the victim stays in the relationship because she enjoys the abuse. However, the public still holds the victim responsible for preventing the abuse or leaving the relationship. People say that the "victim not leaving" is a primary reason why domestic violence continues to be a problem ("Florida's Perspective on Domestic Violence" 1999). The most common interventions suggested by the public are various types of counseling and the victim leaving the relationship—and she is typically held responsible for taking all the actions needed to leave.

The Abuser

Although people have learned more about victims, they appear to know far less about abusers. In one study, individuals participating in focus groups were asked, "Why do men beat women?" According to the researchers, "Many people reacted with a long pause or asked us to clarify the question. Some attempted to shift the focus to the previous conversation. Others shied away from answering the direct question" (Klein et al. 1997:32). The majority of people said they did not know why men would abuse their partners. When people did talk about abusers, they most often referred to alcohol and childhood abuse as reasons why they abuse (ibid.). I also discovered through my interviews that people are most likely to discuss alcohol and childhood abuse as the reasons why abusers use violence. The following are some examples from my interviews of how people talk about abusers.

Lori said that she thought the abuser was usually drunk, although she was not sure why she had this opinion. She thought it might be connected to media images:

> I do think of a man who drinks. I don't know why, I just do. That could be from watching TV. I do remember *The Burning Bed*. I can't remember anything specifically but usually the man would be drunk or he would go out drinking and then come back.

Jackie said that she usually thinks of "the drunk husband and the battered wife." She said that she gets these ideas from television shows but that it also makes sense to her because she cannot imagine her own husband abusing her. It is striking that the main reason she does not imagine her husband being an abuser is because he is not a heavy drinker:

> I can't understand how someone could do that unless they are affected by other factors like alcohol because I can't understand my husband ever abusing me. It is conceivable that he might divorce me but I can't imagine him ever hitting me. He'd storm out before that. But he doesn't drink heavily either. I've seen alcohol alter people's personalities a lot. Most of the time the abuser in TV shows is drunk.

James thought that if we could eradicate alcohol and drug use, then "domestic violence overnight would probably be half of what it is today." Doug also connected alcohol and drug use with domestic violence. In his opinion, not only does alcohol use cause the abuser to abuse more, but alcohol can cause a victim to provoke the abuse. He depicted a typical scene that he had heard about from friends and police:

> Anywhere you have a situation where drug and alcohol are being used by both parties, you have a situation that could occur. They both get drunk. They start yelling at each other. The guy being the stronger, bigger person, beating the hell out of the female. In that situation, they're both drunk, the wife, or female, could have said something to the guy to get him started back

and forth. It may not have happened if she hadn't been drunk. I've just heard about this from friends and police.

Another common factor people cited to explain the problem was that the abuser was a victim of child abuse. Maria said that from the movies she learned that when a child is abused, there is a good chance he or she will become abusive as an adult. James and Jerrad both elaborated on why observing abuse as a child can cause someone to be abusive.

James: Observing abusive relationships as a child is a key factor. It just makes children learn these things. There are other factors to it certainly. But I think a learned behavior—seeing your father do it or your grandfather do it— makes it much more likely that somebody else will do it.

Jerrad: I think I know why some people are more likely to be abusive. Their own personal experience—just being abused at home. That might lead them to be more likely to abuse later in life just because it was more accepted in their household. When they're older, they're expected to do it to their children.

A quote from James best captures the overall opinion on abusers. He thought that someone who has observed abusive relationships as a child and also drinks is at a very high risk for abusing: "If you can do both of those things and not beat on people, then you've really accomplished something."

When discussing victims, the public often holds them personally responsible for the abuse. Victims are blamed for provoking the abuse because of their behavior. They are also blamed for not leaving because they are too weak, not in control, or too passive. These explanations place the blame directly on the victim. However, when discussing the abusers, people use explanations—alcohol use and childhood abuse—that place the blame on factors external to the individual.

Using an Individual Frame to Talk about Domestic Violence

In the past three decades, there has been an explosion of attention and social science research on the topic of domestic violence. While in the 1960s, there were very few articles on domestic violence in academic journals, today there are several journals dedicated to the topic. This research has provided us with information on all aspects of the domestic violence problem. These range from the psychological studies of victims and abusers to sociological and feminist research that has advanced our understanding of how domestic violence relates to structural and cultural factors, such as society's tolerance for violence, structural power arrangements, and gender socialization. Even though academic theories have advanced our understanding of domestic violence to include structural and cultural factors, public understanding of domestic violence focuses primarily on the individual or psychological level.

Using an individual frame of understanding affects public views on policy, which can be seen in the promotion of counseling as the most effective solution. When asked about how we should respond to domestic violence, the majority of the public favor counseling services over alternative policies, such as stiffer penalties for batterers or any changes in structural and cultural factors that foster violence. People think that the victim needs protection and help, but there continues to be a strong emphasis on the privacy of the family, family harmony, and marriage counseling as a solution (Klein et al. 1997; Stalans 1996; "Florida's Perspective on Domestic Violence" 1999).

An individual frame for understanding domestic violence focuses on one or more individuals in the abusive relationship as opposed to also including the structural and cultural levels. Significantly, a dominant focus is on how the victim is causing the abuse or allowing it to continue. Solutions rooted in this frame remain on the individual level and are primarily focused on intervention, not prevention.

Most people do not consider the many other factors involved in domestic violence that come from the interaction of the individual, institutional, cultural, and structural levels of society. People fail to focus on preventative solutions that coexist with intrapersonal and institutional responses yet have the potential to reduce the problem. The public fails to see the need to transform the parts of society that teach and foster acts of domestic violence.

CONCLUSION

Even though most people say domestic violence is not right, people still believe that some situations are "private" and that some circumstances justify the abuse. Furthermore, many people hold the victim personally responsible for solving the problem and, at times, for causing the abuse. People do not have as much to say about the abuser. When people do talk about the abuser, they focus primarily on alcohol use and childhood abuse, factors that do not hold the abuser personally responsible. The general public uses an individual and psychological frame for understanding the problem and does not expand this to include a structural and cultural context. However, as illustrated by the complex landscape of domestic violence, there is much more to this social problem than just the victim not leaving or the abuser using alcohol. An overemphasis has been placed on the individual level of understanding, especially on the victims.

There has been an interesting shift in how people talk about victims of domestic violence. Today it is more common to hear people describe the complexity of the situations faced by abuse victims. They articulate many of the problems that advocates and researchers on domestic violence have been discussing for the past three decades. More people are able to explain why it may be hard for a victim to leave an abusive relationship. However, even when people have more "understanding" about why it is hard to leave, victims are still expected to take responsibility for leaving.

The Family Violence Prevention Fund helped conduct one of the largest national studies on public opinions of domestic violence. It found that people find it easier and perhaps more enjoyable to talk about victims as opposed to talking about abusers. People did not want to focus on the abuser. "It seemed easier to keep him out of the conversation. They were much more comfortable talking about the woman—why she stays, what happens to her, and how they could help her" (Klein et al. 1997:48). Though the authors of the Family Violence Prevention Fund study say that it is a "heartening sign of success for the battered women's movement" to hear that participants express sympathy for abused women, I argue it should also be viewed as a significant finding that the people are not able to talk about abusers or about the social factors related to domestic violence.

Domestic violence has a complicated landscape of issues that could and should be considered when trying to understand the problem. We could view the problem from the cultural and structural level. However, the dominant public understanding focuses only on the individual level. Why is it that the public has such a limited view of this problem? Why does it not have an increased understanding about the abusers or about the social and cultural context involved with violence? To help answer these questions, we turn next to the sources that people use for understanding social problems. As explained in the next chapter, most people rely on the mass media as their main source of information. The public's dominant focus on victims is influenced in large part by how the media frame the problem. There are many possible angles for looking at domestic violence, and yet most often the media lens zooms in on the victim while leaving out the rest of the landscape. How do people use the media to build their opinions about domestic violence? How do people evaluate media messages? These questions are addressed in the next chapter.

NOTES

1. All names in this chapter have been changed to protect the identity of students and interview participants.
2. How to label the problem continues to be debated (e.g., Jones 1994). "Domestic violence" is criticized for not identifying the roles of victim and offender. Simi-

lar terms criticized for this obfuscation include "domestic dispute," "family violence," "conjugal violence," "spouse abuse," "partner abuse," and "marital aggression." Other commonly used terms, such as "battered women," "abused women," "wife abuse," and "wife beating," identify the victim but obscure the offender. Terms like "wife abuse" and "spouse abuse" are criticized for ignoring abuse outside marriage. Many feminists and advocates use the term "battered women," but it implies that a woman's main identity is that of a helpless victim.

3. Gelles and Straus (1988) argue that one of the main causes of family violence is the structure of the family. Factors such as unemployment, poor working conditions, financial problems, and health issues create stress on the family. Norman Denzin provides another sociological view of family violence. Denzin also focuses on the whole family but situates the violence in emotionality and interaction. "Violence occurs within an interactional framework of superordinate and subordinate relationships that tie husbands, wives, and children into the domestic establishment called the home" (1984:486). These interactions reflect economic, cultural, social, and legal issues in society. Denzin argues that these structural processes must be examined from within the family.

4. For example, Mildred Daley Pagelow (1984) describes her use of social learning theory as an integration of differential association and differential reinforcement. Although Pagelow focuses on more types of family violence than just violence against women, her perspective reflects feminist concerns with institutional responses to violence, sex role socialization, and male dominance in society. Boys learn to be aggressive by modeling adult males. Furthermore, if a model's violent behavior has "functional value" in society, this gives observers encouragement to repeat the behavior. Paul Kivel (1992) argues that through popular culture and adult male role models, boys learn roles in which violent behavior has a central part.

5. For more information on intervention programs for men who batter, see Bancroft (2002) and Bennett and Williams (2001).

6. For example, Schwartz and DeKeseredy (1997) use a male peer-support model to explain dating violence. They argue that the four most important factors in explaining sexual assault are the ideologies of familial and courtship patriarchy, alcohol consumption, membership in male support groups, and absence of deterrence. Although aspects of their model are psychological, they argue that focusing only on the individual ignores the broader societal forces that affect individual behaviors such as men growing up in a culture that emphasizes male dominance over women.

7. Feminist theorists argue that violence cannot be understood without looking at gender and power: Violence against women is a result of patriarchal attitudes held by individuals and institutions as opposed to some psychopathic sickness on the part of the abuser. Rather than being a "sickness," battering women is a normalized outcome of the male socialization process, in which domination over women is expected and taught (Dobash and Dobash 1992). "The right of men to control the female body is a cornerstone of patriarchy" (Sheffield 1995:1). Most feminist theorists believe that all forms of violence against women are interrelated and are strategies of a patriarchal system to control, dominate, and silence women (MacKinnon 1993; Dobash and Dobash 1979; Yllö 1993; Caputi 1987). This position argues that male violence against women and the fear of that violence maintains

the patriarchal definition of a woman's place. Some theorists describe this process as sexual terrorism (Sheffield 1995) or domestic terrorism (Marcus 1994). Forms of violence against women that contribute to sexual terrorism include rape, battering of women, sexual harassment, femicide, incest, stalking, obscene phone calls, pornography, and prostitution (Sheffield 1995; Marcus 1994; MacKinnon 1993; Russell 1993; Caputi 1987; Itzin 1992).

8. For an overview of the criminal justice system's response to domestic violence see Iovanni and Miller (2001). For an explanation of the Violence Against Women Act of 1994 see Valente, Hart, Zeya, and Malefyt (2001).

9. Some scholars study family violence on both an interpersonal level and an international level. This perspective not only embraces the culture of violence perspective for family relations, but shows how violence in the family leads to other human rights violations. Riane Eisler (1997) argues that research needs to consider interpersonal violence as a natural link to global human rights violations. She illustrates how violence in family relations socializes people to accept other human rights violations as normal. In order to fight violence on an international level, we need to recognize and solve the abuse in intimate relations. The distinctions made between the public and private spheres has prevented us from doing this. See also Michele Beasley and Dorothy Thomas (1994); and Bond and Phillips (2001).

10. See Renzetti (1992, 1997) for more on gay and lesbian battering. See Crenshaw (1994) for more on race and domestic violence.

11. For example, Gelles and Straus (1988) argue that many people learn that violence in the family is an acceptable means to resolve conflict. Through cultural images, including television, movies, sports, and fairy tales, individuals learn that the cultural rules often legitimate or require violence (Gelles 1993).

12. For more information on the role of alcohol and family violence and rape see, for example, Jasinski (2001) and Schwartz and DeKeseredy (1997).

13. For example, in a survey conducted in Florida ("Florida's Perspective on Domestic Violence" 1999), respondents were given the following definition: "Domestic violence is defined as any physical act of violence by a man toward his wife or girlfriend." One of the reasons that these surveys may have limited the definition is because most research and advocacy reports indicate that the majority of victims are women. This point will be discussed more in Chapter 6, as there continues to be controversy and debate over the question of gender and victimization. A second reason might be that people's opinions about domestic violence may vary greatly depending on how they are defining the problem. For example, people might have dramatically different opinions about men's violence against women versus gay and lesbian violence or women's violence against men. In order to get a clearer picture of what people think, surveys narrow the scope of the questions.

14. Individuals ranged in age from twenty to the mid-fifties and all but two individuals were white. Everyone had at least a high school education and most had college degrees, ranging from associate's to master's.

3

"I Get My Experience from the Media": Using Media to Understand Social Problems

How do you learn about domestic violence or other social problems, like juvenile delinquency, rape, corporate crime, homelessness, poverty, or pollution? Have you experienced these problems firsthand? How much of your knowledge is from the media? The sources of information that we use to help understand social problems can be thought of as tour guides that lead us through the complex social problem landscapes. When people visit a city they do not know, they may go on a tour to get an overview of the community. Imagine that they decide to take two tours. Their first tour guide highlights the tourist attractions, while the second guide focuses on the extreme class differences present in the city's various neighborhoods. These two tours would be quite different even though they focused on the same city. In the same way, depending on the guide, tours through a social problem landscape can depict different pictures of the problem.

Media have become popular tour guides for people in their process of learning about social problems. Research studies find that most people rely on the media as a main source of information.[1] For many issues, people use the media as their *only* resource for thinking about social problems. This is not surprising if you just look around. Think of the easy access we have to television, radio, newspapers, movies, internet, books, and magazines. From these resources, individuals construct their own conceptions of what is normal and acceptable.[2] James and Shirley, two people I interviewed, illustrate how the media serve as their tour guide.

James has had no firsthand experience with abuse. For this single forty-one-year-old male, television and newspapers are the main source of information on domestic violence. James says that his first memory of learning about domestic violence is *The Burning Bed*. This 1984 television movie is based on a book about a battered woman who, after years of abuse, set fire to her husband's bed while he was sleeping. James describes the story:

> It was just a horrible experience a woman went through with her husband. Physical and emotional abuse that he had put towards her. I don't know if he beat the kids or not too, but he controlled her from day one when they first met. It was just total control. I guess her self-esteem or whatever wasn't enough to fight back until it just built up enough until it exploded and I guess she killed him.

James says that after seeing that movie, he realized that victims cannot just easily leave a relationship, because they are dependent and have low self-esteem.

Shirley, a forty-two-year-old married mother of three, also has no first-hand experience with abuse. Like James, she says that her main source of information on domestic violence is the media, and one of her earliest memories about domestic violence is also *The Burning Bed*. Shirley learns even more about domestic violence from women's magazines:

> I get my women's magazines and I read those. There are articles in there usually every month on one woman's story. It's sometimes about violence. That's one of the categories that you see women writing about in the magazines. The [*Ladies' Home*] *Journal* is the main one. Usually there are stories about women who have actually been able to do something about their situation. I don't know that I ever read a story that's, like, I'm in this terrible situation and I can't do anything about it. Usually they are women who have somehow found the courage and support to actually get themselves out of the situation. So they are encouraging stories that other women could probably relate to and see somebody else's success.

By reading women's magazine articles, Shirley learned that the problem is very complicated. Although it is easy to think "Just leave," she knows now that it is not so simple. "When you read these stories there is a lot of the woman's emotion in the story, a lot of her feelings, trying to explain—not even trying to explain but just 'this is the way it was.' It made me realize that it is a lot more complicated and harder." Shirley said that watching *ER* and other dramas showed her the reality of the situation.

Both James and Shirley had no firsthand experience with domestic violence, so their "experience" with domestic violence came from media. And some of those experiences really stayed with them, such as watching *The Burning Bed*—a movie that first came out over fifteen years before I talked to them. Most people who have no firsthand experience with social problems use the media as their main source of information. Although there are many academic theories about domestic violence as well as claims by advocates and professionals who work in the area, most people learn about domestic violence from the popular media. The media are the most common and influential tour guides for exploring the landscapes of social problems.

MEDIA EFFECTS

Many people believe that the media have an effect on social problems, such as juvenile delinquency, child abuse, and violent crime. Newspaper reporters, researchers, politicians, and other claims-makers warn us that exposure to particular kinds of media will cause people to do bad things. For example, some people argue that children who watch too much television are likely to engage in violence, or teenagers who listen to heavy metal music may commit suicide. Or, to give an old example that now sounds silly, during the 1950s Congress investigated how comic books lead to juvenile delinquency.[3] In all of these examples it is suggested that media cause people, or at least influence them, to engage in dangerous, violent, or at-risk behavior.[4]

There is another way that the media are connected to social problems, one that may not be as obvious. The media shape the way people *think* about social problems; for many people, in fact, the media are how they *experience* social problems. Let me give you an example from one of my courses. In my juvenile delinquency class, we were discussing research about boot camps. One of the students told me that she disagreed with the research findings from the reading assignment because she had seen juvenile delinquents on *Sally Jessy Raphael* and they were not like the juvenile delinquents presented in the studies. Students often question research findings because they do not reflect their own personal experience, but this student was questioning the results based upon her *media experience*. Because she had no firsthand experience with the topic we were studying, her way of thinking about the topic had been shaped by the media. Notice that Sally did not influence this student to *commit* juvenile delinquency. Instead, it influenced how she *thought* about juvenile delinquency.

Analyzing how the media affect the way we think about social problems is important not just because people bring perspectives developed from the media to college classes, but because they also bring them to roles that influence public policy. For instance, someone like my student may one day serve on a jury hearing a case involving youth crime and may view the case through a perspective she developed, in part, from talk shows. She may choose in the voting booth between politicians with different views on how to deal with juvenile delinquents. She may be a police officer, a juvenile probation officer, school board member, or judge. She may become a newspaper or television reporter whose own stories are shaped by the images she has seen in other media.

People understand social problems through their experiences. Their view of the landscape of a social problem depends on the particular angles and images that their experience provides them. The media are a primary source of these images for most people. However, there are other ways to learn about social problems. For example, you may have firsthand experience with a problem such as domestic violence because you are a victim or abuser. And some people have secondhand experience—they know victims and abusers or they work with them, as is the case for some police officers, social workers, shelter advocates, lawyers, judges, clergy, and medical personnel. People might also gather other views of the problem through doing research, taking classes, or using other sources of information.

My focus in this book is how the media play a significant role in shaping people's opinions. In Chapter 1, I illustrated in Figure 1 that people receive media stories through a filtering process that they use to evaluate the messages. Those "other ways of knowing" besides media experience play a crucial role in evaluating the media messages. In this chapter, I explain how people use the media as a source for understanding domestic violence, and how they evaluate the media. Then I discuss how media simplify the problem by comparing those people who use the media as a main source with those who rely on their lived experience with abuse.[5] To illustrate these points, I draw on the in-depth interviews introduced in Chapter 2.

USING THE MEDIA

During their interviews, people who had no firsthand experience with abuse were most likely to use the media as a main source of information. Sometimes people spoke of these shows as their "only experience" with abuse and the primary source of information about the problem. "I watch a lot of news shows on TV like *Dateline, 20/20*," Kathy said. "That's where I form a lot of my opinions really." Maria claimed that "whatever knowledge I have gained about domestic violence, it is from the [Lifetime channel] movies."

The most common media source of information mentioned was television, including news magazine programs like *20/20*, *COPS* (which shows "real footage" of police work), talk shows such as *Oprah*, dramatic shows, soap operas, and television movies. The specific television movie discussed most frequently was *The Burning Bed* (which starred Farrah Fawcett as a battered woman) and it is interesting that it continues to be such a significant reference for people who first saw it almost two decades ago. Perhaps because it was the *first* movie many of them saw (and indeed one of the first TV programs about domestic violence), the memory is stronger for them.

Individuals may remember specific television programs more easily than specific newspaper articles because of the visual images. Curtis, for instance, said it was hard not to believe the movie because of its strong and persuasive images. Specifically, he said that he could remember Farrah Fawcett's "bruised body" from *The Burning Bed:*

> It has a lot to do with television probably because of the visual component where the pictures of domestic violence are pretty graphic. Both in news reports and entertainment. I can remember Farrah Fawcett in a movie on domestic violence. I can remember that for some reason. I can remember seeing her bruised body at one point.

Other than television, the two most common media sources were magazines and newspapers. When they discussed these media, people were often less specific about their examples. They referred to "reading it somewhere" or giving examples of possible magazines but not knowing which magazine or paper they had read. Ron explained that he picks up any newspaper or magazine when he gets a chance to read, including women's magazines:

> I read the newspapers and some of the magazines. I'll be sitting anywhere and I'll grab a magazine. It could be a *McCall's* or *Woman's Day* or anything. I'll just pick it up and start reading it if I have nothing else to do, and I read quickly. I like to absorb a lot of information. Some of it sticks and some of it goes in and out.

As Ron suggested, people often "pick up" magazines they may not subscribe to or read on a regular basis. The audiences for magazines and newspapers are larger than just those who subscribe. People read copies in waiting rooms, friends' homes, coffee shops, libraries, and other public places. It is difficult to accurately know the "readership" of any particular magazine because of this secondary audience.

Some of the people I interviewed could describe specific themes about domestic violence that they remembered reading. Ann described the letters in the magazines that were about abuse. Most magazines have sections where readers can send questions to an "expert" who then gives advice in a column. Most of these columns deal with relationships. Ann remembered a question from a woman asking whether the person who was hitting her would change. Ann said that the expert usually told the victim to leave the relationship:

I used to read *Seventeen* when I was in high school. I used to read *Cosmopolitan* last year. There were letters that people had written. Like, "Will he change? He hits me occasionally and then he always says he's sorry. He'll be nice for awhile before it happens again and I always want to believe that he'll change." The advice columnist usually always says "Get out."

Even television advertising or previews for movies can be a source of reference for people. Sheri said that she remembers an advertisement for a movie on domestic violence in which a man was the victim. As illustrated in the following excerpt, she did not actually see the movie but remembered it from the previews. At least in her memory of the preview, she is able to describe quite a few details:

I do remember that there was a movie—I didn't watch it—but I remember seeing advertisements for a movie on TV and that was the premise of it. This lady was manic depressive and she'd be OK and everybody thought they had this wonderful relationship, but if things didn't go right and the pressure got to her she'd start throwing things, you know, like knives and dishes and stuff. And this guy loved his wife and never thought of it that way. I think it was called something like *Men Don't Tell*. I saw it advertised. But I didn't see it. I avoid those things like the plague.

Even though Sheri claimed that she avoids television movies "like the plague," she still remembered the advertisement and used it as a reference for talking about domestic violence.

I have provided a few examples to illustrate particular shows and sources that people use for thinking about social problems. It is important to understand not just what media people use, but *how* people use the media stories they encounter. Do they simply believe everything they see and hear, or are they able to critique it? And if so, how do people evaluate the media?

EVALUATING THE MEDIA

In my social problems class, students learn that social issues are never as simple as most media portrayals suggest.[6] After spending a semester learning about the construction of social problems, they are more equipped to critically evaluate how the media and others frame problems and to understand that there is almost always a lot more to the story. But this knowledge comes at a cost. Many students complain that it is no longer as much "fun" to watch media because they find themselves analyzing the framing process. Furthermore, they often feel overwhelmed and frustrated because social problems become much more complex for them. They realize that

there is not just one profile of an abuser or drug deal[...]
They understand that solutions are not simple. I try [...]
saying that understanding the complexities of social [...]
more effective teachers, journalists, lawyers, docto[...]
ever, they are right. It can be overwhelming and diff[...]
social problems after learning how complex they are[...]

Learning more about a social problem and gaini[...]
cally evaluate media messages do not happen only in a classroom. People
who are involved with social problems, such as victims, advocates, or
friends of victims, also learn a lot more about a social problem than just
what is in the media. These additional experiences help them to evaluate
media portrayals because they have something with which to compare
them. This became very clear to one of my students when she thought
about how her father, a lawyer, was able to critically evaluate legal television shows such as *Law & Order* but would not have the same ability to critique *ER*, a show about emergency rooms. People read and receive media
messages differently depending on their background experiences.

So how do people evaluate media messages? Are people able to be critical about how the media are portraying a social problem such as domestic violence? These questions have been investigated for many years.
Different media-effect models have provided different explanations for
how people can resist or critically evaluate media messages. The earliest
models gave the public very little credit (and sometimes no credit) for
evaluating media. For instance, Lazerfeld's two-step flow model, popular
in the late 1940s and 1950s, implied that the public had no resistance to
dominant media messages, which were transmitted through public opinion leaders (Lazarsfeld, Berelson, and Gaudet 1944; Katz and Lazarsfeld
1955; Golline 1988). Starting in the 1980s, other researchers began to
develop models that were more complex in explaining how people used
the media. Some scholars argue that people use the media for different reasons and that they have multiple interpretations, which vary according to
their backgrounds (Morley 1986; Radway 1984; Ang 1985; Kellner 1995;
Fiske 1987). For example, Morley, in his study of family television viewing,
argues that people's position in society influences how people use and
evaluate the media (Morley 1986). However, these models still do not go
far enough in explaining how individuals are able to resist the dominant
media message, what role personal experience plays in this resistance, and
what factors, such as lack of experience, may make some individuals more
susceptible than others to media messages.

In the following pages, I argue that unless people have experiences
other than media, they have difficulty critically evaluating what media say
about domestic violence or any other issue. First, I explain how those without firsthand experience use a hierarchy of credibility and are more likely

to evaluate the format rather than the content of the messages. Second, I argue that for many people it does not seem to matter that they often cannot remember where they have heard or read something. Even if the source of the information is forgotten, individuals may use those references to construct their own opinions. Furthermore, it may be that these images are even more powerful because they become "common knowledge." Finally, I will show how firsthand, and even secondhand, experiences help people critique media messages.

Hierarchy of Credibility

People have a hierarchy of credibility that helps them evaluate media. Elements of these hierarchies include general categories of media (e.g., print news vs. television), types of shows within media (e.g., tabloid talk shows vs. news), and whether the media are based on fiction or true stories.[7] Most of the people I interviewed thought that magazines and newspapers were more credible than television, even if television is the source of information most often referred to. According to Maria, "Whenever you read, you get the facts." Ann said that if she reads something in the *Chicago Tribune*, it must be pretty accurate. Shirley had a similar reaction to her women's magazine: "When I read the articles in the [*Ladies' Home*] *Journal*, I don't find myself doubting those stories. It's hard to understand the different issues, but I don't really doubt that they're true." Carol even has a hierarchy of credibility for magazines. She discusses how some tabloid magazines, which she calls "rag mags," are much less credible than *Good Housekeeping*. She believes the articles in *Good Housekeeping* are presented "honestly" and in "good taste." In general, Carol believes that magazines are more credible than newspapers, but both print sources are more credible than television. Like other individuals, Carol discussed her evaluation of media with terms like "good taste," "gory details," "emotionally manipulative," and "sensational":

> I think [women's magazine articles] are written in pretty good taste. *Good Housekeeping* is honest in the way they present their articles. I don't think they get into really gory, gory details. They are not like what they call these "rag mags" like you get in a grocery store that get into the graphic details. They [*Good Housekeeping*] present their articles honestly and are meant to educate people and hopefully try to get things turned around.

The "rag mags," though, printed "gory details," such as police photographs from the O. J. Simpson trial, which Carol thought were too sensational. Some news magazines and most talk shows were also considered too sensational to be credible. As Carol explains, the exception is *Oprah*, which many individuals believed was more credible than other talk shows.

Some of these network shows like *Hard Copy* are more sensational than TV news shows like *48 Hours*. If I am home, I will watch *Oprah*, but most of the rest of them, like *Jenny Jones*, is just garbage. Oprah has a different approach to all of this. It's not cheap and sensational and trying to dig up all the dirt they can. She discusses issues. She is very credible. Her shows are really worthwhile.

People also criticized media portrayals they thought were "overkill." As Sheri indicated, when people believe there is too much coverage of a problem, they evaluate those stories negatively:

> They are so emotionally manipulative. Not that this is necessarily a bad thing because that's what propaganda is. I think they have their place but it went from being "Oh my gosh, did you see that movie" to where they were just cranking them out. It was kind of overkill.

Coverage of the O. J. Simpson case was often given as an example of overkill and people claimed they learned little from it. According to Kathy:

> It got so long and so dragged out that you just get sick of hearing about it. I don't want to deal with it. I don't care anymore. If you get drowned out with this stuff in the media, you start to tune it out.

Another important factor people used in evaluating the media is whether or not media accounts are labeled as being based on true stories. While news stories are assumed to be based on reality, even if they are sensationalized, TV movies come in two versions: "based on true stories" and "fiction." People attributed much more credibility to the former. What is most important here is the label "true story" rather than how comprehensive and accurate the story is. "Based on a true story" does not mean that all the details are true. Still, seeing these words at the beginning of a show seems to matter for many people. Individuals often made a point of mentioning that a movie that they were using as a source of information was based on a true story. Although Maria has not observed any abusive relationships that she can compare to media portrayals, she does rely on the validity of "true stories." When describing a show that she had seen, Maria always indicated whether or not it was a true story. If it was not a true story, then she could not be sure how accurate it was. For instance, she is not sure whether men are really victims of domestic violence:

> All the movies I watch are all based on true stories so naturally I believe that there is violence. There is only one movie that I saw—and that was not based on a true story—that was the other way around. The wife was abusing the husband. So to me it seems that there is 100 percent abuse from men's side rather than women's side. There may be some, I'm sure there would be. But

in all the movies I've seen, the husband is abusing wife. The movie where I saw wife abusing husband wasn't based on true story. So I guess that does not count.

Although people attempt to judge media based on a hierarchy of credibility, their inability to remember the sources of information results in referring to "stories" and "facts" without remembering the specific source. Much of people's understanding of domestic violence seems to be constructed from forgotten sources.

Constructing Common Knowledge

It seems that when people hear something often enough, or perhaps when they forget where they heard it, they simply label that source as "common knowledge" or even "common sense." Although people have systems of evaluating sources of information, they often use information from forgotten sources. The very fact that sources are forgotten can give the information greater credibility as "common knowledge." Some media researchers have attempted to understand the path that media influence takes to impact individuals.[8] Theories about media influence often suggest that it matters who is talking in determining how much influence the message has on others. Certainly I agree that some people in our culture are granted more credibility than others. However, even if people are not able to remember the source of information, they may still use it. Michel Foucault, who wrote a lot about the connections between knowledge and power, argues that it does not matter so much who says something, but simply that it was said.[9] It matters more that ideas are in popular media than it matters who introduced those ideas. Even if the source of the information was forgotten, individuals use those references to construct their own opinions. As Foucault suggests, it does not seem to matter that individuals often cannot remember where they heard or read something. Even though individuals have a hierarchy of credibility for media sources, when asked about their understanding of domestic violence, they used any past references they could remember, even if they forgot the source. Sometimes media-based experiences even become "common knowledge."

Often the individuals in this study accepted as "fact" information apparently gleaned from media for which they can remember no specific media source. When asked where they had heard something or why they had that opinion, most people could not recount where they heard it. They just referred to "the media." Sheri mentioned that information on domestic violence will just "work into your consciousness." Later in the interview, she stopped and reflected on how she got her information: "It's funny because sometimes I'm sitting here thinking 'Where do I hear this stuff? Do I read it?'" Upon reflecting on where she gets her information, Sheri also wondered whether her opinion is her own or someone else's:

As I'm getting older I'm finding myself thinking, "Now is this what I really think or is this what I saw in the movie. And the heroine who I admired said it and now I think that." But it makes sense. If there is something in there that says that's right, that's right.

Similarly, Tim mentioned that he had a sense that his reference for answering the questions was a "generic news story." He could not remember specific people or stories, but rather had stock images in his head from which he drew:

I have this vague sense that I've been answering these questions based on what I've been picking up in the media. But I really still don't have a specific remembrance of some actual news story. I just have this vague generic news story in my head. I can't remember specific persons, or pictures but just sort of the stock news story about this kind of thing. And there have been many of them, which is why I probably can't remember one specifically.

Nevertheless, individuals provided "facts" about domestic violence from forgotten media sources. For instance:

Curtis: I think it is a significant problem. I can guess on numbers. Every fifteen minutes a woman is beaten. I don't know where I saw that or heard it. I don't even know if it is right. And I can't cite any specific examples, but perhaps the newspaper has given me some idea on how widespread it is.

Jackie: I don't have any specific examples but I know I have seen programs where they have made a correlation between an abusive person and someone who was abused when they were a child. And I've seen plenty of things where alcohol and drugs were involved.

Information from forgotten media sources, conversations with friends, and things that "just make sense" or are "common knowledge" blend together.[10] For instance, Carol talked about "natural born victims." When asked where she had heard this term, she had difficulty remembering, but was sold on the idea that there are "natural born victims":

I'm sure I've read it somewhere. I don't know if I've ever heard it discussed on television shows or just discussing things with coworkers that we've heard from various sources. I probably read about it from reference books like health books and self-help books.

Likewise, Ron says, "I think it is pretty common knowledge that the people who are abusers were most likely abused themselves as children." Even though Ron's information may have been derived from one or more television shows or magazine articles, labeling it "common knowledge" transforms it from a media claim to something that everyone knows. Forgetting the specific source, then, may actually give the information more credibility.

Using Other Experiences to Evaluate the Media

The people I interviewed who had firsthand experience with abuse were less likely to use the media as a main source of information and had a greater variety of experiences to draw upon to understand domestic violence. These sources include their own abuse, stories from friends, their experience with advocates and other professionals, as well as references from the media. This variety of experience allows them to have a more complex interpretation of media messages. Even people who had secondhand experiences with abuse were able to use those to evaluate the media.

The victims of domestic violence critiqued the content of the media rather than just using a hierarchy of credibility. Their critique of media portrayals of domestic violence included concerns that the media contribute to the normalization of abuse, are not proactive enough, and do not portray the "average person." Gina, who uses her own experience to critique the way television portrays abuse, is especially concerned about the normalization of abuse in relationships that the media tend to portray:

> In these shows [nighttime dramas] or even the daytime soaps, it's like somebody strikes somebody out of anger. It's like "You little bitch. Pow." And then the soap goes on and you don't see the victim ever go, "That's it. I'm out of here." So the day-to-day role models on television, nobody ever has the attitude of "If you ever strike me once—and that's all it takes is once—I'm out of here." There's always the rationalizations to stay in. So I think that's bad from the media point of view. It's like "there is physical violence in all relationships and that's just the way things are."

Gina not only criticized the way some media portray abuse, but also discussed how the media could be better used for reducing domestic violence:

> I think that the commercials that they have on—the little kid watching mom and dad fight—those kind of public service announcements are good. They are very effective. They do play low and dirty and pull on the heart strings. The public service announcements are important but it seems like they are only on in the evening. I think they should be run all the time—in the middle of the soaps, and in the middle of kids' cartoons.

Gina explained that the "constant things like commercials" would be better than the half-hour news report or the two-hour made-for-TV movie. She said that it is a "subconscious factor." She says that commercials on domestic violence may send subliminal messages to people like "in the soap operas where somebody gets slapped and the relationship goes on because that's just the way it is."

Like Gina, Jerrad—whose mother abused him as a child—criticized the media for not being proactive in its coverage of domestic violence: "It seems like the only time it [domestic violence] is brought up is when something goes wrong. They [media] don't try to deal with it before. So you never see how we can deal with the situation until it happens." Jerrad also criticizes the media for spending so much time covering sports heroes instead of "the average person":

> They [media] seem to think that it's worse if a sports figure does it than an average person—like they are somehow different. They always put them up on a pedestal and they're like role models and don't do anything wrong. When they do, they're shunned upon. So they get all this coverage while Joe Schmoe down the street is beating his wife and it probably won't even get an article in the paper.

People use their own firsthand experience to point out particular media portrayals of domestic violence that they thought were right on track. Barbara identified with scenes from *The Burning Bed*:

> I remember once that *Burning Bed* story that was a long time ago. The way her parents were is a perfect example of how some people look at it. Law enforcement. Men on the police force tend to look at it as she deserved it or he had a reason for it. It's ignorance. A lack of self-esteem on their [police's] part that they think it is necessary.

Even having secondhand experience with abuse enabled the interviewees to have more complex evaluations of the media. Having experiences beyond the media allowed them to compare and validate, or invalidate, their media-based experiences. Two of the men interviewed used secondhand experience to help gauge whether or not the media were accurate in their depiction of domestic violence. Doug doubted that the movie *Rosewood* was a realistic portrayal of abuse because of his cousin's abusive experience. He said that his cousin was hit a lot in the stomach and ribs where you couldn't see it. He contrasted that to the movie:

> Probably the most recent one was *Rosewood*. I think [domestic violence] was portrayed pretty well. Guy punching, kicking, hitting a girl. It showed her black and blue with a broken nose. I think that it probably is not as realistic as some of the more common abuse. [More common is] probably unseen, punching in the stomach. Abuse that can't be seen by the public.

James thought media depictions were accurate when they mirrored personal observations:

I think for the most part it is accurate. Especially when you can see it in print and on TV and then see it happen in the workplace situation. Then, it's like oh, that's true. Then you have a personal experience of it.

Those with firsthand experience were more likely to avoid media portrayals, especially television movies. Barbara, for instance, who has experienced abuse in an adult relationship, described how she did not like watching TV movies about domestic violence because they caused her to relive her pain through television:

The stalker stories. They are documentaries. They are real life. I don't want to watch them. I realize that there are bad things in the world like that but it's just too hard for me. I live alone and I've had some serious problems myself and I don't need that. It's just too sad. It's vivid. You can see it happening. Words are not as explicit as seeing blood. I don't like horror movies and that is a mild form of horror movie. I just don't feel that is necessary in my life. I know what it is.

Other research shows that women with firsthand experience with violence "objected to the portrayal of violence against women as 'entertainment' and resented how such representations elicited painful memories" (Schlesinger, Dobash, Dobash, and Weaver 1992:15). Women with personal experience were more likely to critique the media portrayal of violence against women than those with no firsthand experience. "Viewers with such life-experience were more sensitive to televised violence, more subtle and complex in their readings, more concerned about possible effects and more demanding in their expectations of the producers of such content" (ibid.:165). Also, women with personal experience were less likely to accept excuses offered for men's violence against women than those women with no firsthand experience with violence.

My interviews with people with first- or secondhand experience show how they are able to critique the media using their experience. They also suggest that the more experience people have with abuse, the more critical they are of the media. These findings provide a contrast to the more limited critical abilities of those with only media-based experience. The next section continues to explore how victims of abuse understand domestic violence compared to those people who rely on their media experience.

COMPARING THE TOUR GUIDES: MEDIA VS. LIVED EXPERIENCE

One way to explore how the media influence public opinion is to compare those people who use the media as their main source of information with those who instead rely on their lived experience. The main point I want to make here is that people with lived experience have a harder time "making sense" of the social problem. They appear to see more of the landscape of domestic violence and have a more complex understanding of the problem compared to those who rely on the media for their information. Those who use the media have an easier time "making sense" of the problem—at least in making sense of the victims. People who use the media but have little other information to help critique the media use simpler frames to explain why victims stay. Their explanations reflect the "official reality" of the problem that is disseminated through the media.

Victims Talk about Domestic Violence

Gina, a thirty-one-year-old woman, has already been a victim in several abusive relationships. Her first abusive experience was with her first high school boyfriend. Gina often expresses wonder about why victims stay in abusive relationships, even though she has experienced several herself. She wonders, "Why does it take so long for people to get out? It's kind of sad that people get so sad and desperate that they cling to little nuggets of goodness." The topic of "why victims stay" came up at other points in the interview. When asked when she could remember first hearing about domestic violence, Gina referred to what she believed would have been a typical reaction of a child after seeing domestic violence on TV. Although she seems to be recreating this image, what is striking is her understanding that "logical assumptions" would lead a child to ask about why the victim stays in a relationship rather than why someone would be so abusive:

> [The first time I heard about domestic violence was] probably watching a movie or something on TV as a kid and somebody is being horrible to somebody else. "Why don't they just leave?" The innocent question from the child, "Why don't they just leave?" I remember no clear incident but I'm sure, or I'm following logical assumptions, that you'd ask something like that to your parents.

Gina said that many of her conversations with friends who had also experienced abuse focused on why they stayed in the relationship:

> I think the conversations with friends have been telling war stories—personal stories or this happened to my friend kind of thing. There was a lot of "How the hell could we have been so stupid." "I can't believe I stayed in this relationship for two and a half years and it took until getting to this point before I got out." Later when I got into another abusive relationship, I didn't wait for it to get that bad.

Gina's focus on her own victimization rather than the abuser came through in her description of her first abusive relationship. Gina said that as far as she knew, her boyfriend had not abused any of his other girl-friends, so she wondered why she was different. Also, when asked what she thought caused domestic violence, Gina turned the question into a focus on the victims:

> Hard to tell. In some ways that's like, "What causes some people to be vic-tims?" Who knows? Maybe it's fate. Some of it is like that's what the person grew up with and they're just walking in the shoes of their parents.

Like Gina, the other individuals who had experienced abuse in an adult relationship discussed how they still could not understand why it takes so long for victims to leave the abusive relationship. Randy said that when he thought about his first marriage, in which his wife was abusive, he won-dered why he stayed for so many years. He said, "I should have ended my marriage on the honeymoon. It just got off to a bad start. I wonder why people stay in situations where they're not happy."

Although Barbara wonders why "men do it"—referring to the abuse—she also continues to wonder "why women let men do it":

> I don't understand why women let men do it to them and I don't understand why men find it necessary to do it. I just can't understand that. I have a brother-in-law who married his second wife. She was a very assertive woman. Put together. She knew what she was doing, knew where she was going or so it seemed to me. I saw her at my daughter's wedding and they'd been married for at least ten years now. She was a mouse. She had turned into this person who just didn't have the self confidence anymore. I was so shocked. And it was my brother-in-law who did it to her. And she let him.

Linda talked about a neighbor she knew who was in an abusive rela-tionship. She thought it was odd that this woman would endure the abuse. When asked if she still thought it was odd that the neighbor stayed after she herself had experienced abuse, she said,

> I still thought less of this neighbor for having gone through it than I would have if I thought she didn't endure it. Somehow there was a criticism within me of her because she did submit herself to that.

Those who have firsthand experience are not just focusing on the vic-tim's behavior in analyzing the problem. Other research studies, including the public opinion surveys discussed in Chapter 2, also show that victims have a greater awareness of the social and cultural factors involved com-pared to those who only rely on the media. Victims are more likely than nonvictims to believe that cultural and social factors contribute to domes-tic violence. For example, abused women were more likely to believe that factors such as a man's desire to control women, people accepting violence toward woman as normal, people not offering to help abused women, and cultural norms tolerating family violence are major contributors to domestic violence (Nabi and Horner 2001). Another major difference between victims and nonvictims is that victims are more likely to favor legal intervention that protects the victim and punishes the abuser. People who have been victims of domestic violence believe that the criminal justice system should emphasize protection of the victim more than keeping the family together. People who have not been victims of abuse are more likely to support policies that emphasize family preservation. Victims of domestic violence are also more likely to want harsher penalties for batterers, an increase of guilty verdicts, and restraining orders against men who commit domestic violence even without a prior history of abuse (Stalans and Lurigio 1995).

Those who have experienced abuse were not explicitly blaming victims for staying in the relationship, but rather their questions and comments reflect the complexity of the problem as interpreted through lived experience. One way to think about the difference between media experience and lived experience is to consider how a football player understands a game in which he played compared to a fan who watches the game's highlights on ESPN. The fan who watches the game's highlights may learn the score of the game, some select "key" plays, controversial calls by officials, and maybe some statistics for a couple of the players. The player, though, has a much more complex understanding of the game. Though the player also knows the score of the game, he might not feel the score tells the whole story. He might disagree with the "key" plays that the ESPN producers chose to tell the story. The ESPN highlights simplify the game so that it is easier to make sense of what happened at the game. People who use the media to understand domestic violence are able to explain some highlights of the problem, but the person who has actually experienced the problem knows that there is much more to it than what the media highlights.

Do the Media Simplify the Story?

Media and advocates help shape what Loseke calls the "official reality" of domestic violence (Loseke 1998). A significant claims-maker in shaping the official reality of domestic violence is the battered women movement. This movement has helped spread the "reasons" why victims have trouble leaving abusive relationships. Most individuals who used the media as a main source of information are able to repeat these reasons, including financial problems, love, guilt, threats, and no social support. These ideas emerged out of early psychological and sociological research on battered women and were disseminated through the media after the late 1970s, when the battered women movement helped to gain public, scholarly, and media attention on the subject. Though not all researchers agree on these "reasons," they have become "common knowledge" in the sense that they are found regularly in the media.

People with no firsthand experience reflect the "official reality" of abuse. As I explained in the previous chapter, even people with no experience of domestic violence have increased their "understanding" of victims over the past several decades. Their descriptions of the problem are more clear-cut, formal, and typified than those who have firsthand experience with abuse. While individuals with no domestic violence experience are able to repeat justifications of battered women's behavior found in the media, former victims continue to wonder why victims stay in abusive relationships. Victims do not have a neatly packaged explanation for why victims stay. They articulate the problem as consisting of complex, confusing events. This finding supports Loseke's research on the confrontation between battered women's personal realities and a shelter's official reality. She finds that at the level of lived experience, the troubles are not easily understood and are often "experienced as a bewildering complex tangle of events" (Loseke 1998:294). However, it is the official reality, the neatly packaged explanations, that are most powerful in the media.

People with firsthand experience with abuse have a harder time "making sense" of domestic violence compared to those who primarily use the media to understand the issue. Similarly to the experience of my students, the more people learn about a social problem through life experience, the more complicated their understanding of the problem becomes. Though people with firsthand experience did not have the neatly packaged explanations of why victims stay, their questions and comments reflect the complexity of abusive relationships. Part of this complexity can be seen in the ability of individuals with firsthand experience to critique the content of media portrayals of domestic violence. They react against these neatly packaged descriptions of domestic violence. I do not think they are "blaming" victims (or themselves) for staying, but rather are more aware of how complicated the problem is and that the simpler media frames do not make sense to them. It is the official reality, the neatly packaged explanations, that are most powerful in the media. Therefore, it is these simpler frames that most people use to understand the problem, and, thus, they miss much of the landscape of any complex social problem.

CONCLUSION

It is important to understand that most people are not "doing research" on social problems when they watch movies or read magazine articles. They are not necessarily seeking out information and then using television movies as their main source. If they need to do a presentation on a topic, or if they have a friend who needs help, they may be more likely to search the Internet, call an advocate at the local domestic violence shelter, or go to the library to check out a book. I am not suggesting that these are always better sources, but they are more likely to offer a broader range of perspectives. However, we absorb information about social problems through the media even if we are not always aware of it or deliberately seeking out information. This information becomes part of our "experience," and we come back to it when we need to make decisions or interpret new situations. Television movies, magazine articles, and advertising are all part of the media culture in which we live. The media culture "helps shape everyday life, influencing how people think and behave, how they see themselves and other people, and how they construct their identities" (Kellner 1995:2). Newspaper columns, magazine articles, films, made-for-TV movies, television special reports, and talk shows are all public arenas where images of domestic violence and other social problems are framed. The stories that the media tell are likely to be the stories people use to talk about domestic violence. The media are the most common tour guides that many people use for learning about this problem.

It is not always the case that people use only mass media to understand social problems. For example, I hope that students in my domestic violence class use their course texts and our class discussions to understand the problem rather than just renting movies on the topic. Furthermore, victims are more likely to draw from their own firsthand experience or from professionals to understand the problem than to just rely on the media. And people whose work involves domestic violence, such as police officers, lawyers, counselors, and advocates, may use work-related experiences to help them understand the problem. However, even for all these people, media references are available and likely help shape their understanding of the problem.

What people experience, whether firsthand or through the media, serves as a foundation of knowledge from which they make sense of social problems like domestic violence. From these resources, individuals construct their own conceptions of what is normal and acceptable. These conceptions, which Cicourel calls "background expectancies," govern all social interaction. These background expectancies enable individuals "to search for 'valid' explanations of 'what happened' and justify decisions" (Cicourel 1968:53). We use existing frames of social problems to help interpret new experiences. If you are called to sit on a jury involving a case about domestic violence, you will draw on your background expectancies to help figure out "what's going on."

During my interviews, I was fascinated to hear so many people describe how the media have helped them learn about the complications that abuse victims face. They articulated many of the problems that advocates and researchers on domestic violence have been discussing for the past three

decades. Most of the individuals I spoke to showed an increased understanding of the dynamics of abusive relationships—for the victim. However, they also reflect the absence—or at least minimal presence—of
popular discourse on abusers. Although there are many academic theories
about domestic violence, most people use the popular media to get their
information. Talk shows, movies, popular magazines, television news
shows, and newspapers all construct images of domestic violence. Why is
it that people who use the media know more about the victim but also continue to hold the victim responsible for solving the problem? Because the
media are such a significant source of information, we need to investigate
how the media frame domestic violence. What are these media stories saying about domestic violence and who is being held responsible for solving
the problem? The next few chapters investigate how and why the media
portray domestic violence.

NOTES

1. To read more about the role of media in shaping people's perceptions see
Croteau and Hoynes (2000), Altheide (2002), Holstein and Miller (1993), Sasson
(1995), Gamson and Modigliani (1989), Berger (1991), Gamson (1992), Kellner
(1995).

2. I borrow from Aaron Cicourel's (1968) concept of background expectancies.
Cicourel says that we all have background expectancies that we acquire through
experience that we then use to make sense of new situations and to make decisions.

3. For more information on comic books and juvenile delinquency see Nyberg
(1998).

4. For an overview of the research on media effects see Surette (1998).

5. I did not set out to compare victims of abuse with those who had no firsthand
experience with abuse. However, in listening to the individuals discuss how they
have come to understand domestic violence, it became clear that the differences
in experience shaped how they used the media and how they talked about the
problem.

6. In this course I use the following texts: Loseke (2003), Loseke and Best (2003),
and Best (2001).

7. Donileen Loseke (2003) uses the concept of hierarchy of credibility to explain
that audiences of social problems hold some claims-makers as more credible than
others. Here I use the term to explain how individuals judge some types of media
as more credible than others.

8. To read about earlier theories on media effects see, for example, Lazarsfeld et
al. (1944) and Gamson (1992).

9. I borrow from Foucault's work on knowledge and power. "What Matter
Who Is Speaking; Someone Has Said: What Matter Who Is Speaking" (Foucault
1991:72; see also Foucault 1979).

10. Gamson (1992) treats popular wisdom as an independent source of information that people use to evaluate media. But this study suggests that "popular
wisdom" cannot easily be separated from the media.

4

Women's Magazines:
The Victim Empowerment Frame

During an episode of the *Sally Jessy Raphael* show, three wives tell the host and audience about their controlling husbands. One by one the women are brought on stage to talk about the abuse and control their husbands inflict on them. When their husbands are eventually brought out, the audience boos them and Sally reads each of them the riot act. The last ten minutes of the show are spent with the "expert" who is there to give the couples advice. The expert says that although she is concerned about the husbands, she is more concerned about the wives. She asks them where along the way they lost their power. Why did they allow their men to abuse them? The audience cheers and claps as the expert "empowers" the victims. The victims struggle to answer the question. They struggle to figure out how they ever had power. Eventually, most of them seem to agree that they must have lost their power and that was why their husbands are abusing them.

The show just described illustrates a particular framing of domestic violence that I call victim empowerment. Not only is domestic violence portrayed as a private problem, but most often it is the *victim's* problem, and she has the responsibility for solving it. It locates the victim's experiences within a frame that ignores not only the role of the abuser, but also that of society. The victim empowerment perspective tells "it happened to me" stories that show how the victim got herself into the situation and how she solved it. It is sympathetic to the victims, but they continue to be held responsible for solving the problem. They are told to find solutions within themselves: "Change your personality." "Increase your self-esteem." "Take control of your life." "Refuse to be a victim." "You have the power to end the abuse." The dominant focus is on victims' needs, "syndromes," stories, and responsibilities. Once you become familiar with it, I predict you will notice the frequent use of victim empowerment on television talk shows, made-for-TV movies, women's magazines, the Internet, classrooms, and everyday conversations. In this chapter, I will illustrate the dominance of the victim empowerment frame over other possible frames through a comprehensive analysis of women's magazines. I focus in-depth on women's magazines, not because victim empowerment is necessarily more dominant there than other media, but in order to show changes over time (I analyzed articles from the past thirty years), to compare how different genres cover domestic violence (Chapters 6 and 7 look at men's and political magazines), and to follow the editorial process that shapes the articles, which is examined in the next chapter.

WHO IS RESPONSIBLE? FRAMING DOMESTIC VIOLENCE AS THE VICTIM'S PROBLEM

When analyzing media portrayals of social problems, I am particularly interested in the issues of cause and solution. Who is held responsible for causing the problem? Who is responsible for solving it? I use the term *frame of responsibility* to describe the way responsibility is assigned in these articles, which impacts what solutions are suggested (e.g., women leaving the abusive relationship, tougher punishment for abusers). After doing a careful analysis of 139 articles about domestic violence in women's magazines, I discovered four frames of responsibility: (1) individuals, i.e., the victims and/or abusers involved; (2) institutions, such as the legal and medical systems; (3) cultural and structural factors, such as societal attitudes, gender role socialization, and the economy; and (4) an integrated analysis focusing on the interaction among individual, institutional, cultural, and structural factors. In this chapter I describe each of these frames in more detail and illustrate them with quotes from articles.

In my analysis of women's magazine articles on domestic violence, I found that 67 percent of the articles use the frame of individual responsibility, and the majority of these articles focus on what I call the victim empowerment perspective. Other articles may not rely entirely on the victim empowerment perspective, but still focus on the victim. Responsibility for solving domestic violence is placed on victims by highlighting the "victim's problem" as the main story. Victims are also held responsible for getting into the abusive relationship in the first place and for provoking the abuse, which is part of the story told when discussing the "couple's problem." A few alternative story lines show up in women's magazines that place the responsibility for domestic violence on institutional, structural, and cultural issues, but they are overshadowed by the more dominant "victim's problem" story line.

I tell you about these four frames of responsibility for two reasons. One is to give a better sense of how I approached the analysis and to show the dominance of the one frame over the others. But the more important reason is to point out that there are ways to write an article about domestic violence, or other social problems, without using an individual frame of responsibility. The dominance of the individual frame of responsibility is an issue not only for women's magazines, but other media as well.

Women's Magazines

Women's magazines are those that are written for and about women and are usually described as "women's magazines" in market-related publications (Endres and Lueck 1995; Gage and Coppess 1994; Holm 1997). Women's magazines offer an interesting perspective on women's issues, often introducing social problems and issues in more detail than other mass media. They also try to capture the changing roles and responsibilities of women. The magazines I use in this study are listed along with the number of articles on domestic violence indicated in parentheses: *Essence* (20), *Glamour* (27), *Good Housekeeping* (18), *Ladies' Home Journal* (28), *Mademoiselle* (7), *McCall's* (10), *Redbook* (12), *Seventeen* (5), *'Teen* (8), and *Vogue* (4). I read all the articles that had domestic violence as their main topic for the time period 1970–2002.[1] There are fourteen articles from 1970 to 1979, thirty-six articles from 1980 to 1989, seventy-five articles from 1990 to 1999, and fourteen articles from 2000 to 2002. I focused on these particular women's magazines for two reasons. First, they all existed from 1970 through 2002, with the exception of *McCall's,* which became *Rosie* in 2001 and subsequently went out of business. The 1970–2002 time frame is important because it covers the emergence of domestic violence as a problem since the battered women movement of the 1970s. A second criterion I used was a large circulation because I wanted to get a sense of how mass media portray domestic violence. All these magazines reached a paid circulation level of 750,000 by 1985.

For my analysis, domestic violence is defined as physical, sexual, and/or psychological abuse that occurs between two adults in an intimate relationship regardless of marital status or sexual orientation.[2] However, all of the articles in these magazines focused primarily on heterosexual relationships.[3]

THE INDIVIDUAL FRAME OF RESPONSIBILITY

The individual frame of responsibility places responsibility for domestic violence on one or more individuals in the abusive relationship. This frame, which was found in 67 percent of all articles, commonly includes case histories of relationships and descriptions of individual actions. Solutions rooted in this frame remain on the individual level and are primarily focused on intervention, not prevention. The most common solutions suggested in these articles are counseling and the woman leaving the relationship—and typically hold her responsible for taking all the actions needed to leave. Though placing responsibility on the individual level could include casting blame on abusers, these articles downplay the role of abusers. Only two articles using this frame focus primarily on abusers.

There are three different categories of articles within the individual frame: (1) victim empowerment perspective, (2) focus on the couple, and (3) focus on the batterer. Victims are held responsible for solving the problem of domestic violence in both the victim empowerment and the couple categories. In "the couple's story," which accounts for 20 percent of the articles in the individual frame, the victims are blamed for provoking the abuse. In the empowerment perspective, which includes 77 percent of articles in this frame, victims are called to end the abuse or prevent it. All together, victims are held responsible for the problem in over 97 percent of all articles using an individual frame. When including all articles from all four frames, the individual focus of *victim* responsibility shows up 65 percent of the time, that is, in approximately two out of every three articles.

Victim Empowerment

In the victim empowerment perspective, power is defined as a personal choice. Women are told they need to "take back the power" to "take charge of their lives." Victims are held responsible in a "sympathetic" way that is often described as "empowering." In a typical domestic violence article in women's magazines, the reader learns about an abuse victim's horrible situation, including the history of how the couple got together and the early signs of abuse. Then we learn at some point what happened to give the victim the "courage" to end the abuse. Usually the abuse ends because the victim got counseling and changed her behavior or because she left the relationship. Five common themes are found in this perspective: (1) how victims should solve their own problems; (2) how "potential victims" should prevent abuse; (3) battered women who kill their abusers; (4) how friends and family can help victims; and (5) "life after abuse" stories. All of these themes focus on the responsibility of victims.

How Victims Should Solve Their Own Problems. Attributing responsibility to the victim for solving the problem of domestic violence is typified by the *Good Housekeeping* series "My Problem and How I Solved It," in which an anonymous woman relates a case history of an abusive marriage and what she did to solve this problem.[4] The first "My Problem and How I Solved It" article focusing on domestic violence appeared in 1972. In it a woman tells her story of being in an abusive marriage and what she did to put an end to that abuse. A counselor told her that she had been challenging her husband too much and that was contributing to the abuse.

> One important clue, to us, came when the counselor pointed out that every time Jim and I had fought physically, it had been when I had challenged his "control" of a situation. And this, the counselor showed us, was especially crucial in our case because it was so terribly important to Jim to have the feeling that he was in control of his domestic life. ("Our Home Was a Battlefield" 1972:86)

With the help of a counselor, she says that she better understood what she was doing to provoke her husband, as well as how she could alleviate his pressure. At the end of the story, she tells how they are still together and working toward solving the problem. This particular article focuses more on how the victim needed to change her own behavior to *save* the marriage. Typically, this advice is found more often in "the couple" stories, which are explained later.

Though that first article focused on a couple that is still together, most "My Problem and How I Solved It" articles on domestic violence end with the victim telling how she left the abusive relationship. In 1996, *Good Housekeeping* published a "My Problem and How I Solved It" article focusing on how one woman escaped a marriage riddled with emotional abuse. Though the type of abuse discussed differs—emotional rather than physical—the message remains the same: women are responsible for ending the abuse.

Other magazines also publish articles that indicate the victim needs to change her behavior in order to save the marriage. In an early *Glamour* article, a battered woman wished she had seen the signs earlier and tried to work through the problems in her marriage:

> Now, I look back and see clearly the signs I missed, signs that, if heeded, might have allowed us to get help to work through the problems and begin again. Besides being alert for all these factors, I would—and this is important—*pay attention*. Instead of looking at anything but the bruises, as I did, I would stop everything at the first shove or kick or punch. It is a problem. It has a solution. And I would try to admit that, we, *not he*, had problems that needed fixing. (Bedard 1978:85-86)

Most women's magazine articles on domestic violence include a couple's historical section on how the victim allowed herself to get into the abusive relationship. These articles also explain why women stay with men who beat them. The authors often emphasize that victims "choose" to stay with their abusers. In an *Essence* article the author says, "This week

I've received calls from two close friends who have chosen to remain with men who physically batter them" (Weems 1988:81). She later explains why women choose to stay: "A woman chooses to remain with her batterer for various reasons. Some of those reasons have to do with economics. . . . Some reasons are physical: She prefers a busted lip to an empty bed" (Weems 1988:84).

Part of the explanation for why women stay in abusive relationships often includes "women's personalities." In a *Mademoiselle* article on "what no one understands about abused women," the author says that women may be more likely than men to fall prey to mind games and manipulation. She explains why women do not leave, or if they do, why they go back to the abuser:

> The obvious question in the face of such a roller coaster of emotional manipulation is why doesn't the woman just leave? Yet leaving is often the last thing she will consider. Or, if she does, she will again fall for her abuser's charm, believe his promises and apologies and end up right back where she was. (Feeney 1989:268)

Other authors claim that it was love that keeps victims in abusive relationships:

> I know this is incredibly difficult for anybody to understand, Burnham says. It's difficult for me to understand. People always ask: "Why do they stay? What's *wrong* with them? Why didn't they get out?" My explanation to myself is that I was madly in love. (Jetter 1994:106)

One of the reasons most articles discuss the victim's "choice" in staying in the abusive relationship is to set up the next step in the argument: If victims are choosing to stay, then they can choose to leave. These articles are sympathetic to victims. As I said before, the main point is to "empower" the victims. Therefore, these stories are set up to show the victim's role in the abuse. Battered women who have left their abusive relationships give other victims advice and encouragement to do the same thing: "Just get out. The power is within you."

When battered women themselves write for women's magazines, they often discuss what finally made them leave. In a *Glamour* article, this "breaking point" is discussed:

> A woman involved in a violent courtship *can* break that cycle and change her life, if something happens to make her want to. She may be so badly beaten that she fears she will die. Or she may simply wake up one morning and decide that she's had enough. (Baker 1983:367)

Sometimes the breaking point is an escalation of the abuse:

But the marriage had ended for me forever the moment I felt the blade of the knife against my throat. I'd wanted to leave Steve before, but that night I knew I had to leave him. I realized then that it was beyond my power to save him, but that I must save myself. (Lewis 1990:259)

My second trip to the hospital broke down some inner wall of resistance. I knew that if I continued like this, I might lose everything, even my life. (Sales 1995:118)

Most of the articles that encourage victims to end abuse plead with women to take control of their lives and get out. The message is that victims are allowing the abuse to happen and they need to realize that it will not end until they make it end. Authors give advice on how to leave and encourage victims to take control:

Making a decision to leave your home and a life of abuse will be difficult. Your husband may even try to stop you, but you must take action now! Abused wives must come out of the closet and put an end to this terrible practice. (Webb 1987:14)

"Don't be a victim," Dr. Briggs said. I knew he was talking to me. "If you don't like your life, fix it. Don't feel sorry for yourself. It will destroy you. If you want to be happy, accept responsibility for your own lives. (Kays 1997:78)

Women are emphatically told to not allow men to abuse them. One battered woman told her readers, "I'll never shake my fear of him, but if I've learned anything from all of this, it's that women cannot allow themselves to be silenced by abusive men" (Golding and Frishman 1996:69). *'Teen* and *Seventeen,* both magazines aimed at young girls, use this victim focus in all of their articles on dating violence. Young victims are told to stand up for themselves and get the help they need:

If your boyfriend is abusing you, you must tell others immediately. You're in great danger if you keep it hidden, since the violence could get worse. You need to use the resources that are available to you—parents, friends, school counselors—to get the support that you need to break away from him and get yourself back on your feet. (Woodward 1990:84)

Often battered women lament that they could have gotten out sooner had they just realized what was going on—had they paid attention to the warning signs:

I should have known this man was dangerous. We all say that. And maybe
we should have known. Certainly, there were signs—flashes of temper, lies.
But I chose to be blinded by romance. He left his girlfriend for me; he sent
flowers; he was passionate, attentive. (Davis 1998:70)

One victim said she ignored the warning signs because she did not love
herself enough:

"The signs that he would one day attack me were everywhere, but I ignored
them," she says. "I didn't love myself enough to end it. I accepted his 'I'm
sorry's, his tears, his candy, and I went back into the lion's den every time."
(Bowman 1998:146)

Victims say they are angry with themselves for not doing something
sooner:

"A lot of my anger now is directed toward myself," she told me recently. "I'm
mad at *me*, I didn't have to stick around and be abused all those years!"
(Rock 1983:58)

I'm not bitter. I don't blame Jake for everything that happened in our relationship. I hold myself responsible for my own actions and choices. Forgiv-
ing myself has been the hardest part. ("Boyfriend Abuse: Troubled Love"
1995:53)

Victims are often portrayed as being confused as to why they let the
abuse continue. They now realize they did not have to allow the abuse to
happen:

Even now I'm baffled that I allowed the abuse to continue for so long—and
all while I prosecuted other abusers. I now listen to the advice I have so often
given to other women: No one can steal my dignity and self-worth unless I
give them up. (Harrison 1999:94)

Former victims will say that they should have seen the warning signs
and gotten out sooner. But, they say, it is not too late for others to realize
what is happening:

Physical abuse rarely comes as a surprise. It's usually preceded by verbal
abuse—harsh words, name-calling. Then comes a push, a shove, a slap.
There are always signs, and we must be discerning enough to assess whether
someone deserves to have a front-row seat in our life. (Taylor 1994:65)

In many of the articles, the women say that they are telling their stories
to encourage other victims of domestic violence to get help. Frequently,
they are pleading with women to end the abuse:

That's why I decided to write about my experience . . . in the hope that other women who may be secretly suffering as I did will be helped by knowing that they are not alone. There is something that can be done about ending marital violence. ("Our Home Was a Battlefield" 1972:86)

Show yourself some respect by seeking the help that you need to end the abuse. Don't forget: The power to change things is within you! (Woodward 1990:92)

The formerly battered women tell their painful stories because they want to inspire their audience:

These memories are painful to recollect, but perhaps other women out there reading this will sigh in relief to find they are not the only ones who made foolish choices, then even more foolishly stood by them. More important, perhaps they will be moved to get help and get out. (Davis 1998:73)

The stories are designed to inspire other victims to take charge of their life and solve their problem. The endings are positive "success" stories because the woman solves the problem. The victim is her own hero. Most stories show how much better the victim is doing since she left:

I want victims of emotional abuse to know that a new start *is* possible. I didn't realize just how miserable I was until I got out of my abusive situation. Shortly after the divorce, Robert moved away. My friends tell me that I rarely smiled in the later years of my marriage, but now I smile all the time. I've also begun dating. But I no longer tolerate certain behaviors. (Burgdorff and Block 1996:89)

But often this new life includes figuring out why they let the abuse happen. Figuring out why they gave away their power is a central part to their healing:

Seeing a therapist is also crucial to making a new life for myself. It's not enough to just escape Dave. I need to understand who I was when I was with him and why I put up with the abuse if I really want to make sure I never get in that kind of relationship again. I just keep telling myself, "Today I'm strong enough for today, and tomorrow I'll be strong enough for tomorrow." I've been through so much already, and it's time to start living life for me. (Vander Pluym 1999:75)

How "Potential Victims" Should Prevent Abuse. Encouraging victims to solve their problem by ending the abuse is not the only theme that holds people responsible for their own victimization. Another assumption in the victim empowerment perspective is that women should be able to prevent many abusive situations by being aware of the warning signs. Learning how to recognize the warning signs of abuse is a theme that focuses on "potential victims" and places responsibility on them for preventing abuse from happening. Many stories on domestic violence include tips for women on how to recognize abusers and avoid being in an abusive relationship. For example, as I mentioned earlier, most victim empowerment stories include advice on how to leave an abusive relationship; they also warn people to avoid relationships at the first sign of abuse. Learning how to prevent abuse is a particularly common focus in young women's magazines, including 'Teen and Seventeen. Preventing abusive situations is also a common focus for my students and the individuals I interviewed, as I discussed in Chapter 2.

Frequently, articles list characteristics that are common in batterers, such as excessive jealousy, verbal abusiveness, controlling behavior, and inability to control anger. 'Teen lists warning signs for recognizing "loser guys." For example, "A loser guy will hurt you on purpose. If he hits you, twists your arm, kicks you, shoves you, pulls your hair or breaks your favorite things EVEN ONCE, forget him" (Carstens 1996:57). These warning signs are not discussed from the point of view of how to help the batterer change these behaviors but rather on how women have the responsibility for recognizing these warning signs and to then end the relationship:

> If you're seeing someone, and you're wondering if he might become abusive, watch out for jealousy—if he doesn't want you to be with your friends or tries to alienate you from the life you had before you got together with him. Also, anyone who calls you names or puts you down, that's not love. If someone's treating you like that, get out. Don't think that just by telling him to knock it off, he'll stop. (Hamlin 1993:46)

Other articles give advice on how to choose nonabusive relationships from the beginning. In Essence, a columnist gives the following advice for avoiding abusive relationships:

> Take responsibility for creating the relationship you desire. This means being proactive. You'll be clear about what you will and will not accept in a relationship. When you assume responsibility for your level of commitment and participation in your own life, magic happens. You become a partner and contributor rather than a victim. (Vanzant 2002:96)

The articles focus on how the "potential victims" have the responsibility for avoiding these relationships, rather than focusing on how these "potential batterers" should seek help and change their behaviors. Therefore, the responsibility is still being placed on victims—or potential victims.

Battered Women Who Kill Their Abusers.   Killing their abusers is the most extreme example of victims having to solve their own problems. In most articles in women's magazines focusing on this theme, the author argues that judges need to allow the battered woman syndrome into court so that jurors can understand what the women went through. However, these articles still focus on individual responsibility rather than institutional responsibility because there is no suggestion about how institutions can stop murder or abuse. Instead, institutions are encouraged to accept what is portrayed as an unfortunate, but at times inevitable, individual solution of murder.

The first articles focusing on battered women who kill their abusers appeared in 1984—two articles in *Good Housekeeping* and two in *Redbook*. The articles gave detailed descriptions of the abusive relationship, the murders, and the trials. Three of those articles were excerpts from two books—*Shattered Night* and *The Burning Bed*—that describe famous cases of battered women who killed their abusers.

Beginning in 1991, articles began to include a discussion about whether or not these killers should go free, or not even be convicted in the first place. This controversy is illustrated in a *Glamour* article that reported the response to a survey, "Could You Imagine Killing An Abusive Mate?" The following statements were responses to that survey:

> If there is sufficient evidence of abuse, and the situation was at the point of kill or be killed, and the victim escaped by killing, then good for her. Let her have her life and her dignity back.

> Why can't abused women turn to family, friends, clergy or one of the shelters provided for them? There are always other means of escape.

> Men do not deserve to lose their lives because they have a problem. Both partners can seek help before it comes to murder. ("Could You Imagine Killing An Abusive Mate?" 1991:193)

This theme is also illustrated in an introduction to the *Ladies' Home Journal* article "Killer or Victim?"

> For years, Joyce Steiner endured horrendous abuse—and then she killed her husband. She spent almost a year in jail before her sentence was commuted. Did she deserve to go free? (Branan 1991:128)

This article, which is clearly sympathetic to the battered woman, also discusses her life after she was released from prison. *Glamour*'s "Battered Women Who Kill" and *Good Housekeeping*'s "Life after Death" articles continue this theme by describing the lives of battered women after their stay in prison. In these articles, the authors describe in detail the abuse that leads up to the murder, and often explain how this abuse may cause a woman to suffer from what Lenore Walker describes as the battered woman syndrome. In a *Glamour* article, Brenda Aris writes about the abuse that eventually led her to murder her husband:

> In the year before the shooting, my life had deteriorated into a nightmare of pain, fear and helplessness. By now I was 27 years old and suffered from the typical symptoms for what psychologist Lenore Walker, Ph.D., an expert on domestic violence, named battered woman syndrome (BWS): I believed I was worthless and that my husband was all-powerful, that my life depended on my ability to placate him. (Aris 1994:160)

The individual frame of responsibility is still maintained because the discussion rests on how the "victim" felt she had no other option but to kill the abuser. In these articles, there is no responsibility placed on institutions or society in general to stop these murders. The focus often goes back to "Why didn't she leave?"

> In answer to the inevitable question—"Why didn't you just leave?"—Joyce says she did, in fact, try. Several times. But like many battered women, she was more frightened of leaving than of staying. (Branan 1991:198)

Mademoiselle's "Murder Next Door" focused on what neighbors could have done to help the abused woman:

> To see what I could have done differently, I called a local battered women's program and several national organizations on domestic violence. The consensus: Ultimately, it had to be Laurie's decision to leave Bruce. (Lockwood 1995:198)

Notice that in the end the neighbor concluded that it was still up to the victim to get out. The victims in these articles are different in that they used extreme violence to end the abuse. I am not suggesting that these magazines are trying to "empower women to kill." However, the frame of responsibility continues to focus on the victims.

How Family and Friends Can Help the Victim.   Women's magazines have published a few articles that encourage other people to help the victim solve the problem of domestic violence. Significantly, the focus is still on how to help the victim rather than on how to help the abuser. Sometimes, friends of a victim are explaining the problem of domestic violence by reflecting on what they saw their friend go through. The advice generally includes giving the victim information on shelters, orders of protection, and counselors so that she can seek help. These articles do not address how family and friends need to change their attitudes about violence in general; rather, they focus on how to help victims help themselves.

Part of the advice given in *Redbook*'s "When Your Best Friend Is Abused" is, "Give her written information about how she can protect herself." A cautionary warning follows: "The situation is complicated, and people do lose friendships over it. We don't have the prescription to say to someone that if you do these certain things, your friend will have an epiphany" (Buchanan 2001:100). Embedded in the advice given to friends and family is that in the end the victim has to decide to help herself. The "When Your Best Friend Is Abused" article is about a victim who did not take her friend's advice to get out of the relationship. The friend continues to worry and hope that the victim will take care of herself.

"Life after Abuse" Stories. In the 1990s, some articles began appearing in women's magazines that described "what they're doing now." These articles describe the lives of women several years after they got out of abusive relationships. In 1993, *Ladies' Home Journal* wrote about Hedda Nussbaum six years after her case. Hedda Nussbaum was a victim in a high-profile domestic violence case in the late 1980s. In 1987, Joel Steinberg, a defense lawyer, beat to death his adopted daughter, Lisa. Hedda Nussbaum was also in the apartment at the time of Lisa's beating. Even though Hedda was also beaten by Steinberg, resulting in severe damage to her body and face, many media stories questioned why she did not leave and get help for Lisa. *Good Housekeeping* followed up in 1997 with a feature article on how Hedda was doing ten years after Lisa's death.

Good Housekeeping also ran "From Battered Wife to Top Cop," a story about a woman who escaped from an abusive marriage and eventually fought her way to becoming a police chief in a Chicago suburb. Osantowski, the woman in the story, encourages other women to get out of any situation they are not happy with, as in the following quote:

> "People say you have to play the hand that's dealt you, but I don't believe that for a minute," Osantowski declares. "I say, if you don't like the hand, reshuffle the deck." (Rubin 1996:20)

One reason for these "life after abuse" stories is to offer hope to women in abusive relationships. The stories encourage other women to take similar actions to end the abuse and choose a new life.

These stories often recount the abuse the women went through and how they got out of the relationships. Overall though, the main point is to provide an inspirational story about what they are doing with their lives since the abuse. The women in these stories are usually helping other abused women or inspiring other groups of people:

> When people hear about all the difficult things I've gone through and then see where I am now, they tell me it inspires them. I just finished a two-year stint moderating a self-help group for divorced and widowed people. I was able to touch a lot of lives. (Harris 2000:73)

The "life after abuse" stories exemplify what many of the articles start to do; they complete the picture of the battered woman as the hero of her own life. The empowerment perspective frames the victim as heroic—but only if she solves her problem.

Empowering the victim is the most common theme in all women's magazine articles on domestic violence. In the next chapter, I discuss why this theme is so important to women's magazines.

The Couple

So far I have described themes in the women's magazines that for the most part hold women responsible for ending abuse or preventing abuse, but do so with an assumption that the women did not deserve the abuse. Occasionally articles look at how victims provoke abuse, but usually this theme is found more in "couple stories." In these articles, victims are often accused of provoking the abuse and needing to change their own behavior in order to get the abuse to stop. These "couple stories" analyze the relationship from the viewpoints of both the batterer and the victim—and assign responsibility to both parties. Nineteen articles—20 percent of all articles using an individual frame—fit this description, and twelve of those articles are from the *Ladies' Home Journal*'s "Can This Marriage Be Saved?" series. The most common solution given in these articles is counseling. Though the batterer's role is also discussed, typically more emphasis is placed on the victim's role and how she can help end abuse. One of the reasons for the emphasis on the victim even in the discussion of a "couple" is that the "newsworthy" angle of these stories is that the victims have a role in the abuse—they are not just the innocent players. Furthermore, these articles serve to give abusive couples hope that they can save their marriage through counseling and the use of better relationship skills.

Just as "My Problem and How I Solved It" epitomizes individual accountability, couple accountability is typified by the *Ladies' Home Journal* series "Can This Marriage Be Saved?" which was introduced in 1953.[5] Articles in this series consist of three sections. First, the wife explains her side of the story. Then the husband provides his perspective. Finally, as in the case of the domestic violence articles, the couple's counselor explains what caused the abuse and how the couple was able to end the abuse and build a healthy marriage, as in this example:

> Though Joel resisted my suggestions initially, insisting there was nothing about him that needed changing, after a few sessions, he began to see how chauvinistic he was. "I love you, Ellen," he said during one session, "and I'm sorry I've been so bullheaded." Just hearing her husband admit this gave Ellen the encouragement she needed to work on her own problems. The first point we had to focus on was Ellen's incessant talking. Furthermore, Ellen was totally unaware that many of her actions clearly provoked her husband. Her shopping, for instance, *was* excessive. And she *was* often late for important appointments because she had so little confidence in her ability to choose an appropriate outfit. (Werner 1986:18)

The articles in this series assigned blame to both the husband's violence and the wife's behavior that "provoked" him. In the "Can This Marriage Be Saved?" articles that discuss domestic violence, the answer is yes—the marriage can and is saved, at least for the present time. At the end of every article, the couple stayed together because of the successful counseling they received.

A 1994 feature article discussed this series as it relates to domestic violence. Margery D. Rosen, editor of "Can This Marriage Be Saved?" since 1983, wrote that the premise for the series is that "many couples can solve their problems if they are willing to face tough issues, and have the right therapist to guide them" (Rosen 1994:152). However, in this feature article, entitled "The Marriages That Shouldn't Be Saved," Rosen reported that "experts" are split on the question of whether marriage counseling can be effective in abusive situations. All the "experts" in the article were psychologists or psychiatrists. The controversy was over marriage counseling versus separate counseling (batterer counseling and victim counseling). Obviously, the attribution of responsibility never leaves the individual level. Rosen herself wrote a 1996 article, which follows the earlier formula of telling how a couple saved their abusive marriage through counseling. And a 1999 article told the story of a couple who stayed together after they sought help for the husband's violent anger and abusive behaviors.

Many of the articles that take "the couple" approach discuss why victims stay in abusive relationships and why abusers abuse. In some articles, the victim is also held responsible for provoking the abuse.

> While we resist the popular notion that wives are "asking for it"—first, because hurt women deserve sympathy, not condemnation; and second, if we *were* masochists, there'd be no problem—we do have to examine the ways in which women may, unwittingly, up the ante in a fight. Studies confirm what husbands have claimed all along: wives *provoke*. (Cunningham 1982:62)

Even if the articles do not explicitly blame the victim for provoking the abuse, there is more emphasis on what the victim needs to do to solve the problem. For example, in a *Glamour* article on dating violence, we read about the victims, then about the abusers, then about what the victims need to do to break free. So there is some information on why abusers abuse, what strategies they use, but the "solution" goes back to the victims (Finkelstein 1997).

The Batterer

Batterers are not discussed much in women's magazines. The role of the abuser is most often discussed in the "couple articles" in which the victim ends up being held responsible as much or more than the batterer. Significantly, most of the articles that mention the batterer's behavior use story-telling techniques that hold the victim as much or more responsible than the batterer. Only two articles in these women's magazines over the past thirty years—less than 2 percent of articles in the individual frame—place individual responsibility solely on the batterer, rather than on the victim or the couple combined.

In the 1994 *Glamour* article "How I Realized I Was Dangerous," batterers around the country were asked how and why they decided to get counseling. Excerpts from the batterers' letters appeared in the one-page article. For example:

> The turning point for me was when I woke up one morning after we were fighting and my hand was sore from hitting her. And I thought, "Man, if my *hand* is sore, just imagine her face, her body, how she must feel." Now I watch all this stuff on TV about O. J. Simpson, and I think, man, that could have been me. That rage, that rage is something else. (Weinstock 1994:91)

In 2000, *Redbook* published "The Secret Violence of Women," which focuses on female batterers. The point of the article is to raise awareness for the problem of women's violence. This is the most in-depth article on "the abuser" and it focuses on women's violence. The article describes the roots of a female abuser's rage and gives examples of the abuse:

> In the beginning, Melissa would simply smash things: a vase, a beer bottle, a porcelain unicorn she'd painted and repainted to get exactly the design she wanted. Before long, she was slapping and punching Hank, spitting at him, clawing at his face with her long nails, biting, and kicking. "I can't think of anything I didn't do to him," she says. "It was like something in my head was saying, This is too good for me, I don't deserve this, and I need to screw it up." (Decarlo 2000:175)

Finally, in this article, the abuser is being framed as the one needing to "wake up" and do something to end the abuse:

One day Melissa came home from work and flew into a rage over some domestic detail. Although it wasn't her most violent episode, it scared her deeply because this time she and Hank were both stone-cold sober. Hank left the house, and Melissa remembers feeling overwhelmed with remorse. When he returned he sat down with her and told her that he loved her but could no longer live like this. She had to get counseling. "You're right," Melissa answered. "I need help. I cannot handle this on my own." (ibid.)

Though most of the article keeps the focus on the individual level, there is a discussion on the social acceptance of women's violence against men. It is significant that this in-depth article on abusers only focuses on female batterers. The article is reporting a "new problem" of sorts—women's violence. As I discuss more in Chapter 5, one of the reasons for focusing so much on women—whether as victims or abusers—is that the target audience for these magazines is women. For other reasons, many political magazines, which are discussed in Chapter 6, also focus on women's violence.

Other articles in women's magazines have sections that discuss characteristics of abusers, but those articles are not framing the batterers as being responsible for solving the problem. Usually, when the batterer is discussed it is in the context of the couple, or in a discussion of what institutions need to do to intervene in abusive situations. For example, in a feature article in *Redbook*, abusers' behaviors are described, but it is in the context of how difficult it is for the legal system to prosecute batterers (Polaneczky 1998). As you will read shortly, other articles that focus on cultural issues include a discussion of men's violence. I am not saying this is a bad way to talk about abusers; it is certainly a good beginning for understanding violence. What I want to stress is the contrast between how little we read about abusers compared to the dominant focus on victims.

BEYOND THE INDIVIDUAL: ALTERNATIVE
FRAMES OF RESPONSIBILITY

There are alternative story lines in women's magazines that place the responsibility for domestic violence on institutional, structural, and cultural issues. These alternative frames appear less frequently and are overshadowed by the more dominant "victim's problem" story line. The articles that use frames other than the individual perspective are found in fewer magazines and tend to be short. Furthermore, these alternative frames were more common in the 1970s and 1980s when the problem of domestic violence was a "new" topic to cover. These three alternative frames—institutional, cultural/structural, and integrational—zoom in on other parts of the landscape.

Institutional Frame of Responsibility

The institutional frame of responsibility accounts for 15 percent of the total articles in women's magazines. This frame places responsibility at the institutional level by locating the causes of and solutions for domestic violence within institutions, such as legal, medical, and religious ones. Most of the articles focus entirely or in part on the immediate needs of the victim and continue to imply that domestic violence is a "victim's issue" and institutions need to focus on the victims over the abusers. The authors argue that either the system failed to intervene and protect victims of domestic violence or that more laws and training are needed for more effective intervention.

For instance, a *Glamour* editorial argued that battered women who had killed their abusers did so because they had no other alternatives. "The appalling fact remains that these women were pushed over the edge of endurance by the unresponsiveness and inadequacy of our justice and social service systems" ("Scarred Lives of Battered Women" 1980:56). The editorial called for better laws to protect victims of abuse and to punish abusers:

> More states must enact laws that give the police greater power to arrest batterers, that enable the courts to evict batterers from their homes, and that make spouse abuse a separate criminal offense in order to encourage prosecution. (ibid.)

Other articles have argued that the legal system fails to protect victims. An example is *Ladies' Home Journal*'s "No Way Out," which claims that "Each year, hundreds of women are killed by ex-husbands or boyfriends who stalk them obsessively, undeterred by police or court orders," and asks, "Why has our legal system failed to protect them?" The article includes the following example:

> Though she'd obtained a restraining order barring him from contacting her or their four-year-old daughter, Brandi, the harassment continued, making her life a living hell. . . . He had allegedly chased her on an interstate highway at 100 mph, waving a gun out of his car window. Again, Dawn pressed charges. And once again, pending a trial, Randall was released. On the day before Dawn was to testify against her husband in court, she found a bullet lodged in her computer at work; someone had fired through the window opposite her desk. Badly shaken, Dawn broke down at the hearing, and the judge dropped the charge on grounds of insufficient evidence. The roses arrived the following week. Four days later, prosecutors say, Randall Jolly shot Dawn four times as she sat in her car outside Brandi's day-care center. (Chittum, Bauman, and Nyborg-Andersen 1990:126)

The Lorena and John Bobbitt and O. J. Simpson and Nicole Brown Simpson cases inspired many articles, which began appearing in 1994. As described in Chapter 2, O. J. Simpson's history of domestic violence, and the 1994 murder of his ex-wife, garnered significant media attention. One of the outcries from Simpson's acquittal included his gaining custody of his children. Critics argued that someone with a history of abuse should not gain custody of children. Shortly before the O. J. Simpson case, Lorena and John Bobbitt became a high-profile case. In 1993, Lorena Bobbitt, an abuse victim at the hands of John, fought back one night and cut off his penis. Lorena was found innocent by reason of insanity. During the trial, evidence of John Bobbitt's previous sexual assaults and violence toward Lorena was given. These cases resulted in more media attention, including the focus on marital rape and abusers getting custody of children.

A new theme appeared in *Good Housekeeping*'s 1997 article "No Place to Hide." In the article, George Lardner, Jr., tells about his daughter being murdered by her abusive ex-boyfriend. The father argues that had the legal system done its job, his daughter would still be alive. Other magazines started to write more about dating violence in the late 1990s.

Although the articles change over time in terms of keeping up-to-date with new laws and bills, some of the same themes and frustrations with the system appear from 1975 into the late 1990s. A 1997 *Good Housekeeping* article about the ineffectiveness of orders of protection mirrors the frustration with court injunctions in a 1975 *McCall's* article. However, a 2002 article in *Glamour* raises a new theme in these magazines, which is described in the title: "Should Women Be Punished for Returning to the Men Who Abuse Them?" The short article discusses poll results on whether or not women should be arrested for returning to their abusers after seeking orders of protection (Glatzer 2002).

Bringing attention to the needs of victims is crucial. However, few articles have given sole attention to tougher punishment for the batterer or even getting help for the batterer. The system's responsibility for arresting, punishing, counseling, preventing, or condemning abusers remains largely ignored. Furthermore, women's magazines do not discuss or demand that institutions—such as the legal, medical, religious, educational, and social service systems—should be working toward *preventing* abuse.

Cultural and Structural Frame of Responsibility

Only 12 percent of women's magazine articles use the cultural/structural frame. According to articles using this frame, factors such as social attitudes, sexism, socialization, violence in the media, societal tolerance of violence, poverty, and family structure all help to foster an environment that may encourage or at least tolerate violence. This frame includes socio-logical and feminist ideas that place domestic violence in an explanatory framework that includes the impact of social structures on individuals' behavior. Unlike the individual and institutional frames, the cultural/ structural frame proposes solutions that are often based in prevention. Half of the articles that focus on cultural/structural factors appeared after the famous Bobbitt and Simpson cases.

One of the themes in this frame is societal attitudes about domestic vio-lence and the need to get people to take abuse seriously. *Glamour* pub-lished an editorial about how most people ignore the abuse they see going on in other families:

> Most of us can easily identify with the neighbor who hears screams next door but doesn't want to get involved; or with the teacher who repeatedly sees bruises on a child's face but fears adverse professional consequences if she confronts the parents; or with the relative who sees a family member being victimized but remains silent rather than break familial ranks. ("I Just Didn't Think It Was Any of My Business" 1988:82)

Redbook's feature article on a domestic murder told the story from the view of the couple's friends. The author says that they learned their lesson about not paying enough attention to the problems in the couple's abusive marriage. "You can't back away from confrontation. You have to be will-ing to risk the friendship, to ask the hard questions" (Alexander 1998:308). But this was hard because the abuser was just like them, he said. We were "Catholic school, altar boys, good grades, did what was right." So how were they supposed to imagine that he could break his lover's wrist, bruise her face, and hammer her to death? So the lesson they learned was to wonder what secrets a couple might have and to reach out when any suspicions arise.

After the highly publicized case of Lorena and John Bobbitt in June 1993, *Ladies' Home Journal* published an article on attitudes about marriage and marital rape. The focus of the article is that society needs to change its attitudes about marriage—starting with teaching our children:

> We [need to] raise our children to have higher self-esteem so that girls would not fall into relationships with boys who manhandled them, and boys would [know] they did not have to beat a woman up or rape her to prove their man-hood. (Gross 1993:170)

Another theme is "sports culture." In the midst of the media blitz regarding the O. J. Simpson case, *Redbook* featured an article on athletes and wife abuse. In "Why Sports Heroes Abuse Their Wives," Joan Ryan reports cases of prominent athletes involved in domestic violence and the connection between their professional and private behavior. She also points out that the sports culture makes it easier for abusers to "get away with abuse" because of their celebrity status:

> After Robin Givens went to court in 1989 to divorce heavyweight champion Mike Tyson, who she claims assaulted her on several occasions, the judge invited Tyson into his chambers to pose with him and his mother for a picture. (Ryan 1995:131)

Of the sixteen articles that use a cultural/structural frame, six of them have appeared in *Essence,* which is a magazine for black women. bell hooks wrote two articles for *Essence* that focused on cultural factors that relate to domestic violence. In "When Brothers Are Batterers," she discussed some cultural attitudes that foster violence against women:

> When I was hit by my longtime Black male companion, who was a quiet, mild-mannered academic guy, friends, family and strangers alike were all quick to ask: "What did you do?" Clearly, in their minds, any time a woman is attacked by her mate, either verbally or physically, there must be something she has done to provoke or incite him. We are to blame. It is this type of sexist and misogynistic thinking that has made violence against females acceptable in our communities. There has long been an attitude that backhand licks from our husbands or lovers to "keep her in line," "to show who's boss" or just "to let her know her place" are not only acceptable but *deserved.* (hooks 1994:148)

Essence has published two articles written from a male point of view that focus on masculine culture and domestic violence:

> That Daddy would ever abuse Mama still seems incomprehensible to me. But masculinity in our community has always been synonymous with male domination of women. (Campbell 1996:48)

Another article points out how domestic violence is embedded in cultural entertainment and social attitudes. Oliver Williams, the author, also calls for men to learn nonviolent ways for resolving conflict:

> What's more, many of us don't even recognize domestic violence for what it is. Consider how easily we dance to music that calls for knocking women around, or how often we've heard a man say, even jokingly, that he needed to "pimp-slap" his woman. Sadly, many believe that conflict—just about any kind of conflict—is a justification for violence. It can play out like this: *I wouldn't have hit her, but she disrespected me.* Perhaps she *was* disrespectful. But we need to ask ourselves: What was *our* role in the conflict that led to the violence in the first place? And can't we find other ways of resolving conflict—

or simply walk away from a relationship that demeans us? (Williams 2002:252)

Most articles in the cultural/structural frame of responsibility explain how domestic violence is tolerated or encouraged because of a particular cultural or structural factor. The solution lies in changing or eradicating those factors.

Integrational Frame of Responsibility

There have also been a few articles that try to integrate the various levels of responsibility by focusing on the interaction of the individual, institutional, cultural, and structural sources of responsibility. However, only 6 percent of articles in these women's magazines take this approach, and two-thirds of those articles appeared in the 1970s and 1980s. The integrational frame calls for preventative solutions that coexist with intrapersonal and institutional responses, yet have the potential to reduce the need for these interventions. This frame explains how individuals are affected by cultural attitudes and stereotypes relating to domestic violence that affect decision-making and social support.

In 1976 *Mademoiselle* and *McCall's* each published short, but rather comprehensive articles that incorporated many complicated factors about domestic violence. The interaction of law and cultural attitudes is illustrated in *Mademoiselle*'s article:

> In her book, Del Martin points out that less than a hundred years ago, there were laws on the books defining *the degree to which a husband might legitimately chastise*—i.e. beat—*his wife*. The laws have been struck down, but the mentality that produced them, and the power structure that enforced them, remain largely unchanged. (Durbin 1976:66)

The *McCall's* article also pointed out the many problems that battered women face when trying to escape abuse:

> But shelter for the victims is not enough. At La Casa de Las Madres in San Francisco, for example, each victim is assigned a staff member who sits down with her and finds out what she needs—welfare check, medical care, job training, legal assistance in pressing charges or getting a divorce, low-cost housing, marriage counseling. (Pascoe 1976:51)

In 1977 *Glamour* ran a short article outlining various solutions needed to fight domestic violence, including shelters, formal training of police, destigmatization of battered women, legislation, and public awareness. In 1979 *Essence* ran an article illustrating the interaction between individual beliefs and police practices:

It is also important to note that the large majority of police officers are men and are subject to the same attitudes about wife abuse that afflict the general public. If these attitudes are carried over into their work, police officers responding to domestic disturbance calls are likely to consider such problems private family matters and wasteful of their time. (Breiter 1979:126)

In 1987, *McCall's* published an article similar to its 1976 one that discusses the multiple problems concerning domestic violence that are interrelated in our society:

The multiple problems confronting the wife-mother en route to freedom: She has to go on relief or find a job, locate affordable housing and appropriate child care, almost insurmountable obstacles for those already worn out by bouts of violence. Meanwhile, her family, friends and clergyman may be appealing to her not to break up her home. (Eckman 1987:159)

Many of the articles using this frame appeared in the 1970s and 1980s. The problem was "new" during this time. The women's movement pushed domestic violence into the spotlight. Because it was considered new, writing an article that described the broad scope and complex issues related to domestic violence was acceptable. However, as I discuss more in Chapter 5, today's writers are encouraged to focus on a particular, even narrow, angle. Once domestic violence became a "known issue," magazine editors may have discouraged comprehensive articles on the topic. Though the integrational framing of the problem is less likely to appear now, we still see a few articles that use this approach. Now, though, when the integrational frame of responsibility is used, it is in reporting a "new" kind of violence, such as the honor killings in countries like India. In *Glamour's* "A Horror Story Every Woman Must Read," the complex problems related to honor violence are examined. Individual attitudes, religion, cultural attitudes about women and family, state laws tolerating violence, and tolerated social practices that encourage the violence are a few of the issues that are allowing this type of violence to continue.

The articles using a more integrational perspective often explain how individuals are affected by cultural attitudes and stereotypes that affect decision-making and social support relating to domestic violence. The solutions in this frame are complex—incorporating the needs for intervention and prevention. Many of the articles emphasize how we need the criminal justice system to enforce laws against batterers, shelters to house victims, employers to provide adequate training and pay, families to offer support, schools to teach conflict resolution tactics, and individuals to change their attitudes toward domestic violence. Though this frame offers the most comprehensive view of domestic violence, it is the frame least used in women's magazines.

VICTIM EMPOWERMENT IN OTHER MEDIA

The victim empowerment perspective is pervasive not just in women's magazines but also on television talk shows, made-for-TV movies, the Internet, classrooms, and everyday conversations. Many made-for-TV movies on domestic violence focus on one woman's story about how she escaped the abuse. The most famous one may be *The Burning Bed*, which I described in Chapter 2 as the movie that most of the people I interviewed remembered. Hollywood movies on domestic violence, such as *Sleeping with the Enemy* and *Enough*, also focus on the victim's problem and how she solved it.

"How a victim allows the abuse" is also one of the themes that saturates television talk shows. Victims are told that they need to reclaim their power and acknowledge how they are allowing themselves to be abused. Sometimes they are criticized for actually provoking the abuse. Other times the victim's role in the abuse is portrayed as more subtle in that the victim sends signals to an abuser that it is alright to abuse her and that she will not resist.

It is common to hear hosts and experts on talk shows ask victims of abuse what they do to tell their abuser that it is alright to abuse them. A prominent example is Phil McGraw, also known as Dr. Phil, a "life strategist" with a television talk show and several best-selling books. Before he got his own show, Dr. Phil was a regular guest on *Oprah*. During one episode, Oprah and Dr. Phil were discussing emotional abuse. Dr. Phil asked women who were being emotionally abused by their partners what they were doing that told the men they could do this. He assumed that the men were "getting away" with the abuse because they were getting signals from their victims that it was alright. Oprah echoed these same questions and encouraged the women to stand up for themselves and regain their power. In the following excerpt you can see that Dr. Phil begins by addressing the abuser but then quickly turns to the victim's role in the abuse:

> Dr. Phil: "Any man who goes home and closes a door and abuses his wife and children is a coward and a bully. Do you get that?
>
> Jimmy: "I get it."
>
> Dr. Phil: "You get that. If you do that, you're nothing but a coward and a bully and you choose where to do it where it's safe, because you don't do it down at some biker bar, do you? You don't do it at [your] job where they can fire you. You don't do it with somebody like me. You want to abuse me? That's not going to happen, is it? Because I don't teach you to do that. And you've [looking to the victim] taught him to do that and you need to teach him otherwise. And it isn't about being six-four and 230. It's about having a

spirit that says 'I'm not going to take this from you.' And more importantly, Jimmy, you've got to say 'I'm not going to take this from me.' Because when you look in the mirror after that, how do you feel?"

Jimmy: "I feel bad." (*Oprah Winfrey Show* 2002:16)

To be fair, Dr. Phil does put some responsibility on the abuser to stop his behavior. But it is clear that he places a lot of responsibility on the victim for "teaching" her abuser that he could go ahead and abuse her. The show continued with Dr. Phil turning to the victim and asking her what she had done to create this situation. Oprah Winfrey also joins in with a forceful voice on victim responsibility:

Unidentified woman: Honestly, I don't know what I've done to create this. I mean, I know that . . .

Dr. Phil: You have to figure out what am I doing to set this up that way, because you can send a message. You can send a message, treat me with dignity and respect or not.

Unidentified woman: I don't know. I really don't know how I've set it all up.

Oprah: Doggone it, this ticks me off. You know why? It ticks me off because you're not taking responsibility for your own life and your own situation. (*Oprah Winfrey Show* 2002:17)

Holding the victim responsible for the problem intensifies when Dr. Phil invites the abuser to blame the victim for his actions:

Dr. Phil: Tell us, Jimmy, why do you do this at home instead of at work?

Jimmy: Because she stays there and takes it.

Dr. Phil: Duh! (ibid.)

One of the common themes on television talk shows like *Oprah* and *Dr. Phil* is that people need to take control of their lives and change what they do not like. Victims are told they give their abusers messages that say it is alright to abuse them. Oprah and Dr. Phil claim that victims teach their abusers to abuse them and that they need to take responsibility for this.

CONCLUSION

Most of the articles in women's magazines as well as messages found in other media portray domestic violence as a private problem. And not only is it portrayed as a private problem, but most often it is the *victim's* problem, and she has the responsibility for solving it. People may be shocked by the explicit blame put on the victims with questions such as, What did she do to provoke him? or statements like, She deserved it. However, the attention placed on victims in most women's magazine articles is more implicit. They tell nice "it happened to me" stories that place the responsibility on victims for solving the problem, as in the "My Problem and How I Solved It" articles. Victims are told to find solutions within themselves: "Change your personality." "Increase your self-esteem." "Take control of your life." "Refuse to be a victim." "You have the power to end the abuse." The dominant focus is on victims' needs, "syndromes," stories, and responsibility. These magazines locate the victims' experiences within a context that most often downplays not only the role of the abuser but also of society. A significant problem with the dominance of the victim empowerment frame is that it severely limits our view of the domestic violence landscape. In Chapter 8, I explain further why this framing is too narrow and how it obscures much about domestic violence including the abuser, the violence, and the cultural and structural contexts involved.

Women's magazines, television movies, and talk shows are part of the mass entertainment media, which is the most common media source that people use for understanding social problems. The mass media influence large numbers of the public and thus have a great influence in dictating what will become the dominant public understanding of a problem. Therefore, the dominant victim focus in mass media greatly influences public perception of domestic violence. There are other perspectives in the media, but many of those tend to be in smaller and particularized media such as political magazines, alternative newspapers, and specialized television programming. These media, such as the political media analyzed in Chapters 6 and 7, tend to have niche markets and smaller circulation. For example, *Good Housekeeping* and *Ladies' Home Journal* each have over four *million* paid subscribers, which dwarfs the number of paid subscriptions at *The Nation* and *National Review* (each at 150,000) and *The Progressive* and *The New Republic* (each at 60,000).[6]

Those who produce media stories transform social problems to fit their own needs. Editors and producers interpret and transform social problems in a way that helps to sell magazines or television shows. Why are victims so important to women's magazines? Why do the mass entertainment media in general focus more on the individual level than the cultural and structural context? The next chapter examines these questions by analyzing how and why the mass media use social problems and by identifying the processes and guidelines by which entertainment media create stories.

NOTES

1. I included only articles that were at least one page long, excluding small "boxes" or "news bits."

2. Though children are certainly victims of domestic violence, I did not include articles that focused exclusively on child abuse. The public often separates "child abuse" from "domestic violence," and I was most interested in how media portray domestic violence among adults. Media coverage of child abuse differs in important ways from how adult family violence is covered. These differences and the implications of media coverage of child abuse, though important, are beyond the scope of this book.

3. I say that all articles are primarily about heterosexual relationships because some articles discussed domestic violence in general, but the examples they used were clearly of heterosexual relationships.

4. McCracken (1993) argues that the "My Problem and How I Solved It" stories are not true stories, as *Good Housekeeping* may have you believe. She argues that no author claims responsibility for the feature story and that most likely fiction and real life are blended together to create the story. Although each story is written as if it is about one woman, it is true that none of these "My Problem and How I Solved It" articles on domestic violence attributed authorship to anyone until the May 1996 article "Invisible Bruises" by Lauri Burgdorff as told to Jean Libman Block.

5. "Can This Marriage Be Saved?" was one of the series of articles that prompted a group of feminists to take over the editorial offices of the *Ladies' Home Journal* on March 18, 1970. In a sit-in that lasted eleven hours, more than one hundred feminists demanded that then editor John Mack Carter be replaced by a woman editor. They called for a revamping of editorial policy to support the goals of the current feminist movement. Although these demands were not met, the *Journal* did allow feminists to publish a section of the August issue of *Ladies' Home Journal* (Hunter 1990).

6. Figures for *Good Housekeeping* and *Ladies' Home Journal* are based on reports ending June 30, 2002 as reported by the Audit Bureau of Circulations. Figures for the political magazines are for 2003 and are based on phone interviews with editors at the magazines.

5

Social Problems As Inspiration, Entertainment, and Emotion: Women's Magazines and Other Entertainment Media

Magazine articles, television shows, movies, newspaper columns, and press releases do not just magically appear one day for thousands or millions of people to see. Media institutions, such as television networks and newspaper and magazine publishers, have guidelines that they use when deciding what stories they will cover (and which ones they will not) and how the stories will be presented. In my classes, I talk with students about how the media have a significant amount of power and control over the news and the images they use to portray social issues. I discuss how commercialism and the drive for ratings often overshadow journalistic integrity and solid investigative research. The journalism students in my classes are often offended when I critique the media in this way. Many of my journalism students feel that they have integrity and ideals that they will use when writing and covering the news. What my students usually come to see by the end of the semester is that it is not just the individual reporter who decides what story he or she is going to write for the front page of the newspaper. It is not just the freelance author who chooses the stories for *Ladies' Home Journal*. It is not just anyone who decides they want to write a column for *Penthouse* or for *The New Republic*. It is not the individual news reporter who shapes the final story for the local or national news show. The creation of a published media story involves decisions made by a number of people and is often driven by our cultural obsession with entertainment, drama, and speed.

Those who produce media images and stories shape the stories to fit their own needs, including ratings and politics. Social problems are an important source of information for the media. The media depend on activists' and experts' claims about social problems for many of their stories (Best 1999). However, the media interpret and transform these problems in a way that helps to sell magazines or television shows. This chapter focuses on the guidelines that help shape stories about social problems in the mass media—the media filtering process illustrated in Figure 1 in Chapter 1. First I describe four major guidelines that shape social problems into uplifting, inspiring stories for media such as women's magazines. For this section, I draw from in-depth interviews with editors from *Ladies' Home Journal, McCall's, Seventeen, Essence,* and *Good Housekeeping.*[1] Then I discuss how commercialism, the focus on entertainment, and the loss of investigative research have impacted journalistic reporting and the media coverage of social problems. To illustrate this shift in journalism, I draw from other studies on media production and from my research of advice books written primarily for freelance writers spanning from the 1940s to the late 1990s.

SOCIAL PROBLEMS AS INSPIRATION: EMPOWERING THE VICTIMS

If you want to write successfully about social problems for women's magazines or for many other media, no matter what your topic is, it is important for your story to empower the victims, be primarily about one person, and have an upbeat and inspiring ending. You might be wondering, How do you write a story on domestic violence that is uplifting and inspiring? How do you keep domestic violence from being a downer? Or think about how you would write upbeat endings for topics such as sexual abuse, child abuse, homelessness, poverty, or drug abuse to name a few. There are so many social problems we could list that differ so much and yet seem to have one thing in common: they are not uplifting! In fact, in my class on family violence, I have students who write in their evaluations that the class is too depressing. I respond that it is hard to teach a class on violence that is both accurate *and* inspiring. Yet this is the requirement for women's magazines. Why is that? And how do they pull it off?

Guidelines That Shape Social Problems As Inspiration

In Chapter 4, I discussed a dominant perspective that empowers victims. This perspective can be found frequently in television, movies, magazines, the internet, and conversations. This frame is sympathetic to the victim's problems and wants to empower the victims. However, the victim continues to be held responsible for solving the problem. This empowering-the-victim perspective saturates women's magazines regarding all kinds of topics, including domestic violence. After analyzing articles in women's magazines, I realized that there was a common formula for writing about domestic violence. I wanted to find out more about how the editors thought about domestic violence when they were shaping these articles.

After interviewing editors and reading their advice for writers, I found four major guidelines that shape almost all articles for women's magazines, not just those on domestic violence. First, women's magazines are *service magazines.* The editors I interviewed described their mission as service-oriented magazines: they are there to provide resources, tools, inspiration, and hope for their readers. The main way they think they can serve women is by *empowering* them, which is the second guideline. The next main guideline editors follow is *keeping it personal*: focusing on one woman's story rather than more comprehensive, social complexities of any issue. Keeping the articles primarily about one woman helps achieve their goal of empowering women and maintaining uplifting endings, which is the fourth guideline. Having *uplifting, positive resolutions* for all the articles is very important for women's magazines. This also ties into the other goals of service and empowerment. These four main guidelines capture the essence of the victim empowerment model and why social problems are turned into "inspiration."

Providing a Service.   Part of the mission for women's magazines is to provide a service to their readers. As an editor for *Essence* described, they do not just want to provide sensational and titillating articles, but rather a service. She said they would always "include some kind of resource or resources that would help people figure out how to get help or prevent abuse or how to see signs in the people you might be associated with and that kind of stuff."

Directly related to their idea of service, editors of these magazines feel that their readers want to be inspired, entertained, and uplifted after reading the magazine. At *Ladies' Home Journal,* an editor said of their mission: "We inform, inspire, and educate women. That is really our goal." The *Good Housekeeping* editor connected the mission of being a service magazine with empowerment. She defines the mission of *Good Housekeeping*:

> It is a service magazine for women and today universally we would define service as tools, information, and understanding. Not just recipes, though we do a very good job on recipes. Issues that help them be better consumers, citizens and probably most important, because I think women themselves see this as an important role, caretakers for their families.

As in all the women's magazines, service is defined in terms of how women can take care of themselves and their family on an individual basis. This connects to empowerment and keeping the stories personal rather than focusing on social and cultural issues.

Essence's editor told me that all articles need to include some sort of service. The magazine ran a profile of a *20/20* reporter, and the editor told the writer that she needed to add a "service sidebar" on the profile because they are a service magazine. So the writer created a service sidebar talking about how to get ahead in your career. Everything, especially something like domestic violence, needs to have a service component. She said "It's just not a poignant story of a woman who was in an abusive relationship, or who died in it, or who got out of it. It's not simply a story for the sake of the story. It is the story for the sake of serving 1.8 million readers."

Empowerment.

> It's not enough to write about a problem. You must also describe how the reader can solve it. The most important key on your typewriter is the "you." Don't tell the reader about "some people." Instead, say *"You* may find that . . . ," or *"You* should watch for the following symptoms." (Shimberg 1988:175)

The above quote is taken from a guidebook on writing for women's magazines and helps to illustrate one of the most important editorial guidelines for women's magazine articles: empowering the readers. Empowering victims also helps keep articles upbeat and provides inspiration for readers.

A *Good Housekeeping* editor told me that domestic violence was a very important issue for the magazine and it would continually cover it. As part of its coverage, she describes empowerment as a central goal:

> We're doing it [covering domestic violence] to raise awareness, which is one of our missions. And the other thing, which is absolutely core to our mission at *Good Housekeeping,* is to empower readers. I'm not crazy about the word "empower" but it really is the word.

I asked her to explain what she meant by empower. She defined it in the following way: "Tools, resources, understanding, knowledge to make the best decisions for their lives. This is true whether they are buying a washing machine or seeing their daughter in an abusive dating relationship." This is tied in directly to its mission as a service magazine.

According to an editor from *Ladies' Home Journal,* "I think that with this issue [domestic violence] the most important thing to say [is] that if you are a victim, don't take it anymore. Get out. Get out of the situation."

Though she did not use the word "empower" here, clearly it is the same message that women need to take control and stop the abuse.

Young women's magazines such as *Seventeen* and *'Teen* also follow this victim empowerment formula and focus on helping teens solve their problems. These magazines seek articles that focus on intimate relationships and also articles that are inspirational or about personal experiences. *Seventeen* and *'Teen* editors encourage writers to focus on "helpfulness" and "empathy."[2] Teenage girls' magazines reinforce the idea that domestic violence is a private problem that you have to solve primarily on your own.

The *Seventeen* editor told me how the magazine is a resource for young girls: "In doing any kind of article for *Seventeen,* it is the idea of empowerment." She wanted to let young girls know that they can make their voices be heard and regain power in abusive situations. She spoke of a specific article that she worked on, "No: 12 ways to make that little word hurt." She explained,

> The rationale behind it, which was a really fine line to walk, was to alert girls to the contributing factors to date rape, whether it be mixed messages or low self-esteem or drugs or alcohol. And to give them the tools that would help them recognize a perilous situation and to try and disengage and assert themselves in that situation.

She described it as a "step-by-step article" telling girls what they can do and say to avoid a date rape situation.

The *Seventeen* editor referred to empowerment as part of both the pop cultural girl power movement as well as third-wave feminism. She captured this movement by saying, "It is no longer taboo to say life isn't something that just happens to you. You have a role in this."

I asked her if she was concerned about putting too much responsibility on the girls for preventing or ending abuse. She said that it was a concern and she tried to have a balance. I noticed that often during the interview she would say things like "Is it the girl's fault? No. But can she do something about it? Absolutely." She said that it was not contradictory to say that a girl is not at fault for being in an abusive relationship and yet that there are things girls can do to avoid these situations. This is indeed a tricky balance that puzzles many people. I am not making light of this editor's attempt to balance this. It is a good example of how victims are given sympathy but yet held responsible.

Seventeen's editor explained that empowerment has been a central principle in her own life:

> And that's been my life as well. I was lucky I grew up with really great parents who told me I could do anything and told me from a very early age to

stand up for myself no matter what. When I was eighteen years old I went off traveling to Europe for three years and my dad said, 'Here is one thing I'm going to tell you. Whenever you are in a situation where you think you should get out of, get out of it." So I had parents who, unwittingly perhaps, filled me with advice to trust myself and to see myself as powerful and I exercise those tools. And you know what, for the most part they worked.

This is an example of how people's prior experience and background expectancies shape the way they see social issues such as domestic violence. The idea of empowerment and taking control of situations has worked for this editor so it makes sense to her that it should work for everyone.

The editors' goals for encouraging women to take control of their situations is clearly reflected in the articles. As described in Chapter 4, the battered women who are writing for magazines say that they are telling their stories to encourage other victims of domestic violence to get help. In many cases, they are pleading with women to end the abuse:

> Making a decision to leave your home and a life of abuse will be difficult. Your husband may even try to stop you, but you must take action now! Abused wives must come out of the closet and put an end to this terrible practice. (Webb 1987:14)

> "Don't be a victim," Dr. Briggs said. I knew he was talking to me. "If you don't like your life, fix it. Don't feel sorry for yourself. It will destroy you. If you want to be happy, accept responsibility for your own lives." (Kays 1997:78)

> Show yourself some respect by seeking the help that you need to end the abuse. Don't forget: The power to change things is within you! (Woodward 1990:92)

I call this perspective "empowering the victims" because I think it best captures the essence of it. I refer to the people being abused in a relationship as victims, but many of the editors want to take away that label and not portray them as victims. An editor from *McCall's* said, "Editors don't want to portray women as victims. They want to empower women, keep it interesting, and keep it on an individual level rather than calling for social action and change." She implies that being labeled a victim keeps women from being empowered. So rather than treat them as victims, these magazines want to focus on empowerment: on helping women figure out how to solve the problem. Who then is the victim in this social problem? Without a victim it is easy to forget there is a perpetrator, especially when the victim is the one being told how to solve the problem.

Keeping It Personal: Avoiding the "Social" Part of Social Problems.   It comes as no surprise that a majority of the domestic violence articles in women's magazines are about individual stories, thereby obscuring the cultural and structural context of the problem. Our culture is saturated with individualism and our media thrive on personal drama. *Good Housekeeping*'s editor summarized this trend in the following quote:

> I think we are very much in an era of personal journalism. Not just in women's magazines but turn on the television and the large number of news programs, *Dateline, 20/20, Primetime,* have almost always a very strong personal narrative running through. *Sunday Times* magazine similarly; the cover story is almost always a one-person story. It is a trend; a style of storytelling; of getting information out and I think that is the era we are in.

As with other media, editors of magazines argue that keeping social problems personal is absolutely essential for their audience. The following are some of those editors' explanations for why the individual stories are so important.

An editor from *McCall's* explained that she, and others at the magazine, thought readers would be overwhelmed by reading about all the cultural and structural forces related to a problem like domestic violence. She thought that readers just wanted simple steps that would help them get out of a problem:

> The subtext of many of these stories is that the individual can solve her problem. These magazines are not looking at problems of these kinds in a societal or cultural context. They're just not. I would imagine that editors think it would be too overwhelming for readers to think that there are all these cultural forces kind of arrayed against them. They don't want to hear that we live in a culture of violence. They like to know that by doing steps one through five they can get out of a lousy situation.

I asked her how she knew that readers just want steps one through five rather than knowledge about the larger social and cultural problems. She said her perspective on that was based on talking to readers. She did not necessarily agree that it was the best approach to covering domestic violence, but that that was what readers wanted. She gave a hypothetical story of a reader who is working in an insurance office in Akron part-time, has three kids, and her husband is drinking and abusing the family. She said that probably that woman does not want to fight all of society. She just wants to get through the day, protect her kids, and not have this happening with her husband. If she can read a magazine article that gives steps on how to do that, then that is a benefit for her. This is part of the magazine's service-oriented philosophy.

The *McCall's* editor connected the personal perspective with the politics of the magazine and their readers. She said that many of the *McCall's* readers are extremely conservative, and that any approach that focused on a more social, cultural, or political view of domestic violence would be considered a feminist approach. She claimed that "a majority of our readers consider 'feminist' a dirty word."

The emphasis on individual stories or personal narratives is an important factor that shapes the victim empowerment model. Some editors refer to this storytelling technique as "one-on-one." They focus on just one individual so the reader has a one-on-one relationship with the person in the story. Editors of *Good Housekeeping* report that they "typically explain the issue through one woman who faced the problem, in a personal, narrative format" (Gage and Coppess 1994:310). Their most popular category of articles is the dramatic narrative where a woman tells about a problem she overcomes to provide an education or inspiration for others who face similar problems. The emphasis is on how the individual overcomes the problem.

When I asked the *Good Housekeeping* editor why there was not more coverage on social and cultural issues related to domestic violence she said, "That's not our role. We are a women's magazine." She said that the magazine focuses on women's lives and is not a sociological magazine.

Many editors believe that their readers would not be interested in a story that was too general or that tried to explain the larger context behind a problem, such as cultural and structural issues. The following quote from an editor at *McCall's* shows how she views the importance of the "one-woman story":

> I think that there are certain topics that remain constant throughout the years and one of those topics would be real-life drama. And that would be a story of a woman who has gone through something and triumphed over it. That is where domestic violence would fit in. My experience at women's magazines has been that readers don't respond too well to kind of general stories on subjects like domestic violence. It does go over better with them, and they will be more interested in the subject if it is framed in terms of one woman's particular story. And that's true I think of most issues like child care, sexual harassment, wage wars. Anything that is very general that doesn't have either any case histories or one great case history tends to be skipped over by readers. I think they feel they come to the magazine essentially for stories.

Seventeen's editor said that it would be impossible to have a story just on the larger social and cultural context that teenagers would find interesting. And for that matter, she was convinced that you could not successfully write that type of article for any audience. She explained that it was too academic. Any social issues needed to be grounded in the stories.

Social and cultural issues could be included by weaving them into the personal narratives.

Essence ran more comprehensive articles in the 1980s about the social and cultural context of domestic violence, but that sort of coverage has diminished through the 1990s. Its editor said that was not a surprise. She attributed the change to the shift in the magazine's audience. People in general think more of their personal needs as opposed to social change now as compared to earlier decades. She thought part of that was the lack of social movements compared to the civil rights and black power movements thirty and forty years ago. She also thought it was difficult to look at societal issues because of the extreme social class group differences within *Essence*'s audience. "There is an extremely upper-class black society and an extremely lower-class black society and how do you talk about both of those groups of folks and all the groups of people in between?"

The *Good Housekeeping* editor also said that this magazine was more likely to publish articles that looked at the larger sociological problem of domestic violence in the 1970s and 1980s than it is now. She said in the 1970s domestic violence was discovered and covered as a big news story:

> It was a "new" topic really when we discovered domestic abuse was not just an issue associated with poverty or crazy people, but that it was really happening in that seemingly ordinary suburban middle-class marriage next door. That was really big news at that time and I think we treated it that way. I don't think we treat it that way today. We know this now. There are other issues that need to be brought forward.

The problem was "new" during this time. The women's movement pushed this problem into the spotlight. Because it was considered new, writing an article that described the broad scope and complex issues related to domestic violence was more acceptable. However, today's writers are encouraged to focus on a particular, even narrow angle. As *Essence*'s editor described it,

> Over time we begin to feel like we've covered this this way. We all know and all have some awareness of the larger issues. How do we approach this in a more personal way? We want things to be personal because that's what people are looking for.

Once domestic violence became a "known issue," magazine editors discouraged comprehensive articles on the topic in favor of the more dramatic personal accounts of the problem.

Upbeat and Positive Endings.   Having an upbeat, positive ending is a central component that completes the story as inspiration and entertainment.

Editors believe that having a positive ending gives readers hope, empowers the victims, and keeps the story from being a "downer." Framing social problems as having positive endings requires selective storytelling. For domestic violence, almost all the stories portrayed abusive relationships where the abuse had ended or at least the woman had gotten out of the relationship. Though this is not an accurate reflection of the problem, it does help meet the goals of the magazines.

Editors explain that they want positive endings so readers will feel hopeful and empowered. *Good Housekeeping*'s editor explained that a positive resolution is so important because it is good storytelling and a part of the empowerment message. "If you leave people unresolved and adrift, it is not going to give the reader the sense that she can also take charge in her life." A *McCall's* editor says,

> That positive ending is really important in women's magazines because editors feel that readers need to be given some hope that their situations can be changed. Women readers need to be given some hope that they can solve their problems in some way on their own. Readers don't like downers.

Essence's editor said that a positive resolution is so important because "if you are reading it and you are in an abusive situation, we want you to feel like you can get out. We want people to feel like it is possible to get out of an abusive situation." Later in our conversation she reemphasized the importance of the uplifting ending because it was directly connected to the empowerment and service the magazine offered women. She wanted to make clear that "it is not simply that this is a downer story and we need an uplifting ending. We want women to know that there is something that they can do. It's about service."

Editors shape stories about domestic violence—and most other issues—to fit four important criteria. The stories need to provide a service for individual readers, empower victims, focus on one woman's story to keep it personal, and remain uplifting and inspirational. Because of these criteria, these stories share three other requirements: not just any victim can be empowered, abusers must be kept in the background, and advertisers' interests must be maintained.

Not Just Any Victim Can Be Empowered

I have explained how the women's magazines focus primarily on the victim when writing about domestic violence. However, it is not just *any* victim that is used in these stories. Victims must not be offensive to the readers, and they must be the type of victims who can "easily" be held responsible for their situations. Women's magazines do not readily write about the elderly or children as victims because they are not easily empowered. In order for their victim empowerment formula to work, the audience needs to believe that the victim can indeed be held responsible for ending her abusive situation; that way the story can be believable and uplifting. Editors assume that their readers would not as easily accept stories that hold elderly victims and child victims responsible for their abuse. (It is difficult to expect younger adult women to be able to end the abuse because of the social and cultural barriers involved, but the readers of these stories seem to accept it.)

Writing about victims of abuse who are more obviously "helpless" is too depressing for women's magazines. The *McCall's* editor said that she proposed doing a story on elder abuse, but her boss said that it was just "too much of a downer." Also, as I mentioned above in discussing upbeat endings, victims in these stories have almost always left the relationship or ended the abuse somehow. There are not stories about women who continue to be in the abusive relationships. This connects both to the empowerment and inspirational goals of the women's magazines. It is a "downer" to read about someone who is currently in an abusive relationship.

Not only do editors choose victims who fit their "empowerment" model, but they also choose "nonoffensive" victims. In general, they say that they choose stories they feel their readers will understand. The *McCall's* editor was more blunt than most about how they choose their stories:

> I would say other criteria we take into consideration in selecting people to be covered in the magazine is [*sic*] probably not the poor, not with awful backgrounds, and this is my own personal opinion, but not those who are too fat or ugly. I think the feeling is that as far as class goes and circumstances, in other words where people are on the economic scale and what they have in their past, i.e., arrests, drug use or whatever, readers find it very easy to distance themselves from someone who has had a less than utopian life. So we're doing a story about a woman who was abused, I can't imagine us doing a story about a woman who was a drug user and abused because we know from letters that readers would say, "What did she expect?"

These stories are about heterosexual women who are not too poor, not drug users, not prostitutes, and do not have any other characteristics that editors think would cause their readers to blame the victim. For example, the editor from *Essence* said the magazine would most likely not do a story about a drug addict who was being abused because the audience might feel the abuse was justified:

> If we had a choice between a person who was a drug addict and in an abusive situation and a person who wasn't, honestly we would probably choose the person who wasn't. The reason for that is that it goes back to: can the audience relate? Because what we wouldn't want to do is have a situation

where the reader reads this thing and feels like, well, this person was messing up anyway. Therefore the husband or boyfriend might have been justified or frustrated.

She went on to discuss a particular situation she knew about that she thought would be too difficult to include in the magazine:

> I know of a situation where a woman is a crack addict. She is married and is a mother and goes out and turns tricks to support her habit. She's been hit by her husband. In the family there is a lot of ambivalence about that because on the one hand, it's like, you know, I wish I could hit her. On the other hand, we know that he shouldn't. But we kind of understand why he did. Those are the kinds of complexities that you want to get at. But we have to be careful in the tone of the story because you don't want to seem to be condoning domestic violence because you don't condone domestic violence even when in your heart of hearts you understand.

Not only do women's magazines limit the portrayal of domestic violence by only focusing on the victims, they also create a narrow framing of "acceptable victims." This selection of "appropriate victims" reflects the finding in public opinion research that indicates a public acceptance of some violence because the victims might be deserving.

Keeping Abusers in the Background

Why is it that these magazines do not write more about abusers? Stories about the perpetrator could be personal and dramatic. The main reason they ignore abusers is the belief that their audience does not want to read about them. Editors at the women's magazines do not think their readers, who they assume are mostly women, want to read about men. Furthermore, they worry that reading about the abuser is more depressing. The perspective used in these magazines assumes that the majority of victims are women and the majority of abusers are men. Therefore, they think that writing about women, and thus victims, is what their readers want. An editor from *Ladies' Home Journal* said that her magazine's readers are going to see things from "a woman's point of view, which typically is going to be the victim in the abusive situation." A *McCall's* editor said that "anything that explores the problems of men is actually not of much interest."

The editor at *Ladies' Home Journal* went further in describing why there are no articles about the abusers. Essentially she did not see the point. There is no payoff for the magazine:

> Doing an article on "Here's Fred. He abuses his wife. Here's why he thinks he does it." What does that get you in the end? Again, I think you also have to look at what is the end of the story. If you have a story about a man who

is abusing his wife or kids and there's no change, like he hasn't done anything to change, what do you gain by publishing that article? If you could show in the story that he really did reform himself, and he was talking about here's what we need to do—if it was from his perspective on why this country has such a terrible record on this and here's what I think we should do, maybe that would have some real information and value to readers. But just to say here is somebody who abuses and isn't that too bad, I'm not sure that really gains you anything.

This editor is again very focused on having an uplifting, inspiring story. The scenario that she describes—a man who abuses and why—could be very educational, but probably not very happy. It is clear from her words that if it is a story about how someone changed, and thus has a happy ending, then she might consider publishing it.

Another concern that several editors emphasized was a legal one. According to a *Ladies' Home Journal* editor,

You also have to worry about his rights, frankly. When you're going to press and saying so and so abuses his wife, that's a pretty serious charge and you better have enough evidence to back that up.

Though editors use this reason to explain why it is harder to write about abusers, they could write a "composite" story about abusers the way they do about the victims. Many of the articles in women's magazines are not about one particular victim. They are about a generalized victim with details taken from several different cases.

Keeping the Audience and the Advertisers Happy

Advertisers are still the dominant source of revenue for much of the media. "Media are in the business of delivering audiences to advertisers" (Croteau and Hoynes 2000:63). This is also the case for popular women's magazines. I asked editors if advertisers restricted how they wrote about social issues such as domestic violence. All of them said that the advertisers did not really place limitations on how they covered issues. How can that be their perception when they readily admit that advertisers are crucial for the existence of their magazine? The answer is that advertising affects journalists not story by story but rather in the overall vision and mission of a magazine, TV show, or other medium. As other scholars have argued, reporters and editors more likely react to advertisers' influence through self-censorship. "Self-censorship refers to the ways reporters doubt themselves, tone down their work, omit small items, or drop entire stories to avoid pressure, eliminate any perception of bias, or advance their careers" (ibid.:70). So it may be true that advertisers rarely tell editors they cannot do a particular story. Most likely the editors and producers are already aware of the desires of the advertisers and prevent any problems from occurring at the level of an individual article.

The editor from *McCall's* gives more insight into this process. She said that advertisers do not put limitations on her. However, she said it is "just sort of understood" what advertisers want. She said that a company like Proctor and Gamble would not come and say, "Don't write a story about anybody over fifty." The advertising sales staff at her magazine already know the realities of the marketplace and they know that advertisers target women in their thirties and forties. Therefore, she says, "Even though, in fact, a woman's magazine has probably millions of women over sixty reading them, they're not really covered in the magazine. They're like the invisible readers."

Magazine editors think about what their audience wants to read (and in particular what they do *not* want to read) as they decide how to write their stories. They are concerned with their audience because they are subscribers, but also because they are the advertisers' interest. Editors do not want to write about topics they perceive would be depressing, because they believe their audience wants to be uplifted. They do not write about men because they think their audience, largely women, does not want to read articles about men. Because the producers are already focused on ratings and entertaining their audience, their coverage of social issues stays fairly safe and nonoffensive. These goals are compatible with keeping advertisers happy.

Alternative media such as political magazines have a more specific audience and do not have to deal with advertisers in the same way. "Media supported by wealthy benefactors rather than advertising (as are many political magazines such as *The Nation, The New Republic,* and the *National Review*) escape the constraints of the marketplace" (Schudson 2003:128). This freedom from advertising is part of the reason political media often have more variety and fewer "entertainment-driven" frames in their coverage of social problems. Political media, however, have other guidelines that shape the way they frame social problems, as I discuss in Chapters 6 and 7.

THE SHIFT FROM INVESTIGATIVE REPORTING TO ENTERTAINMENT AND EMOTION

Social problems are transformed into entertainment not only in women's magazines but also in other media, including television. There has been an increasing shift in journalistic reporting to focus more on entertainment and less on providing information. Some people refer to this type of programming as "infotainment" (Fishman and Cavender 1998). Altheide argues that commercialism drives this entertainment format, which he describes as the primary frame media use to shape social problems such as crime and violence. "Commercialism has contributed to the blurring distinctions between journalist and entertainer" (2002:112). Increased competition, corporate mergers of media businesses, and a drive for profit have all contributed to the shift toward entertainment. "The result is that newspaper editors, increasingly trained in the world of business instead of news reporting, focus more on marketing and packaging the news" (Croteau and Hoynes 2000:63).

Criticism of news focusing too much on entertainment is not new. Yellow journalism, tabloid reporting, and strategies for making news entertaining and sensational date back to the nineteenth century (Schudson 2003). However, the drive to make news entertaining arguably has crossed the line into news *as* entertainment. There is little to no difference between news programs and other media. There used to be a distinction between "news" and "nonnews," but that difference is shrinking because of the focus on entertainment, which dominates the "postjournalism era" (Altheide and Snow 1991).

The connections between entertainment and news are increasing. Altheide gives the example of how news coverage foreshadows future TV movies. "In this way, TV news becomes a kind of preview or advertisement for coming attractions. News as a form of knowledge is transformed through news as entertainment into news as advertising" (Altheide 2002:47). Also, the past three decades have seen the rise in social problems as entertainment in the form of tabloid news shows such as *Hard Copy, A Current Affair*, and reality crime shows such as *COPS, America's Most Wanted*, and *Unsolved Mysteries* (Fishman and Cavender 1998). Public opinion surveys indicate that people's perceptions of crime and violence are influenced by these types of shows. Furthermore, the production techniques used by "reality shows" and tabloid news magazines are now being used by more mainstream news programs (Schudson 2003).

When television and other media adopted the entertainment format, emphasis shifted from gathering information to getting emotional reactions and great, albeit short, quotes.

> Capturing a sob, seeing tears flow down cheeks, looking into the eyes of the interviewee during tight camera shots merged as critical features of the message and, in some cases, the most important part of the report. (Altheide 2002:108)

Altheide also argues that television journalists are taught to go into interviews not only knowing the questions, but also knowing the answers—or at least the answers needed to create the entertainment frame:

TV journalists are trained to focus on certain themes and angles of topics for interviews. This means that they enter the interview with a well-defined sense of what the story is, what the parts will be, and, with exceptions, the individual being interviewed is merely playing a part in completing the picture. (ibid.:107)

This is a stark contrast from past journalistic values that saw interviews as information gathering and believed that the story should be shaped based on what the interviewee told the reporter. Altheide describes this shift in journalistic interviewing as "a transformation from information to an impact orientation" (ibid.:101). Media producers have become more concerned with making dramatic impacts on their audiences to support the entertainment format rather than informing their audience. As other scholars have described it, "The emphasis of interviewing has shifted from information gathering to satisfying production values stressing impact, shock, morality play scenarios, and 'big conclusions'" (Holstein and Gubrium 1995).

This shift from gathering and disseminating information to producing entertainment can also be seen in the advice given to people writing for popular magazines. The dominant trend in advice books for freelance writers has shifted from in-depth research and using experts for information to less rigorous research and using experts for legitimation.

Writing for Magazines

If you walk into any large bookstore, such as Barnes & Noble or Borders, you can find a section on writing. In this section are many books that give suggestions on how to write and publish for various media, including novels, crime books, nonfiction, and magazines. In order to get published, authors need to meet the editors' and publishers' expectations, which are often outlined in these books. These guidebooks are written primarily for freelance writers, who often write a majority of articles in popular magazines. For example, 40 to 95 percent of articles in women's magazines are written by freelance authors (Holm 1997; Deimling 1984). I analyzed writing guidebooks from the 1940s through the 1990s to discover how the advice for doing research and using experts has changed.

In the 1940s and the 1950s, guidebooks emphasized conducting thorough and in-depth research on your topic. Clear emphasis is given on learning as much as possible on the subject. It is important to become your "own expert" on the subject by learning from the authorities in that field (Brennecke 1942; Campbell 1944; Neal 1949). In the 1960s and 1970s, there is a transition to doing minimal, "economic" research to save time. Some advice books that have appeared since the 1970s are even more blunt about not doing much research. "Unless you've discovered a way to eat bylines, it doesn't make much sense to spend 40 hours researching and ten hours writing an article for which you'll be paid only $40. So, how much research should you do? The answer is: *As little as possible!*" (Kelley 1978:41, emphasis in original). The trend toward advising authors to do minimal research became dominant in the guidebooks for the 1980s and 1990s. One guidebook author warns writers that collecting too much research can complicate your writing. "Taking on a complex subject about which you know relatively little is one of the largest psychological hurdles—as well as a practical problem—for beginning writers" (Stuller 1988:34).

The shift from in-depth research to economical research also affects how authors are advised to use experts. Experts are often self-identified individuals who "believe that their understandings should be used to educate and assist those who are less knowledgeable and fortunate" (Loseke and Cahill 1984:296). These individuals claim their expertise based on intellectual study, practical experience in social service provision, or both, and include academics, social service providers, political activists, and journalists. In the 1940s and 1950s, authors of advice books on writing for magazines emphasize using experts to learn about the topic about which you are writing. Writers are encouraged to soak up the expert's information. Writers are told not to talk too much during an interview so that the expert has time to give his or her expert opinions (Patterson 1939). Authors are also encouraged to speak to many authorities to "become an expert" so that you can check authorities against each other (Patterson 1939; Brennecke 1942; Campbell 1944).

During the 1960s and 1970s there is a shift in how to use experts. Even though experts are still used as sources of information, authors begin to take on more ownership of the article (Weisbord 1965). During this shift, starting in the late 1960s, authors are told to gain information from experts, but less emphasis is placed on learning all you can. Authors are advised to gather enough information to support their theme. During this decade there is a shift from learning about the topic from the expert to gathering information to support or legitimate the author's predetermined theme (Bird 1967). The author is working under the assumption that readers will take the story more seriously if "experts" are quoted in the article rather than just giving the author's opinion. Increasingly it seems that many authors go into a story knowing what they want to say and only consult experts who will give them a quote to support their predetermined theme.

In the 1980s, guidebooks begin to be more explicit about using experts for legitimating stories. Editors strongly encourage getting the support of experts. "Your articles need the support of expert opinion, quotes, moving anecdotes, etc. These are important because they substantiate *your* ideas" (Shimberg 1988:176, emphasis added). In *Get Published: 100 Top Magazine*

Editors Tell You How, an entire chapter is dedicated to finding and inter-viewing experts (Gage and Coppess 1994). Experts are viewed more as a tool for legitimating an article than as a source of information that might change the article's focus. "The role of an expert is to give the article cred-ibility and to tell the audience the most important points." Writers should know before the interview "what you want your subject to tell you, or the direction in which you want the questions to lead." Writers should not get trapped in a long-winded interview. "Remember, he or she may be the expert on the topic, but you're the writer and the one who decides what to include in the article" (ibid.:72). The most important part of interviewing experts is "getting good quotes." Some writers call their interview sources to review their quotes. However, writers are told not to send their sources the entire article because "experts tend to want to add information or rewrite paragraphs that do not include their quotes" (ibid.:77).

After interviewing experts, the writer decides on the most vital pieces of information to include within the narrow space constraints. Therefore, even if an expert tries to discuss the multiple dimensions of a social issue such as domestic violence, the author of the magazine article will only choose the quotes that legitimate his or her particular angle. For example, David France quoted Ann Jones in his *Good Housekeeping* article on domes-tic violence. France uses Jones's quote to support the idea that since the first shelter for battered women opened, homicide rates have dropped. "'If a woman has an escape hatch, she'll take it,' says Ann Jones, author of *Next Time, She'll Be Dead: Battering and How to Stop It*" (France 1995:150). This is the only time he quotes Jones. France failed to explain that Jones's argu-ment also includes structural, cultural, and institutional barriers that keep women from leaving a relationship. The quote France uses does not rep-resent Jones's theory or expertise. It simply legitimizes his article. Most of the time, authors of magazine articles in this study use only one quote per expert. This minimum usage of an expert's knowledge leads to a misrep-resentation of that expert's total knowledge and understanding.

Exploiting Guests and Evoking Emotions

The entertainment frame not only affects how journalists interview experts, but also their guests on talk shows and news shows. Producers and interviewers often conduct interviews to get the most drama and sen-sationalism out of a story. Even when subjects do not want to see them-selves as victims, some media stories frame them that way. Carol Ronai describes her experience with a news show that wanted to interview her for a story about children of mentally retarded parents (Ronai 1997). Ronai says that she was assured the story would not frame her mother, a men-tally retarded woman, in any way that would be negative or harmful to the family. Ronai wanted to do the interview in order to raise awareness of the needs and difficulties mentally challenged parents faced when raising children. She quickly learned that the news program wanted to cast her as a victim and portray her mother as a terrible parent who should have never been allowed to have children. The news show used a variety of tactics to elicit emotion and dramatic stories from her that allowed them to frame the problem as a tragic victim's tale.

Television talk shows have also relied on the exploitation of social problems for the bulk of their shows. Kathleen Lowney explains that talk shows use social problems not only to provide entertainment, but also the drama, personal confessions, and salvation reminiscent of the early religious revivals. These goals are achieved through the exposure of individuals' deviant lifestyles. Talk shows personalize social problems through the production and framing of victims and victimizers. As with other media, talk shows are driven by commercialism and focus on ratings. Producers see "conflict" and "emotion" as a key to getting people to watch their shows. "Talk show staffs see social actors in conflict as creating 'good television,' for their disputes often involve dramatic tension, confrontation, and emotion" (Lowney 1999:40).

Laura Grindstaff worked at two talk shows while conducting ethnographic research on television talk shows and described the production process in *The Money Shot*. She says that talk shows are using social problems as entertainment:

> Critics are right when they suggest that producers have an instrumental stance toward guests and their problems, that, as much as hosts or producers might stress educational, informational, or therapeutic goals, talk shows are making entertainment out of ordinary people's lives, using their transgressions and hardships to garner ratings. (2002:247)

Grindstaff explains that talk shows are produced with one goal in mind: the money shot, which she defines as "concrete, physical evidence of real, raw emotion" (ibid.:116). Producers work hard to lead guests to emotional outbursts, often achieved with surprise information, challenging viewpoints, and most importantly, the exploitation of sensitive, intimate, and volatile topics.

In an interesting comparison, Grindstaff points out that news programs portray social problems in similar ways to the talk shows "by decontextualizing issues and events, privileging individual solutions to complex, social problems, creating drama by juxtaposing opposing viewpoints, and emphasizing deviance, conflict, and violence over normal consensual relations" (ibid.:249). One of the experts that she interviewed described being interviewed by a news program as worse than a talk show. "I could be on a national network news program for fifteen to twenty seconds," he said, "and I've been on a [talk show] for an hour! So which is tabloid, which one is ethical? Well, from my point of view, I'd rather be on [a talk show]" (ibid.:250).

Altheide also argues that news reporters push the people they interview in order to get the dramatic and emotional images in news interviews. "It is about generating conflict and drama and emotional tugs that touch audiences and let them participate: a public degradation ritual. It is about ratings and money" (Altheide 2002:120).

CONCLUSION

Stories about social problems that are written for women's magazines are shaped by the editorial guidelines of service, empowerment, personal drama, and uplifting endings. Framing social problems in a way that leaves readers inspired, uplifted, and entertained may help magazines and television shows sell stories, but it gives a skewed perspective of the problem of domestic violence. Empowering individuals and having upbeat endings with positive resolutions are important to women's magazines. In order to do this, they almost always use profiles of women who have successfully ended their abuse—either through counseling or leaving the relationship. This does not accurately reflect the millions of women who continue to be in abusive relationships. It does not reflect the women who have left countless times only to be drawn back into the relationship for a variety of reasons. This style of storytelling also does not inform people that leaving an abusive relationship can be very dangerous. Studies show that victims' attempts to leave a relationship often result in escalated violence because the abuser becomes more desperate to maintain control. So this perspective is trying to "empower victims" but is doing so without giving them all the information. By ignoring the social and cultural context of the problem, it leaves out very important understandings of why it is not so easy for victims to just leave. And what about those victims who face so many barriers that they are not able to leave in steps 1, 2, and 3? Are they left thinking that if it is all up to them to end the abuse and they cannot do it, then there is no other alternative? Chapter 8 expands on the implications of using a victim empowerment perspective.

Guidelines that emphasize individual drama are found in other mass media as well. There has been an increasing shift in journalistic reporting to focus more on entertainment and less on providing information. An analysis of writer's guidebooks shows that in the past few decades advice has shifted to doing less research and using experts to legitimate a preconceived story. Commercialism, the focus on entertainment and emotion, and the loss of investigative research have impacted journalistic reporting and the media coverage of social problems. The entertainment media transform and personalize social problems in ways that will help attract a large audience. When people are entertained or inspired by stories about victims who overcome their problems, they are also learning about the causes and solutions for these problems as framed through entertainment. Complex social problems are reduced to emotion, drama, and heroic tales. Stories about social problems that are shaped to be inspiring and entertaining are usually simplistic and focus on just the individuals involved, which does not reflect the complexity of the problem. Editors feel it would be too overwhelming and depressing for readers to know about all the social, cultural, and structural factors related to social problems.

However, there are other types of stories in the media, such as those found in the political media, which I discuss in the next two chapters. These magazines are driven by political orientations more than consumerism and entertainment. Their political agendas help shape the stories. Therefore, we find quite different portrayals of domestic violence in the political media compared to entertainment media. Political media target a much smaller audience who seek political analyses of issues from a particular perspective. Though these frames are quite different, it is important to remember that the number of readers or viewers for many political frames are dwarfed by the *millions* of people who consume the mass entertainment media.

NOTES

1. Unless indicated differently in the text, all of the quotes from editors are from interviews I conducted with top editors at women's magazines. For each quote, I indicate which magazine the editor works for, but I am not including names to protect their identity.

2. For more information on editorial advice on writing for magazines see advice books such as Holm (1997).

6

Men's and Conservative Political Magazines: The Antifeminist Frame

While reading a political magazine that occasionally writes about domestic violence, I come across the following image. On page 139, there is a woman sitting on a fur rug completely naked—except for the high heels and a collar around her neck attached to a leash. She is running her hands through her hair while seemingly growling at the viewer. Do you think I am describing a picture from *Playboy* or *National Review*? It may seem obvious that the pornographic picture I described belongs to *Playboy* and not *National Review*, but you cannot tell the difference between these magazines when reading their articles on domestic violence. It is an old joke to say that people get *Playboy* and *Penthouse* "for the articles." Although best known for their nude pictures, both of these popular men's magazines do contain articles on social problems, such as domestic violence, that reach millions of readers. Though these men's magazines are usually categorized as "entertainment" rather than "political," they certainly play a role in the politics of framing domestic violence. Because politics, rather than entertainment, shapes their domestic violence articles, I include the men's magazines in the category of *political media*.

It may come as a surprise to some that *Playboy* and *Penthouse* are remarkably similar to the *National Review* and *The New Republic* in how they frame domestic violence. I did not go about analyzing these different magazines thinking that they would be so similar. However, I discovered through my research that men's magazines such as *Playboy* and *Penthouse* use the same perspective on domestic violence as *The New Republic*, *National Review*, and *Reason*. Because they tell the same story, I discuss these magazines together to illustrate an antifeminist frame of domestic

violence. I refer to this perspective as antifeminist because, as I will illustrate, countering the feminist battered women movement is its primary
agenda. This political agenda shapes social problems such as domestic
violence in a similar way as the drive for entertainment and ratings shape
mass media portrayals of social problems. Political media frame particular parts of the landscape in order to promote their agendas.

The stories on domestic violence in the antifeminist frame are not uplifting or inspirational as are those in women's magazines. When writing
about social problems, these editors are less interested in "the money shot"
but rather look for the political angles that support their politics while
debunking the "other side." These magazines are also looking for controversial angles to stories that are not reported in other mass media stories.

Why can these magazines focus on politics and not be as concerned
with "entertainment" and ratings?

> Obviously it is a sex magazine so there are girls who are in sexy pictures.
> That's the main reason people buy it, but we have also found over the many
> years of business that they also like the kind of investigative reporting we do
> because we are kind of in your face on the edge. Bob [Guccione, the pub-
> lisher] loves to be sued. He loves to win, but he loves to be sued. He is a com-
> bative type of guy so that's kind of the profile of the magazine. (editor of
> *Penthouse*)[1]

This editor at *Penthouse* describes the magazine's journalism as "in your
face on the edge" and "combative." Though he thinks the readers enjoy
this type of writing, he points out that it is a "sex magazine" and that is
why people buy it. In a sense, the pornographic pictures at magazines like
Penthouse and *Playboy* give their publishers and editors a forum for their
political views on social issues. They do not have to worry as much about
their audience and advertisers in terms of what the articles say. The "sexy
pictures" subsidize their politics. This argument is further illustrated by
Penthouse's recent bankruptcy. Now that pornography can be easily
attained through the internet, traditional pornographic magazines like
Penthouse are facing stiff competition. Their sales are dependent primarily
on the market for their pornography, not their politics. However, it is their
politics that shapes the articles.

Not all magazines have to rely on pornography to subsidize their political viewpoints. Other political magazines such as *National Review* and *The
New Republic*, and their liberal counterparts *The Nation* and *The Progressive*,
are also subsidized and do not rely on advertising as a major source of
income. These magazines have wealthy benefactors who support the magazine in lieu of advertisers (Schudson 2003). The people who fund these
magazines are expecting stories that are political in nature and geared for

the political interests of the targeted audience. While mass entertainment media are driven by consumerism, these magazines are driven by political orientations. Therefore, we find quite different portrayals of domestic violence in the political media compared to entertainment media. They target a smaller audience, which seeks political analyses of issues from a particular perspective. Within political media there are two contrasting frames of domestic violence: the antifeminist frame and the social justice frame. In this chapter I describe the antifeminist frame and draw from my interviews with editors at *The New Republic* and *Penthouse* to explain how their coverage of domestic violence, and other social problems, is shaped more by the editorial staff's political philosophy and their search for "new" information on the issues rather than from the need to sell entertaining stories. Then I discuss implications the antifeminist frame has for social policy and for understanding domestic violence. Chapter 7 discusses the social justice frame.

ANTIFEMINIST FRAME: REFRAMING THE PROBLEM

Victims in stories that use the empowerment frame are treated sympathetically, but they are still held responsible for ending the abuse. The antifeminist frame tells a different story of domestic violence, yet also holds the victim responsible for the problem—at least female victims. Furthermore, this frame emphasizes the responsibility of female abusers and battered women activists. The antifeminist frame found in men's and conservative political magazines is actively trying to reframe the way the battered women movement has constructed the problem. While women's magazine articles define the problem as the actual acts of domestic violence, the articles using an antifeminist perspective define the problem as the battered women movement's construction of the problem. In other words, these articles do not try to understand domestic violence or what the victims or abusers go through, but attempt to resist the battered women movement.

What is the battered women movement? In Chapter 8 I will give a more detailed overview of the emergence of this movement. Here, I will just briefly summarize the battered women movement to help illustrate what these magazines are countering. The battered women movement of the 1970s jump-started the public discussion, academic research, and media attention given to domestic violence. This feminist movement frames domestic violence with the following three assumptions: First, victims should not be blamed for the abuse they receive. Second, domestic violence is primarily a problem of men abusing women. And finally, domestic violence is one component of a patriarchal system that includes other forms of discrimination against women.

To illustrate the antifeminist frame, I draw from the following magazines (the number of domestic violence articles is in parentheses): *Playboy*
(4), *Penthouse* (10) (two of the *Penthouse* articles use a social justice frame,
which I describe in the next chapter), *National Review* (11), *The New Republic* (5), and *Reason* (3). I reviewed all the articles on domestic violence in
these magazines for the time period 1970–2002. However, there were no
domestic violence articles published in these magazines in the 1970s, and
only five articles in the 1980s. Over 84 percent of the articles were published in the 1990s. Furthermore, 40 percent of the articles were published
in 1994 and 1995, which is the time period of the O. J. Simpson trial, which
brought significant attention to the issue of domestic violence and the justice system in general.

Five main themes describe this frame: First, the antifeminist frame
reframes the problem as "human violence" by claiming that men and
women are equally violent. However, in discussing abuser responsibility,
these articles focus only on female abusers. Second, the antifeminist frame
holds female victims responsible for their own victimization, claiming that
they are not innocent bystanders and that some victims may actually enjoy
the abuse. Third, the antifeminist frame critiques society's tolerance for
women's violence, but does not include the same kind of analysis of men's
violence. Fourth, it focuses on men's rights and discrimination against
men in the legal system and violence legislation. And finally, the fifth
theme blames feminist advocates for the problems our society is experiencing related to domestic violence. The antifeminist frame reframes the
problem—the problem is no longer domestic violence; rather it is battered
women advocates.

"Human Violence"

The antifeminist perspective attempts to reframe the problem in a way
that removes gender from the problem. The most common method for
doing this is to refer to the problem as "human violence." The following
quotes from *Penthouse* and *Playboy* illustrate this theme:

> Domestic violence is neither a male nor a female issue—it's simply a human
> issue. (Brott 1993:40)

> Domestic violence is neither solely a men's nor a women's issue. Both sexes
> are involved in provoking and causing injury to each other. (Siller 1996:22)

> Domestic violence is not an either-or phenomenon. It is not either the man's
> fault or the woman's. It is a both-and problem. (Sherven and Sniechowski
> 1994:45)

Although these articles often give examples of female violence to support the "human violence" argument, they rely mostly on official statistics

and sociological studies to defend their argument—especially Richard Gelles and Murray Straus's research on domestic violence. Gelles and Straus are sociologists who have conducted large survey studies of family violence.[2] For instance, in her article in *The New Republic* (1994), Katherine Dunn accuses the media and "advocacy groups" of abusing domestic violence statistics because they state that women are the majority of abuse victims. She claims: "We are not being told the truth about domestic violence. For starters, it is nowhere near as extensive as the media is claiming." She argues that these statistics are wrong and cites studies such as Straus and Gelles that give different numbers. She uses this research to argue that men and women are equally violent:

> Straus and Gelles are two of the many researchers who have found domestic violence distributed equally between the sexes. In about half the cases of mutual battering, women were the instigators—the ones who slapped, slugged or swung weapons first. (1994:16)

The same strategy and sources illustrated in *The New Republic* article are repeated in *Playboy, Penthouse,* and *National Review.* In *Playboy*'s "Women are Responsible, Too," Judith Sherven and James Sniechowski cite several studies that show women and men are equally violent. They begin the list of studies with the word "Facts":

> Half of spousal murders are committed by wives, a statistic that has been stable over time.
>
> The findings of the 1985 National Family Violence Survey . . . revealed that women and men physically abuse each other in roughly equal numbers.
>
> While 1.8 million women annually suffered one or more assaults from a husband or boyfriend, slightly more than 2 million men were assaulted by a wife or girlfriend, according to a 1985 study on U.S. family violence published in the *Journal of Marriage and the Family.*
>
> *Social Work: Journal of the National Association of Social Workers* found in 1986 that among teenagers who date, girls were violent more frequently than boys.
>
> Mothers abuse their children at a rate approaching twice that of fathers. (Sherven and Sniechowski 1994:45)

Two years later, in 1996, Sidney Siller repeated this list of "facts," with a few minor changes, in his *Penthouse* column. Other authors use the Gelles and Straus research on domestic violence along with other studies to argue that women are as violent as men:

> The same survey that found that a woman is beaten every 15 seconds also found that a man is battered every 14 seconds. This research indicates that 54

percent of all "severe" domestic violence is committed by women. (McElroy 1995:88)

In addition to statistics, some articles include examples of female violence against men. Brott points out that not all men are physically stronger than women, as the stereotype would have it:

> But not all men are bigger than their wives. On one occasion, Stanley, whose wife weighed more than 200 pounds, locked himself in his car to keep her from attacking him. She managed to get in anyway. Once inside she shoved him face down into the passenger seat and jumped on him, putting her knees in his back. He reached for the cellular phone to call for help, but she wrestled it away from him and hit him several times on the side of the head with it. (Brott 1993:32)

In her article in *The New Republic*, Dunn gives examples of female violence that failed to trigger a national discussion of how dangerous female abusers can be. One of those examples included a mother setting her children on fire:

> Let us note that on February 22, Maria Montalvo, a registered nurse in New Jersey, punished her husband for moving out after she had assaulted him. She drove their two preschool children to her husband's parents' house, where he was staying, and parked the car out front. She then doused the toddlers with gasoline and set them on fire. (Dunn 1994:16)

Asa Baber, the one-time writer of *Playboy*'s "Men" column, often discusses his own victimization as an example of female violence:

> I lived with a woman who physically abused me. It didn't start out that way. Like all romances, it began optimistically, but something soured, and her response to what she soon considered my unacceptable presence was to go on the attack. She raged, slapped, kicked, scratched, hit. Once, I woke up with a knife in the mattress beside me. (Baber 1986:29)

The antifeminist perspective argues that there are as many male victims as female victims because of the mutual violence between men and women. However, the female abusers are highlighted in all these articles while the male abusers are ignored. And interestingly, though the authors seem to believe that men are just as likely to be victims, the concerns about their victimization are rarely discussed. The articles focus on women's violence, but not on the needs of male victims. When the authors turn their attention to victims, it is in the context of female victims and their role in the abuse.

There has been much more research that compares men and women's victimization rates than what is portrayed by the antifeminist frame. There continue to be important debates over how to best measure victimization and violence, which I will discuss later in this chapter.

Victims Are Not So Innocent

The antifeminist frame challenges female victims' innocence by holding them responsible for their role in their own victimization. Some of the claims even suggest that victims enjoy "the dance" of an abusive relationship. One of the main arguments is that women are not as "innocent" as they are usually portrayed—and men are not as "evil":

> In the fight against domestic violence, men are almost always presumed guilty. The image of the battered woman is a firm one in the American mind. The print and electronic media portray men as brutal perpetrators of domestic violence, while at the same time depicting women as sympathetic, innocent victims. (Siller 1996:22)

Asa Baber uses the O. J. and Nicole Simpson case as an example of this "innocence vs. evil" campaign:

> The cant from the feminist community has been: Men alone are vile abusers; the women they bully are blameless prisoners. Throughout O. J. and Nicole's marriage (and after their divorce), he was nothing but a cad and brute, while she was an angel. Complex human interactions? There were none. It is time for us to challenge this superficial analysis. (1996:33)

The female victims are criticized in these articles for not leaving because they may actually enjoy the relationship too much, denying their own role in the "dance of mutual destructiveness," and not protecting other people. Furthermore, articles in *The New Republic* and *National Review* downplay both the severity and extent of female victimization.

Stanton Peele suggests that battered women do not leave a relationship because they like the "intensity of their spouses' feelings":

> Quite often, the abuse victims and the men they kill seem to have been involved in consensual relationships, from which the women derived basic emotional gratification. The women refused to leave the relationships when given a real opportunity to do so because they welcomed the intensity of their spouses' feelings. (1991:40)

A *National Review* editorial used the case of Hedda Nussbaum, Joel Steinberg, and Lisa Steinberg to argue that Hedda stayed in the abusive relationship because she was a masochist. She is then blamed in part for the torture of her daughter Lisa:

> If a masochist submits to inhuman abuse, that is perhaps his (or her) business. But the moment a third party is involved, we pass beyond the realm of different strokes for different folks. Miss Nussbaum, at the very least, acquiesced in the prolonged torture of Lisa Steinberg. As an adult (however disturbed), she bears a portion of the blame. Whatever deals the legal system may have made with her cannot expunge her own moral culpability. ("Lisa Steinberg's Torturers" 1988:19)

Sherven and Sniechowski do not have such explicit reasons for why women stay, but they clearly state that victims must be held responsible for their role in the abuse. Although they give the obligatory nod to men's responsibility, the main point of the story is told in the title—"Women Are Responsible, Too"—and illustrated in the following quote:

> If women are not expected to think and act for themselves, if their self-esteem is in shambles and their dependency is characterized as feminine, the fault cannot be laid at the feet of men. (1994:45)

Although the following excerpts are from different articles and are written by different authors two years apart, both describe domestic violence as a dance that *needs* two people:

> Both the male and the female are bound in their dance of mutual destructiveness and in their incapacity for intimacy and appreciation of differences. They need each other to perpetuate personal and collective dramas of victimization and lovelessness, and so, regrettably, neither can leave. (ibid.)

> The pathology of any abusive relationship includes a victim who is deeply infatuated with the process. That is part of the sickness, and it's one of the reasons the victim finds it so difficult to disengage from the dance. This is one truth about domestic violence that we do not want to hear: *It takes two to tango.* Domestic abuse is a dance, sometimes a dance of death, and it takes two people to do it. (Baber 1996:33, emphasis in original)

Baber applies this idea to the O. J. and Nicole Simpson case by quoting attorney Melanie Lomax: "Nicole was involved in this dance with O. J. Simpson. She has to bear her share of the responsibility." He warns his readers that some people will be offended by that statement and "will dismiss it as a classic example of blaming the victim. But her words are accurate" (Baber 1996:33).

Baber himself was the victim in a violent relationship and reports that until he accepted the fact that he was partially responsible for the violence, he could not get out:

Until I accepted the fact that I was a player and part of the process of domestic violence, I was paralyzed. There was something perversely intriguing about my situation. As if I were hypnotized or drugged, I entered into a daily ritual with my abuser. But I was unwilling to take responsibility for my part in it. After all, she was the one on the attack. She was the aggressor and potential killer. I never hit her, never got physical, so I assumed that I had virtue on my side. It was a tremendously self-righteous position, and it felt good. (ibid.)

Baber says that whether you are a man or a woman in an abusive relationship, "Please get the hell out now. If you do not, it's a decision you will have to live—or die—with" (ibid.). Although Baber uses his own experience as a victim, the primary focus of the article is on women's responsibility.

The antifeminist frame focuses on women when discussing the responsibility victims have to end the violence. However, when shifting their attention to the perpetrator and the social context of violence, the focus is on women's violence.

Social Attitudes about Women's Violence

The antifeminist frame critiques society's tolerance for women's violence but does not include the same kind of analysis for men's violence. Many articles in these magazines discuss why society does not hold women responsible for their violence. One theory put forth says that there are two sets of rules concerning violence. Brott supports this idea:

When it comes to domestic violence, society seems to have one set of rules for men and another for women. Perhaps it's because we have been socialized to view women's violence as somehow less "real" (and consequently more acceptable) than men's violence. (1993:34)

Brott argues that our society teaches girls that it is alright to be physically violent and that people applaud women striking back:

Women are subtly encouraged to be more violent. Dr. Straus found that "a large number of girls have been told by their mothers, 'If he gets fresh, slap him.'" Images of women kicking, punching, and slapping men with complete impunity are not only widespread in movies, TV, and books, but the viewer's or reader's reaction is usually, "Good for her." (ibid.)

On the other hand, men are told to "never hit a girl" and if they are hit to "take it like a man." Brott argues that this type of socialization leads male victims of abuse to not protect themselves. Because of how men are socialized, they are reluctant to report being victims of abuse. "Men are trained not to ask for help, and a man's not being able to solve his own

problems is seen as a sign of weakness" (ibid.). Brott gives an example of
how male victims are treated when they do come forward:

> Take Skip, who participated in a program on domestic violence aired on the
> short-lived Jesse Jackson show in 1991. Skip related how his wife repeatedly
> hit him and attacked him with knives and scissors. The audience's reaction
> was exactly what male victims who go public fear most—laughter and con-
> stant, derisive snickering. Even when they are severely injured, men will go
> to great lengths to avoid telling anyone what they've been through. (ibid.:32)

Most of the articles suggest that in order to stop domestic violence, society must acknowledge and hold female abusers accountable. In the following quote, women are singled out as needing to be held responsible:

> The women's movement claims that its goal is equal rights for women.
> Women, therefore, should share responsibility for their behavior and their
> contribution to domestic violence. Only the truth will stop the epidemic of
> violence that is destroying our families and our nation. (Sherven and
> Sniechowski 1994:45)

Although this perspective claims that men and women are both violent,
it ignores males abusers and the cultural and structural context that tolerates male violence.

Battered Justice: Discriminating against Men

A fourth theme in the antifeminist frame focuses on the legal system
and violence legislation. However, this frame accuses feminist advocates
of abusing the justice system and discriminating against men. Sidney
Siller, a lawyer and an advocate for men's rights, wrote articles for *Penthouse* that discussed men's legal rights. In his 1983 article, "Wife Rape—
Who Really Gets Screwed," Siller argues that the new movement to make
"wife rape" illegal jeopardizes men's legal rights. False accusations are
one of his concerns with this new concept:

> Your wife can accuse you of rape at any time during your marriage without
> third-party corroboration. In eleven of the fifty states in America, that charge
> can lead to your arrest, prosecution, and incarceration. Your protection
> against this conjugal lie is absolutely nil. It's her word against yours.
> (1983:104)

As a response to the feminist movement's efforts to make wife rape illegal, Siller calls for the organization of a men's group in order to combat
the legal assaults against men and to "preserve the traditional values of
civilization":

The politically sophisticated female organizations now operating will succeed in their revolutionary goals unless men organize in self-defense. Reasonable individuals of both sexes who are not interested in destroying the very underpinnings of our society must surely agree that the time is growing late if we are to preserve the traditional values of civilization. (ibid.:105)

Siller argues that social institutions—inspired by feminists—are unfairly accusing men of being the sole perpetrators of domestic violence and ignoring the men who are victims. "Pigeonholing men as aggressive, animalistic, and brutish, these feminist-inspired cabals broadly and unjustly accuse men of being the sole perpetrators of domestic violence" (Siller 1986:26). Ten years later, Wendy McElroy broadens Siller's argument by accusing "radical feminists" of using domestic violence and rape to create a "new jurisprudence that assesses guilt and imposes punishment based on gender." McElroy claims that men's rights are being violated in this fight against rape and domestic violence:

This sort of injustice is the inevitable consequence of treating men as a separate and antagonistic class, rather than as individuals who share the same humanity as women. Men are not monsters. They are our fathers, brothers, sons, husbands, and lovers. They should not be made to stand before a legal system that presumes their guilt. (1995:88)

Battered women advocates are accused of abusing justice by playing the "victim card." In an article for *The New Republic*, Jean Elshtain points out that "as Nietzsche himself observed, the flip side of an urge to dominate is an urge to submit and then to construe victimization as a claim to privilege" (1992:25). She argues that in the "social world of the radical feminists" battered women are constantly defined as "victimized, deformed, and mutilated." By portraying herself as a victim, she "seeks to attain power through depictions of her victimization":

The voice of the victim gains not only privilege but hegemony—provided she remains a victim, incapable, helpless, demeaned. This can be part and parcel of an explicit power play. Or it may serve as one feature of a strategy of exculpation—evasion of responsibility for a situation or outcome. (ibid.)

Penthouse and *National Review* both published articles attacking the Violence Against Women Act (VAWA). The VAWA is described as unnecessary and a waste of money:

In VAWA, 62 mostly exhausted, cowed senators think they have found an easy way to ingratiate themselves with the "authentic" women's lobby. But the damage this bill can do is not likely to be limited to the money wasted on sensitivity training or the encouragement to added litigation. Much of the education it funds will paradoxically belittle the crime the bill wants to punish, by confusing the real crime of rape with any sexual intercourse the woman regrets the next morning. And at the same time it would officially affirm the most toxic attitude of the "gender feminists" that, as Catharine MacKinnon put it, men are "a group sexually trained to woman-hating violence." (Guttman 1993:47)

The antifeminist frame also claims that the justice system is letting women get away with murder because it considers the battered woman syndrome in cases where victims kill their abusers. When defending battered women who kill their abusers, lawyers use the battered woman syndrome as part of a self-defense argument. Several of these articles claim that this is "battered justice." McElroy argues that this defense shows how our justice system has become warped by the battered women's movement:

The success of "battered woman syndrome" as a defense in murder cases also illustrates how standards of justice have been warped by the politicization of violence against women. Traditionally, a plea of self-defense required imminent danger without the possibility of escape. Today, courts are acquitting women who kill abusive husbands in their sleep. (1995:74)

Caplan argues that the battered woman syndrome is one more way that men are discriminated against. "Reduced to its essence, battered-woman syndrome is not a physician's diagnosis but an advocate's invention. It means: Blame the deceased" (1991:40). This frame claims that acquitting battered women or granting them clemency may encourage more women to kill. The battered woman syndrome is dismissed as an intellectually incoherent concept that hurts women and justice.

Blaming Battered Women Advocates
A fifth theme of the antifeminist frame is blaming battered women advocates for the problems our society is experiencing related to domestic violence. These advocates are accused of spreading myths and false statistics, promoting a "male-bashing campaign," and failing to accept equal responsibility for stopping women's violence. One argument often made in this frame is that "radical women's groups" actively oppose the spreading of any information regarding female violence against men. McElroy says that "in the current climate of hysteria, those who question the conventional wisdom are denounced as enemies of women" (1995:74). Feminists are accused of threatening researchers and others who speak on behalf of male victims.

These magazines argue that not only are the "radical women's groups" opposing any information regarding female violence against men, but are also actively encouraging a "campaign of male-bashing." "And in general the battered-women campaign is powerfully fueled by the radical feminist presumption that all sex is violence, and all men are brutes. Call in the exorcists" ("Killing the Enemy" 1991:13). In 1994—during the O. J. Simpson saga—Baber focused on public attitudes and domestic violence with a specific look at male-bashing: "The Simpson-Goldman murders have highlighted more than one epidemic. Male-bashing is a national disease, and the folks who perpetrate it have it down to a well-funded, well-practiced science" (Baber 1994:36).

Baber gives his readers six suggestions for facing the "current campaign of shame" being lodged against men. Here are three of those suggestions:

(2) Whenever you hear domestic violence described as solely a male problem, remember that women are not immune to violence. Statistics show that women and men are equally capable of brutality in the home.

(3) Although the female of the species is labeled as more peaceful and nurturing than the male, remember that mothers abuse their children at a rate almost double that of fathers.

(5) As long as we believe that men alone need counseling in domestic violence cases, we will be dealing with only half the problem. The stereotype of the abusive husband and the abused wife often falls apart under examination. It should be required by law that both the husband and the wife get counseling after domestic violence complaints. (ibid.)

In this article, Baber does not really give suggestions for solving domestic violence. Rather he targets "male-bashing" as the problem and offers suggestions for resisting the message that men are the majority of abusers.

Siller offers an alternative to this "male-bashing." He calls for more emphasis to be placed on "the value and importance of fatherhood and the presence of a man in the home." Furthermore, he claims that "reducing and eliminating the crime of domestic violence is too important for our national leaders to lay the entire blame at the feet of men." Feminists are blamed for not doing enough to stop women's violence. Therefore, he concludes that they are not taking responsibility for stopping domestic violence (Siller 1996:22).

Some articles using this frame downplay the extent and severity of female victims' injuries. The authors often charge feminist advocates with "abusing statistics" regarding female victims. The statistics given by "advocacy groups" are often described as lies and myths. "Like hydra heads or spreading kudzu, the false statistics keep proliferating" (Young 1994:43). Cathy Young goes even further by arguing that the violence itself is not as bad as you may think. She cites Gelles and Straus's research that estimated about 1.8 million American women suffered at least one incident of severe violence each year. However, Young claims that "only 7 per cent of them required medical care." She also points out that a study published in the *Archives of Internal Medicine* found that "48 percent of 'severe marital aggression' by husbands caused no injury, and 31 percent caused only a 'superficial bruise'" (ibid.:44). Young concludes her article with a sarcastic question for the battered women movement: "Why not just say that 5 out of 4 women are battered by men, and be done with it?" (ibid.:46).

Feminists are also blamed for taking the wrong approach toward treating abusers. Feminists have supported court-ordered counseling programs for batterers. Programs such as Emerge, which was started in 1977 as one of the first batterer programs, assume that men who abuse believe that men are superior and are entitled to dominate and control their partners. Part of the program works at resocializing men and changing their attitudes toward women. The antifeminist frame also challenges this approach to solving the problem of domestic violence. In a *National Review* article, Margaret Hagen describes the programs: "In those counseling programs, the treatment the men are most likely to get is 'gender therapy,' focused on eradicating the male need for power, control, and dominance" (1998:38). She then argues that these programs do nothing to help abusers and instead favors research that could predict who will be abusive. Hagen claims that the feminist push to reform attitudes about women is only getting in the way of effective intervention.

Like Chess Moves: Countering the Battered Women Movement
The antifeminist frame counters claims made by the battered women movement. I illustrated five main themes in this frame. Here I will show how those themes work like moves in a chess game, countering main points of the battered women movement.

1. The battered women movement claims that domestic violence is primarily a problem of men abusing women. The antifeminist perspective reframes the problem as "human violence" by claiming that men and women are equally violent. Furthermore, because its point is to emphasize the existence of women's violence, it only discusses female abusers and ignores male abusers.
2. The battered women movement states that victims should not be blamed for the abuse they receive. The antifeminist view holds female victims responsible for their own victimization, claiming that they are not innocent bystanders and some victims may actually enjoy the abuse.
3. The battered women movement critiques social attitudes that contribute to violence against women. The antifeminist frame critiques society's tolerance for women's violence, but does not include the same kind of analysis for men's violence.

4. One of the central objectives of the battered women movement was to lobby for legislation that would aid victims of domestic violence, such as the Violence Against Women Act. The movement also pushed for educating the court system and police officers so they could more effectively respond to domestic violence situations. The antifeminist frame also focuses on the legal system and violence legislation. However, articles using this frame accuse feminist advocates of abusing the justice system and discriminating against men.
5. The battered women movement consists of advocates who claimed to be fighting violence against women. The antifeminist frame blames these feminist advocates for the problems our society is experiencing related to domestic violence.

As I have illustrated with these five themes, the antifeminist frame is actively trying to reframe the way the battered women movement has constructed the problem of domestic violence. This frame does not focus on trying to understand domestic violence or what the victims or abusers go through, but rather on resisting the battered women movement. Why do these magazines frame the landscape of domestic violence in this way?

WHY THIS FRAME?

The magazines described in this chapter that use the antifeminist frame are more conservative in their political orientation than their more liberal counterparts, *The Nation* and *The Progressive*, which are discussed in the next chapter. Though *The New Republic* claims to be more moderate in its politics, during the time period when most of the domestic violence articles were published, its editor, and thus the magazine, were more conservative than at other times in its history. Conservative politics emphasizes personal responsibility in areas of crime control and prevention and believe that the government cannot and should not solve crime problems and should stay out of people's personal lives (Berger, Free, and Searles 2001). Conservative politics downplays the role of social, cultural, and structural causes of crime and violence. This is in opposition to the assumptions of more progressive movements, including the feminist movement, which situates violence against women in a cultural and structural framework. Conservative politics also emphasizes family preservation and privacy in a way that often seems at odds with the feminist movement's attempts at disclosing the oppression of women within the family.

The antifeminist frame also reflects a larger cultural movement, which has been described by some as a "backlash" to the women's movement. Faludi describes a backlash against the feminist movement as "a powerful counter-assault on women's rights, a backlash, an attempt to retract the handful of small and hard-won victories that the feminist movement did manage to win for women" (1991:xviii). The strategies of this backlash include denouncing feminist research while heralding other scientific research, and blaming the women's movement for many of the problems it is fighting (ibid.). Numerous social issues have been framed within a backlash discourse including the "liberation" of violent women offenders, women's fear of success, infertility, the breakdown of the family, delinquent youth, and tension and conflict between spouses (Wood 1999; Chesney-Lind 1999; Staggenborg 1998; Mednick 1989; Faludi 1991). These problems, and others, have been framed as negative consequences of the women's movement.

The New Republic, **Domestic Violence, and Conservative Politics**

An in-depth look at *The New Republic* illuminates how conservative politics shapes a magazine's coverage of social problems such as domestic violence. Articles about domestic violence in *The New Republic* are similar to those in *National Review* and quite different from the articles found in liberal magazines such as *The Nation* and *The Progressive,* which are described in Chapter 7. However, *The New Republic* is generally considered a moderate magazine that identifies with the Democratic party. Why is its coverage of domestic violence similar to that of its conservative counterpart? The answer is related to the mission of the magazine and the philosophy of its editor during the early 1990s when "Truth Abuse" and "Battered Reason," two of its feature articles on domestic violence, were published.

The New Republic defines its role not as supporting a political movement, but as discovering new angles on public issues and challenging orthodox views across the political spectrum. A senior editor at *The New Republic* describes the magazine as "counterintuitive."

> The magazine likes to surprise people. Magazines want to be fairly counterintuitive on the theory that a less predictable magazine is a more interesting magazine. The magazine has always had a "throwing sand into conventional wisdom" attitude. The magazine definitely has a reputation of trying to be a magazine that rather than telling you what you already think, tells you why what you think may be wrong. I suppose we get carried away with that. We might be so eager to point out the problems that the magazine ends up being more about that than the ideas.[3]

Like all magazines, the politics and mission of a magazine are directly influenced by the people who work there at any given time. This editor claimed that "the magazine represents the collective obsession of the staff." He said that "in general there is a certain political, moral, philosophical universe to which everyone partly belongs. And that tends to define the magazine's mission and ideology."

The politics at *The New Republic* are generally liberal and during the Clinton presidency its advertising copy claimed it was "the in-flight magazine of Air Force One." However, its diverse staff has included conservative writers. From June 1991 to June 1996 the editor was Andrew Sullivan, who seemed to fit the magazine's mission of challenging the status quo.[4] Sometimes described as a gay Catholic conservative, Sullivan was an early advocate of gay marriage who also criticized gay culture and politics. During this period the magazine ran a number of articles critical of liberal positions on cultural issues such as multiculturalism, affirmative action, and gender politics. Sullivan's tenure took place during a time of increased media coverage of "political correctness." According to its critics, political correctness was an intolerant left-wing movement that had gained power in many American universities, especially in the humanities, women studies centers, and multicultural programs. Critics argued its adherents invented facts to support their rigid orthodoxies and attempted to silence their critics with speech codes and mandatory sensitivity training. Many media outlets ran stories challenging the falsehoods supposedly promoted by political correctness. This type of story fit *The New Republic*'s mission of challenging the status quo and the magazine's more conservative politics of the 1990s.

The New Republic's two feature articles on domestic violence were published during Sullivan's reign. These two articles, written by Jean Elshtain and Katherine Dunn, use an antifeminist frame to portray domestic violence. In particular, the authors question and challenge the battered women movement's construction of the problem. A current senior editor at *The New Republic* described the culture of the magazine during the mid-1990s as being critical of liberal causes:

> The magazine during the mid to late 1990s—and rightly or wrongly depending on your political perspective—believed in general that a lot of liberal causes were being promoted somewhat disingenuously by groups that were playing loose with the facts. The magazine certainly during the mid-90s in general had several people who were interested in writing about this and were suspicious of these groups for various reasons. And that is probably why those articles got printed.

Indeed the two articles on domestic violence, "Battered Reason" and "Truth Abuse" both challenge the claims put forth by feminist advocates. However, domestic violence was not the only topic to be framed in this way. During this period the magazine ran articles ridiculing academic women's studies programs (Sommers 1992), critiquing the concept of date rape (Krauthammer 1993), criticizing the Violence Against Women Act (Vachss 1993), and proposing a Darwinian critique of feminism (Wright 1994). A similar list could be compiled of articles challenging standard liberal positions on race and multiculturalism. "Truth Abuse" and "Battered

Reason," although similar to articles found in more conservative political magazines, fit with these other articles from Sullivan's reign in that they criticize feminist orthodoxy, particularly its supposed willingness to invent facts and figures to support its agenda.

During Sullivan's editorship, the magazine ran articles by women like Christiana Hoff Sommers, Camile Paglia, Naomi Wolf, Katherine Dunn, and Jean Bethke Elshtain, who challenged feminist orthodoxy. These writers did not share a common perspective—Paglia and Wolf exchanged ad hominem attacks during an exchange on the relationship between feminism and sex.[5] However, all of them were critical of some aspect of second-wave feminism.

Using women's voices to put forward the antifeminist frame is a strategy used in other media to resist feminist constructions of social problems (Ussher 1997). When Katie Roiphe wrote a book that critiqued the date rape movement, newspapers, magazines, and various interest groups used her voice to fuel their own criticisms of the antirape movement (Roiphe 1993). Although *Playboy* and *Penthouse* relied mostly on male authors, *The New Republic, National Review,* and *Reason* employed female authors in key domestic violence articles. In 1992, *The New Republic* published Jean Elshtain's article "Battered Reason," which challenged the battered woman syndrome defense. Elshtain argued that the feminist movement is playing the victim card and abusing the justice system. In 1994, Katherine Dunn used the antifeminist frame in "Truth Abuse." In the same year, Cathy Young wrote a strikingly similar article for the *National Review* entitled "Abused Statistics." Young also published a major article in 1998 for *Reason* that attacks the battered women movement. In 1995, the *National Review* had Wendy McElroy write about "The Unfair Sex." McElroy attacks the women's movement for "pushing images of women as victims and men as beasts" and "using the issues of domestic violence and rape to create a new jurisprudence that assesses guilt and imposes punishment based on gender" (1995:74). McElroy argues that the battered women movement abuses the justice system and unfairly prosecutes men. Using women's voices is a critical strategy in the antifeminist frame. By having both men and women advocating this frame, the issue of gender is further removed from the social problems, which is an objective of this frame.

A Question of Service

Political magazines, like other media, do cater to their audiences. The stories about social problems are shaped depending on how the editors perceive what their audience needs to know about an issue. To examine the question of service more, I use examples from *The New Republic, Penthouse,* and *Playboy.*

Unless there are people on staff at *The New Republic* who want to use domestic violence as a way to challenge the "conventional wisdom" about issues or to question the feminist movement, the problem of domestic violence does not seem to fit what the staff think of as their mission. I asked a senior editor why *The New Republic* does not cover domestic violence more. He said that domestic violence is not typically seen as a "big issue" that is important to Washington politics, which represents a large share of their target audience.

> The magazine reflects political conversation in Washington. The magazine does tend to write about the "big issues" and by that I mean taxes, economy, and that sort of stuff. Not that domestic violence isn't important but there may be a sense that it is not an issue that Washington and national politics bring much to bear on it. What happens in Washington doesn't make that much of a difference in what happens to domestic violence, for better or worse.

This editor also thought that the mainstream media already covered domestic violence sufficiently so that it was not a topic in need of his magazine's attention.

Most of the articles in *Penthouse* use an antifeminist frame and in particular stress the discrimination against men in the battered women's fight against domestic violence. It sees itself as a "men's magazine" and therefore tries to offer advice and service to its largely male audience. Seven of the ten articles on domestic violence in *Penthouse* were written by Sidney Siller, a lawyer who addressed men's legal rights. *Penthouse*'s editor said that Siller tried to protect men against false accusations of domestic violence:

> [Siller] saw the increasing use of false accusations of domestic violence against men in child custody cases and divorce cases. As a service to our readers who are men, we visited that topic a lot. Telling men what to do to try and protect themselves both before and after getting into that kind of situation.

It is important to point out that *Penthouse* saw the legal rights of men as a more important service than telling men how they can recognize if they are abusers and where to get help for themselves and others. *Penthouse* did publish two articles that focused on men's violence, which are discussed in the next chapter.

Playboy's founder, Hugh Hefner, also sees his magazine as a service to men and as a forum for his own political and social views. A detailed description of Hefner's politics and beliefs can be found in "The Playboy Philosophy"—a document that Hefner published in *Playboy* that describes his views on life and what it means to be a "playboy."[6] Though he is selling pornography, the magazine serves as a forum to discuss a variety of issues from his particular viewpoint. Hefner argues that *Playboy* not only entertains men through the pictures, but serves them through the editorial content and the articles.

We find quite different portrayals of domestic violence in the political media compared to entertainment media. In the conservative political magazines, they target a smaller audience who seek political analyses of issues from a particular perspective. Though the men's magazines are in the business of entertaining men, the guidelines that shape the articles are driven by the politics and mission of the magazines. They rely on the pictures to sell the magazines, which allows them to use the articles to market their politics. In addition to analyzing why the men's and conservative political magazines use an antifeminist frame, it is also important to analyze what implications this has on our understanding of domestic violence.

IT'S NOT REALLY ABOUT THE VIOLENCE: IMPLICATIONS OF THE ANTIFEMINIST FRAME

It might seem that the antifeminist frame broadens our view of the landscape of domestic violence because it focuses on male victims and women's violence, which the victim empowerment frame fails to do. And indeed, women's violence should be taken seriously, and male victims of domestic violence deserve support and protection. Even if male victims are only a minority of the victims, they still deserve help and support. However, the antifeminist frame is not taking women's violence and male victims seriously. These issues are mostly a camouflage for what is primarily a political countermovement to other constructions of domestic violence. I expose these political strategies more clearly in this section and discuss the implications they have on the portrayal of domestic violence.

The antifeminist frame uses two strategies to counter the battered women movement: degendering the problem and gendering the blame. This frame degenders the problem of domestic violence, saying, in effect, that this problem really is not about gender; that both men and women are violent. However, this perspective then genders the blame by criticizing women, especially battered women advocates. When this frame provides examples of domestic violence, they are either examples of women being violent to men or of women victims who are responsible for bringing violence upon themselves.

Degendering the Problem

The antifeminist perspective attempts to reframe domestic violence in a way that removes gender from the problem. The most common method for doing this is to refer to the problem as "human violence." Arguing that men and women are equally violent is necessary for these authors to reframe the problem as "human violence" or to degender the problem. Therefore it is important to examine their use of sociological statistics and the context they leave out in their analysis of men's and women's violence.

The most widely cited family violence research is Richard Gelles and Murray Straus's, which is based on data collected through the 1975 and 1985 National Family Violence Surveys. The surveys used the Conflict Tactics Scales, an instrument that asks one member of a couple to answer questions regarding acts occurring in the past twelve months. Using data from both 1975 and 1985 surveys, Gelles and Straus argue that the rate of wife-to-husband assault was about the same as the husband-to-wife assault rate. However, Gelles and Straus also agree that when it comes to serious injury, women are ten times more likely to be the victims (Gelles 1997). The argument that claims men and women are *equally* violent ignores the limitations of Gelles and Straus's study and other research that shows women are the majority of victims.

Gelles and Straus failed to look at the amount of women's violence that was in self-defense and at the extent of injuries for men and women (Saunders 1988). Perhaps in response to these criticisms, Straus and Gelles have acknowledged that the results of their study can be misleading because the Conflict Tactics Scales used to gather the data did not measure the reason for the violence or the injuries resulting from assaults (Gelles 1997; Straus 1993). Gelles criticizes those who take the data on battered men out of context:

> Unfortunately, almost all of those who try to make the case that there are as many battered men as battered women tend to omit or reduce to a parenthetical phrase the fact that no matter how much violence there is or who initiates the violence, women are as much as 10 times more likely than men to be injured in acts of domestic violence. Thus, although the data . . . show similar rates of hitting, when injury is considered, marital violence is primarily a problem of victimized women. (1997:93)

Even though Straus and Gelles say that women may be violent in the home, they agree that women sustain more physical injury, lose more time from work, and require more medical care (Straus and Gelles 1995). Furthermore, Gelles and Straus's survey data focus on counting acts of violence and do not consider other strategies of control and intimidation such as psychological, sexual, and verbal abuse and the use of threats against children, relatives, and pets.

The argument that men and women are equally violent in the home also ignores contradictory research that indicates that the majority of victims are women.[7] Analyses of police reports, court records, crime victimization surveys, and other surveys reveal that the overwhelming majority of victims are women.[8] Furthermore, some research indicates that men underestimate the perpetration of their own violence while women overestimate their own violence and its consequences (Dobash and Dobash 1998). Empirical and theoretical approaches to domestic violence must take into account the fact that men and women interpret their victimization and their perpetration of violence differently, and that an understanding of domestic violence must be located within the broader context of other intimidation and control strategies and the gendered context in which they occur.[9]

It is clear that not only does the antifeminist frame ignore research that indicates women are much more likely to be victims than men, but it also disregards Gelles and Straus's own warnings about taking the data out of context. This frame selectively uses research in order to argue that violence is "human." One of my students questioned what was wrong with trying to frame domestic violence as a human issue rather than just a "man's issue" or a "woman's issue." She felt that both men and women are involved and it will take both men and women to solve the problem. I agree that both men and women are hurt by domestic violence. The danger in treating violence as "human" is the assumption that violence is somehow "natural." This ignores the social and cultural context within which people learn how to be violent and learn that they can get away with the violence. Arguing violence is "only human" implies that the problem is "human nature" or normal behavior between people without any consideration of gender role socialization or cultural attitudes toward women and men. By removing gender from the framing of the problem, this perspective undermines the role of gender and power in abusive relationships and distorts the bigger picture of domestic violence.[10]

Gendering the Blame and Obscuring Men's Responsibility

Although the antifeminist perspective frames domestic violence as a "human issue" and argues that women and men are equally violent, when it comes to discussing responsibility for ending abuse, the focus is on women. Thus, although violence is degendered, blame is gendered. Not only are female abusers held responsible while male abusers are obscured, but female victims and battered women advocates are also blamed for the problem. First, the antifeminist frame challenges female victims' innocence by holding them responsible for their role in their own victimization. Some of its claims even suggest that victims enjoy "the dance" of an abusive relationship. Second, the antifeminist frame critiques the social tolerance for women's violence but not for men's violence. And finally, battered women advocates are blamed for spreading myths and false statistics, abusing the justice system and discriminating against men, promoting a "male-bashing campaign," and failing to accept equal responsibility for stopping women's violence.

Degendering the problem while gendering the blame diverts attention away from men's responsibility and the cultural and structural factors that oppress women and foster violence.[11] Though this frame does zoom in on the part of the domestic violence landscape that includes our cultural tolerance of women's violence, it still ignores our tolerance of men's violence. Paul Kivel argues that "counterattack and competing victimization" are tactics that men use to avoid responsibility.[12] In the national debate about gender, men are claiming that they are mistreated, cannot speak without being attacked, and are the victims of male bashing. "Those with power have many resources for having their view of reality prevail, and they have a lot at stake in maintaining the status quo" (Kivel 1992:104). He warns that we must be aware of these tactics and be ready to counter them. "If we keep our eyes clearly on the power and the violence, we can see that these tactics are transparent for what they are, attempts to prevent placing responsibility on those who commit and benefit from acts of violence" (ibid.).

Taking Women's Violence and Male Victims Seriously

If magazine publishers and editors were interested in reporting on the seriousness of women's violence and the need to help male victims, the content and framing of the problem would be very different from the articles described above. A 1998 article in *New Man* gives insight into what this perspective might look like if abused men were the center of the concern as opposed to a tool for the political opposition to the battered women movement (Abraham 1998).

Editors at *New Man* claimed that after they published its cover story on abusive husbands, they were "inundated with letters from anonymous husbands begging the magazine to tell the other side of the story" (Thomas 1999:56). In their March/April 1999 issue, *New Man* published "The Husband Abusers." This article claimed that 15 percent of domestic violence victims are men. One of the biggest differences between the *New Man* article and articles using an antifeminist perspective is that it focuses on the question: "What can a man do when his wife is abusive?" As opposed to just blaming women for the bulk of domestic violence, this article tries to help male victims. Though male victims are given advice on an individual level, cultural solutions are also addressed, including the need for churches to take a more proactive position on the problem of all spousal abuse.

It is significant to point out that the types of abuse the article claims husbands face are mainly humiliation, verbal and emotional abuse, and "deliberate withholding of sex." Although physical violence was discussed, most of the examples were of verbal abuse. The article points out that "abuse against women tends to be more severe than that against men" (ibid.:57). And the author claims that men represent only 15 percent of all domestic violence victims. The article also differentiates between types of women's violence:

> The most common grouping are women who use violence as a form of self-defense; the second group consists of women who have themselves been abused and are finally reacting; the third group are women who are stronger than their spouses or who are the "primary physical aggressors." This group is the smallest. (ibid.:58)

I am not suggesting that the problems of emotional and verbal abuse should be taken lightly. Emotional and psychological abuse is devastating to people. I point out that most of the examples of abuse against men are nonphysical to illustrate that the "equality of physical violence" argument that the antifeminist frame uses still misses the problems that male victims face. If the goal of the magazines were to provide a complete picture of men's and women's violence, then a different picture would emerge. However, rather than trying to better understand the problem of violence (by men or women), providing political opposition to the battered women movement appears to be the driving force in the antifeminist frame. Certainly, victims who are male need to be helped and women's violence needs to be taken seriously. However, targeting women's violence only as a strategy to obscure men's violence does not further our understanding of domestic violence—no matter who the victims and perpetrators are.

CONCLUSION

The antifeminist frame is not really focused on the problem of domestic violence itself. Instead it reframes the problem as the battered women movement's construction of domestic violence. The antifeminist frame tells a different story of domestic violence and yet also holds victims responsible—at least female victims. And this frame also emphasizes the responsibility of female abusers and battered women activists. The antifeminist frame degenders the problem of domestic violence, saying, in effect, this problem is not about gender; both men and women are violent. However, even though the violence is seen as "equal opportunity," this frame helps men avoid responsibility for stopping the abuse by placing all blame on women. Thus, the perspective is gendering the blame by focusing intensely on women, whether they are victims, perpetrators, or advocates.

Whether people agree or disagree with the politics described in this chapter, one can see the effects a magazine's mission and politics have on social problems. The conservative political agenda, which includes the goal of countering the feminist movement, tells a particular story about domestic violence, leaving out large parts of the landscape. This political process of shaping the portrayal of social problems is examined further in the next chapter, which focuses on more liberal political media. Furthermore, the social justice frame used in the liberal media gives an alternative frame that goes beyond blaming the victim. Of the three frames on domestic violence found in the media, the social justice frame is the only one to actively resist framing the victim. Why is that, and how does one tell the story of domestic violence without holding the victim responsible?

NOTES

1. All of the quotes from a *Penthouse* editor are from an interview I conducted with a top editor at *Penthouse*. I am not including his name to protect his identity.

2. For more information on Gelles and Straus's research, see Gelles (1997, 1999) and Straus (1993).

3. All of the quotes from *The New Republic*'s editor are from an interview I conducted with a top editor at the magazine. I am not including his name to protect his identity.

4. Sullivan became the acting editor in July 1991 and the editor in October 1991.

5. Wolf (1992:23) accused Paglia of "howling intellectual dishonesty"; Paglia (1992:4) claimed that Wolf's book *The Beauty Myth* was "a perfect example of what has gone wrong with both feminism and Ivy League education."

6. Hugh Hefner originally published "The Playboy Philosophy" in the December 1962 issue of *Playboy*. "The Playboy Philosophy" was approximately 345 pages long.

7. For more information on the problems with the sexual symmetry argument see Dobash, Dobash, Wilson, and Daly (1992).

8. For examples of other studies on domestic violence that challenge the sexual symmetry perspective see Berk, Berk, Loseke, and Rauma (1983), Brush (1990), Dobash and Dobash (1979), Gaquin (1977–78), Schwartz (1987).

9. The sex symmetry perspective also relies heavily on Steinmetz's (1977, 1978) articles about a "battered husband syndrome." Her articles received media coverage in the late 1970s and recurring media coverage in the late 1980s and the 1990s as fuel for the backlash against the battered women movement. Steinmetz (1977b) claimed that her study indicated that 250,000 husbands are battered by their wives each year. Critics challenge Steinmetz's figure of 250,000 battered husbands because she found *no battered husbands*—but four battered wives—in her study of fifty-seven couples (Pagelow 1984; Straton 1997). Steinmetz compared the results of her study to police reports of twenty-six cases in which two of the victims were husbands. Based on this comparison, she argued that only one out of 270 cases of

abuse are reported. Therefore, since there were two police reports of husband abuse, then there could have been 540 incidents of husband battering. She generalized from this number to 250,000—a number that then exploded to twelve million in the media (Pagelow 1984; Straton 1997).

10. Domestic violence is not the only form of violence that is degendered by critics of feminist constructions. Typical cases of men's everyday violence against intimates and acquaintances, including rape and incest, are obscured in the media by sensationalizing less common "stranger abuse" and "sick rapists" (Caringella-MacDonald 1998; Meyers 1997; Smart 1989; Soothill and Walby 1991; Websdale 1999).

11. This counters any attempts to situate social problems within a patriarchal framework. Susan Caringella-MacDonald (1998) argues that it is easier to sell sensationalized stories of rape cases in which the rapists are "sick" rather than writing about male power and everyday sexism. Likewise, portraying men's violence against women as rare or "only human" obscures the patriarchal attitudes and social structure that underlie the problem.

12. Similar media strategies for reporting men's violence occur in other media and cultures. A mainstream Australian newspaper minimized men's responsibility and distanced its own view from feminists when reporting on men's violence against women. The effect of these editorial strategies was to position its critique of men's violence against women within "hegemonic narratives of gender relations in which women acquiesce in domestic violence, feminists vilify men, and men as a group are much-maligned and not to be held accountable for the behavior of a small, aberrant minority" (Howe 1999:153).

7

Liberal Political Magazines:
The Social Justice Frame

Americans don't want to believe that respectable men, much less beloved sports heroes, assault and even kill girlfriends and wives. The contortions that juries put themselves through to acquit these men are truly amazing. (Pollitt 1995:45)

There's no clearer statement of patriarchy than a prayer Orthodox Jewish males recite daily, thanking God for not making them women—a fate worse than death. (Cool 1995:28)

The above quotes are excerpts from articles on domestic violence that do not zoom in on the individual victim but rather target social and cultural factors that foster violence—in particular violence against women. I call this perspective the social justice frame because it goes beyond the individual and calls for social changes to promote justice. This frame raises important points about social problems that need to be discussed in order to make progress in preventing violence. This perspective is hard to find in mass media. However, it is the dominant frame used in liberal political media.

There are two important themes in this chapter. First, the social justice frame is another example of how media guidelines shape stories about social problems. And second, this frame gives an alternative perspective of domestic violence that goes beyond blaming the victim. Of the three major frames on domestic violence found in the media, the social justice frame is the only one to actively resist framing the victim. In Chapter 5 I described how mass media stories focus on personal drama, especially the victim's story. Therefore, stories about domestic violence and other social problems focus on individual responsibility and ignore the political, social, and cultural context within which the violence happens. The entertainment media highlight the individual story because it is assumed that the target audience wants to be uplifted, inspired, and entertained even when the topic is a social problem. Editors and producers of mass entertainment media fear that a focus on the cultural and structural issues becomes too boring, depressing, and overwhelming for the audience. Portraying domestic violence as the victim's problem is the dominant frame in mass media. The dominance of this frame limits the ability of the public to see and understand the greater landscape of domestic violence.

In contrast to the mass media's focus on entertainment and personalized stories, the missions of *The Nation* and *The Progressive* involve investigation of political and social issues. Therefore, their stories about social problems are framed very differently. I refer to this perspective as the social justice frame because it focuses not on the individual level of responsibility but rather on the social and political contexts. The use of this frame is directly related to the editorial guidelines these magazines use. Drawing from my interviews with editors at *The Nation* and *The Progressive*, I describe the mission and politics of those magazines, which shape a social justice frame of domestic violence.[1] After explaining the editors' mission and political orientation, I illustrate the social justice frame with examples from their articles. Later in this chapter, I explain why *Penthouse* also published two articles that use this frame even though the politics behind those stories is dramatically different than that found at *The Nation* and *The Progressive*.

THE MISSION AND POLITICS THAT SHAPE THE SOCIAL JUSTICE FRAME

Magazines have missions: what they are hoping to achieve through their publications. Both *The Nation* and *The Progressive* have missions and political orientations that allow them to focus on domestic violence as something that is wrong and should be addressed, especially from political and social points of view. According to the editor at *The Progressive*, "In the twenty years I have been here, domestic violence has been a subject that we consider part of the progressive agenda—that is to report on and oppose domestic violence. That's what we've tried to do." When writing articles about domestic violence, these editors assume that domestic violence is a problem that needs to be opposed. How they write about the problem is shaped by the overall guidelines at the magazines. I describe three central themes that shape the missions at *The Nation* and *The Progressive*: (1) using a liberal, progressive political orientation, (2) working toward peace and social justice, (3) critiquing the media, and (4) avoiding victim-blaming.

The Nation and *The Progressive* are both self-identified liberal or progressive magazines. *The Progressive* editor said that being liberal includes a strong identification with peace, social justice, civil rights, and civil liberties. He said that the emphasis on civil rights includes women's rights, which are important for the issue of domestic violence. *The Nation*'s editor described part of its mission and progressive politics as "giving voice to people who don't enjoy positions of power and privilege in society." She thought that this part of the mission in particular related to domestic violence. *The Nation* tries to give a voice to the problems of "victims who get obscured or overlooked by mainstream media."

The editor at *The Nation* contrasted how it portrays domestic violence with how a more right-wing magazine such as *National Review* might tell the story. She distinguishes the liberal politics approach as more about the social and economic context compared to the more conservative emphasis on the individual:

> We would definitely emphasize the woman's point of view and the larger social and economic picture and how that influences what happens in the home. Whereas they [right-wing media] might reduce it to a matter of either women's violence or talking about it as some sort of individual occurrence and problem as opposed to seeing the larger systemic issues and how a sexist society creates a fertile environment against women. They would not recognize that the society even is sexist.

Part of the progressive political orientation is an emphasis on peace and social justice. The editor of *The Progressive* said that its mission is "to be a journalistic voice for peace and social justice." He said that domestic violence falls under that purview because it is a form of injustice, discrimination, and violence. An emphasis on peace and social justice obviously shapes concerns about violence. Editors at both *The Nation* and *The Progressive* said that the magazines are interested in fighting against all types of violence. *The Progressive* editor discussed its concern with many types of violence.

> As far as the question of domestic violence goes, we think there needs to be a heightened awareness of abusive power relations. Now if it is male to female, this is a problem of getting at male superiority complexes in this country—traditional chauvinism if you will. And if it is domestic violence outside that paradigm, it is about people recognizing the importance of nonviolence in their personal lives and not to be abusive and bullying. It is about taking more of a holistic view of violence—both societal violence and individual violence.

Both editors said that they would not limit the scope of domestic violence to just men's violence against women, but they see that particular type of violence as the most prevalent.

The editors said that they saw the women's movement as playing an important role in social justice and that their missions are compatible with that movement. *The Progressive*'s editor said, "We believe that feminism and women's liberation and equality for women are an essential piece to social justice. That's right there in the bull's-eye of what we do." The editor at *The Nation* also said that the magazine is sympathetic in principle to the women's movement and what it is trying to do. She said "I think we would be less inclined to engage in harsh criticism of the battered women movement. We are more inclined to be sympathetic." Even though they are supportive of the feminist movement, both editors emphasized that they are independent of other political movements and even critique the battered women movement when appropriate.

Another central aspect of their missions is media criticism. The editor at *The Progressive* said that the founder of the magazine saw media criticism as one of the reasons for establishing the magazine and it continues to analyze and critique media coverage of issues. Media coverage and criticism also has an important place at *The Nation*, which runs a regular media column and annually publishes a detailed report on media ownership.

The social justice frame avoids blaming the victim and does not just focus on a personal narrative, which is a crucial difference between this frame and the victim empowerment and antifeminist frames. It is not by accident that *The Nation* and *The Progressive* avoid holding the victim responsible. Both editors said that it was a priority for them not to blame the victim. *The Nation*'s editor said that she and her staff were always looking for the larger political angle of any story: "The stories of individual victims can come into it and it makes for interesting reading. But we always want to make the article about a larger political issue; that this does not just relate to one person's life." The editors said that it was an intentional decision to avoid holding the victims responsible for their victimization. According to *The Nation*'s editor, it is a high priority for the magazine to be very careful not to blame the victim. She said that although mainstream media and right-wing media may do that, *The Nation* would not. *The Progressive*'s editor said "We are conscious of avoiding the blaming-the-victim trap." He observed that society has a long history of blaming victims. First, victims of domestic violence were ignored, which he called a traditional form of sexist oppression. Then, after domestic violence became a public problem due to the pressure of the feminist movement, he said that victims were portrayed in an unflattering light. Early on, victims were accused of "having it coming to them" and then later they were blamed for not doing enough to get out of the situation. He said that at *The Progressive* "We have tried to educate ourselves over time on this issue and be sure we don't repeat facile and biased descriptions of what happens in circumstances of domestic violence."

When editors and writers at *The Nation* and *The Progressive* are shaping articles about social problems, those stories are filtered through the missions of the magazines, which include a strong emphasis on progressive politics, peace and social justice, media criticism, and the avoidance of victim-blaming. Using these guidelines, the articles on domestic violence zoom in on different parts of the social problem landscape compared to what we find in the victim empowerment and antifeminist frames.

THE SOCIAL JUSTICE FRAME

Now that we have a picture of the mission and political interests of *The Nation* and *The Progressive*, we can explore how these guidelines shape stories about domestic violence. The social justice frame focuses primarily on men's violence against women and emphasizes the political, social, cultural, and structural context of the violence. Following are six examples of themes found in the social justice frame—all of which are drawn from articles published in *The Nation* and *The Progressive*. After describing examples from these magazines, I explore how and why *Penthouse* has used a social justice frame.

"The Media Distort Our Images of Male Violence"

A strong theme in the social justice frame is a critique of media coverage of violence. This is not surprising since media criticism is an important part of the mission of *The Progressive* and *The Nation*. Both magazines have published articles that critique media images of domestic violence. Among their criticisms are that male violence is distorted and presented from only a male point of view and that media are slow to understand the dynamics of domestic violence. For example, Elayne Rapping argues that media coverage of domestic violence is presented from the male point of view:

> Hollywood movies, TV news reporting and drama, and hard rock and rap music have a long and inglorious history of glamorizing male violence and distorting its social and emotional realities. Quite simply, we have not seen images of male violence that accurately target its sources and hold its perpetrators accountable. (Rapping 1994:34)

Rapping discusses how no shows present images of male violence as neither glamorous nor acceptable:

> What the movies show us are male villains who are really not like you and me. They are larger than life, in charm or viciousness—often both—and are, therefore, somehow separate from the "normal" males we actually know, or are. (ibid.)

Although most movies and most television shows present distorted images of male violence, Rapping points out that talk shows and soap operas have been featuring "women's issues" such as domestic violence since the beginning of the women's movement. However, Rapping criticizes the daytime portrayal of male violence because it focuses on the pathos of the woman victim who is helpless against her brutish attacker:

> Somewhere between the hero/demons of the big screen and the heroine/victims of the daytime small screen, there ought to be a space for the true depiction of male violence—as it really occurs, by the kinds of men who really, every single day, every sixteen seconds—do it. (ibid.:36)

Rapping calls for media to start depicting accurate portrayals of male violence against women. Accurate coverage of the problem needs to start focusing on the everyday violence and the culture that supports it:

> Who are the perpetrators? Why do they continue to commit these crimes? And why are those in power so quick to distort, deny, and brush under the rug all traces? (ibid.)

Related to the argument that the media distort violence, these magazines also accuse media of ignoring abusers and the context of violence.

"Mainstream Media Ignore the Abusers"

Another theme in the social justice frame argues that violence against women and children is not taken seriously by network news and political talk shows. In an article in *The Progressive*, Susan Douglas critiques news shows for ignoring violence against women in their discussions on domestic and foreign policy. She argues that media report on victims of violence but ignore abusers:

> More often than not, reporters focus on the woman who is battered, not the batterer, and ask why she doesn't leave instead of why he beats her. Each assault stands alone in the news, each woman a lonely, pathetic spectacle. Individually, their stories are welcome fodder for the news mill. But collectively, violence against women and children—and the mindset that begets it—are ignored or minimized by the pundits as comparatively unimportant in the grand scheme of things. (Douglas 1993:21)

Another article in *The Nation* critiques the media coverage of the John and Lorena Bobbitt case. Lewis Cole writes that he has learned a lot more from *Court TV* than any of the print coverage regarding the case:

> After even an hour or two of watching it [*Court TV*] you were already way beyond the print or television reporters in your understanding: Halfway

through the trial, the *New York Times* was still so cl— — —
tion that had taken place in the courtroom that it pr— — —
ing the case as a curious instance of passion and ma— — —
have made a good folk ballad. (Two weeks later, they — — —
lishing an editorial about Lorena as an abused wife.) (Cole 1994:24)

In a more recent high-profile national case, four soldiers killed their wives within five weeks of each other. Lutz and Elliston wrote an article for *The Nation* that critiques the media and public reaction to these murders. They argue that the murders gained a lot of attention because three of the soldiers had just returned from the war in Afghanistan. The killings raised a lot of questions about the effects of war on soldiers, the role of military values, and the side-effects of teaching people to kill. The authors argue that "on the epidemic of violence against women throughout the United States and on the role of masculinity and misogyny in both military and civilian domestic violence, however, there has been a deafening silence" (Lutz and Elliston 2002:18).

"Public Attitudes Often Ignore or Tolerate Violence against Women"

Critiquing society's reactions to domestic violence is another component of the social justice frame. People's responses range from humor to indignation, disbelief, and ignorance. Jane Slaughter wrote an article in *The Progressive* about the reactions people had to a black eye she received from running into a street sign. They ranged from ignoring the issue, bringing it up in "private" so as not to embarrass her, and reassuring her that it was not her fault whatever happened. Slaughter points out that most people assumed someone hit her without asking what happened. When she did tell people what happened, their responses often turned to joking—both by her and others. She concludes that joking is society's way of dealing with our "preoccupation with sex, violence, and the combination thereof":

> If you haven't been battered, you can make a joke of it and avoid admitting how nasty it is in real life. Women explain innocent cuts and bruises with a catch-phrase: "My other lover's been beating me." Men and women use language that disguises brutality and makes it sound almost playful. "Knock her around, give her a poke." (Slaughter 1987:50)

Using the outcome of the O. J. Simpson case as an example, Katha Pollitt critiques the public attitudes that tolerate male violence:

> Americans don't want to believe that respectable men, much less beloved sports heroes, assault and even kill girlfriends and wives. The contortions that juries put themselves through to acquit these men are truly amazing. "Hey, men and women fight," commented one Queens juror after last May's

acquittal of Karamchand Singh, who stabbed his former girlfriend twelve times and smashed her head with a four-pound piece of cable. Self-defense, said Mr. Singh; besides, she was a slut. Even his lawyer was stunned that the jury bought it. (Pollitt 1995:45)

Related to this argument is that when people and society do pay attention to violence against women, they blame the victim.

"Media and Society Focus Too Much on Women's Responsibility"

Articles using the social justice frame argue that media and society in general place too much focus on women's responsibility for domestic violence. For example, Susan Douglas discusses the absence of public debates on why men beat and why they can get away with it:

> What we need is a much more thorough public examination of why men beat. Even on the *Brinkley* show, which did a decent job of using the Simpson case to draw attention to wife abuse, George Will raised the age-old blame-the-victim question, "Why do women stay?" without asking its obvious antecedent. This led to a discussion about the "battered-wife syndrome," while ignoring the "battering-male syndrome." (1994:15)

Douglas describes a news segment during the O. J. Simpson coverage that focused almost entirely on female responsibility for domestic violence. The family-law attorney featured said that for many women their only alternative is to change their identities and flee. Douglas asks, "But what of the men? Why do they beat and how can they be made to stop?" (ibid.).

Douglas reports that Jeff Greenfield said that the feminist movement is responsible for the media hype of the O. J. Simpson case. She responds that this attitude leads to an exaggerated focus on women's responsibility:

> Once again, the boys are innocent bystanders: The vixens made 'em do it. Greenfield's suggestion is not new—that when any cultural product becomes overcommercialized and full of swill, it has, in fact, been feminized. I guess this is why there's still so much emphasis on the woman's complicity in domestic violence, and so little on the man with the fists, the knife, or the gun. (ibid.)

This argument returns to the emphasis on needing to examine the roots of the violence rather than focusing on the individual victim.

"Class and Race Differences Should Not Be Ignored"

The social justice frame also recognizes class and race differences in how one experiences violence and also the complications for prevention and intervention. Few domestic violence stories using other frames discuss class and race differences in how people experience violence. The feminist movement has also been criticized for focusing too much on white women while obscuring particular needs of minority women. Marcia Smith opens her article in *The Nation* with disgust as she describes how a NOW volunteer calling for donations used the Nicole Brown Simpson death as an example of what they are trying to stop. Smith explains her irritation by giving examples and statistics that indicate that a majority of victims are African-American women. She calls for both NOW and African-American leaders to prioritize the fight against domestic violence since a majority of its victims are black. Furthermore, she discusses different problems that African-Americans face:

> Reliance on police intervention to arrest the perpetrators of domestic violence, for example, has very different implications in African-American communities, in which both men and women bear the brunt of police indifference and abuse, and in which men are frequently targeted for false arrest. (Smith 1997:24)

Smith argues that mainstream women's organizations must acknowledge and address the multiple roots of the domestic violence problem in order to be relevant to women of color.

"Welfare Reform and Immigration Laws Hurt Battered Women"

The social justice frame focuses on structural factors that contribute to the problem of domestic violence. Two examples of these issues are welfare reform and immigration laws. Welfare reform has led to strict time limits that dictate how long recipients have to find a job or get training, which may discourage battered women from leaving abusive relationships if they feel there is no safety net for them any longer. Gonnerman uses the case of Bernice Haynes as an example of a battered woman trying to escape poverty through education and a better job only to have her abuser stand in her way:

> When Bernice Haynes tried to get off welfare by enrolling in a job training program, her boyfriend tossed her textbooks in the trash. He refused to watch their two children while she was in class. And he would pick fights with her when she tried to study. (Gonnerman 1997:21)

Other welfare reform restrictions may be harmful to battered women, including the residency requirement that would penalize a victim for fleeing to another state for safety. Furthermore, the rule that requires welfare recipients to identify their children's father may jeopardize the lives of bat-

tered women. Activists are fighting to get states to adopt the Family Violence Option as part of the welfare legislation, which would identify victims of battering and waive any requirement that unfairly penalizes them.
Although this option is a good beginning, Gonnerman points out the
many stumbling blocks that remain, including how to identify domestic
violence victims.

In an article for *The Progressive*, Catherine Capellaro (1997) adds that
immigration laws do not provide enough resources to help battered immigrant women. Some of the barriers immigrant women face include language problems, no skills, no family, no childcare, and a lack of
transportation. Without these skills and social support, it is difficult to seek
protection from your abuser. Related to the problems with immigration
laws, *The Progressive* also pushes for changes in U.S. law to make it easier to
grant asylum to battered women. The article, "Battered Women: A New
Asylum Case," lays out the barriers the current system poses to battered
women (Shelton 1999). Articles in this frame have also reported on change
in laws that have helped battered women, such as the Violence Against
Women Act. An article in *The Nation* argues that this act has helped the fight
against domestic violence and then raises the concern that a Republican-
controlled Congress may not renew the act (Aldrich 2000).

The Nation and *The Progressive* both consistently use a social justice
frame in covering domestic violence and other social problems. This frame
reflects their missions and politics so it makes sense that it is used. *Penthouse* also has used a social justice frame, though for very different political reasons.

PENTHOUSE ON VIOLENCE AGAINST WOMEN

In 1995, inspired by the O. J. Simpson case, *Penthouse* published two articles that constructed domestic violence as a problem where the victims are
women and the abusers are men and the analysis of the problem reflects
the social justice frame. This is a sharp contrast to its other articles, which
use the antifeminist frame. I focus in-depth on the article about religion to
illustrate how politics at *Penthouse* shaped this story. Drawing from an
interview with the top *Penthouse* editor, I show that politics also shaped
this social justice frame article—even though the magazine's politics is
much different than that which guides *The Nation* and *The Progressive*.

Lisa Collier Cool's article discusses how "religious 'true believers'
preach violence against women" (1995:27). Cool argues that fundamental
Christians, Orthodox Jews, and fundamentalist Muslims are more likely to
tolerate, and in some cases advocate, violence against women than more
moderate Christians, Jews, and Muslims. Cool cites Gelles and Straus's

studies on family violence that indicate "the more fundamentalist and doctrinaire practitioners had the greatest amount of abuse of women and children" (ibid.:28). Cool also quotes Anson Shupe, a sociologist and coauthor of *Violent Men, Violent Couples.* Shupe discusses how in these patriarchal cultures, males run the show and females are inferior:

> There's no clearer statement of patriarchy than a prayer Orthodox Jewish males recite daily, thanking God for not making them women—a fate worse than death. Plenty of Protestant preachers talk as if the weight of the church and the Bible is behind wife abuse because women are told to be humble, acknowledge their inferiority, and give up control to men. A theme of submission runs through this tragedy like a red letter, because once you start telling women they must submit to men, you get the problem of what to do if they don't, which puts you on a slippery slope that invariably leads to violence. (ibid.)

Cool and the experts she quotes argue that these religions need to start acknowledging the abuse that is occurring and then to preach against it. Clergy need to begin to understand the dynamics of domestic violence. She also points out that there need to be battered women's shelters that are equipped to meet the religious and dietary needs of Orthodox women.

The Politics behind the Stories

Penthouse's editor told me that because it is a men's magazine, domestic violence is not "a staple of the types of articles" they do. However, he said that during the O. J. Simpson case "when the whole country kind of exploded," the magazine decided to publish a couple of feature articles on domestic violence:

> I had a discussion with Mr. Guccione about this, that really the problems of domestic violence seemed to go beyond what was out there. That a lot of people were really very conflicted about it. That a lot of people were confused and probably a lot of our readers since they cover the gamut. So we thought that it was worthwhile to do a couple of pieces. Not jumping on the bandwagon like a lot of media saying that all men were suddenly evil; like some of these crazy feminists saying that Super Bowl was a day of violence, but also to explain that there really was a thing like domestic violence and that people could maybe see it in themselves and weren't aware that they were in a violent relationship when they were.

He said that they saw those articles as a public service. "Given the very high profile of all this and given our profile, being one of the top men's magazines in the country if not the world, we sort of saw that as a public service."

The article on how religion fosters violence against women was influenced even more directly by politics. The following quote from the editor shows how he thought about the story:

> Now the story by Lisa is actually a story that is very close to my heart. As you can imagine *Penthouse* is often attacked, especially by radical feminists and people on the far right, as being a publication that instigates violence against women, which is a terrible lie that's hurt us terribly in both our circulation by getting us banned by certain newsstands and getting hidden in newsstands but also it is a real libel. So this article, as I was talking to Lisa about it, let's just look at people who really preach violence against women and cause violence against women. If you look at the societies in which the women are most violated and treated the worst, I would say are societies where you would get your head chopped off if you were to have a copy of *Penthouse*. So clearly there is something else going on in violence against women besides *Penthouse*. So she went out and did this article. It is an article that contains a lot of truth but also puts things a little more into perspective for the people who are attacking us. So I kind of had my heart in that.

Penthouse published this article more for political revenge than for trying to support the fight against domestic violence. The *Penthouse* editor said that he wanted to publish the article on how religion fostered abuse in order to "get back" at the religious critics of his own magazine.

As illustrated in this chapter, different political motivations can shape a similar frame. Nonetheless, the politics of a magazine and the assumed interests and politics of the targeted audience influence the framing of articles. In addition to analyzing why the social justice frame is used, it is important to examine how this frame shapes our understanding of domestic violence.

DOMESTIC VIOLENCE THROUGH THE SOCIAL JUSTICE FRAME

The social justice frame gives us a different view of the domestic violence landscape than we can see from the victim empowerment frame. The differences are good in that they give alternatives for understanding domestic violence. I think that one of the real strengths of the social justice frame is that it challenges us to consider the cultural and structural issues that foster violence. This view of social problems rarely gets heard in the mainstream media, which focus more on entertainment. However, fewer people are exposed to the social justice frame because it generally appears in political media, which have smaller audiences. *The Nation* has approximately 150,000 paid subscribers and *The Progressive* has 60,000. These are small audiences compared to the millions of subscribers for magazines such as *Good Housekeeping*, which has over four million subscribers, or *Playboy*, which has over three million.[2] Even though the audience is small, the social justice frame's emphasis on cultural and structural problems offers a perspective that is critical for shaping our understanding of domestic violence that goes beyond the victim.

There is also a similarity in how the social justice frame and the victim empowerment frame view domestic violence. Both of these frames portray the problem of domestic violence as primarily an issue about men's violence against women. Zooming in on men's violence against women causes other types of violence to be in the shadows, including elderly abuse, women's violence, or gay/lesbian violence. Though the editors of *The Nation* and *The Progressive* both say they see domestic violence as including more than just men's violence against women, they focus on men's violence more because it is more prevalent. These frames have helped shape public perceptions of domestic violence as primarily a problem of men abusing women.

Another part of the domestic violence landscape that is not examined very well even in the social justice frame is the analysis of the individual abuser. Though the antifeminist frame discusses abusers as part of the story, it mainly highlights only female abusers and does so primarily to argue that women are not "innocent." So the antifeminist frame also fails to examine the individual abuser. The victim empowerment frame focuses on the individual level of the problem, but only for victims. The social justice frame zooms in on the political, economic, cultural, and structural forces that may influence abusers, but does not offer an in-depth look at how individuals learn to abuse and what can be done to help them or stop them.

POLITICAL MEDIA AND ACADEMIC RESEARCH

The two political frames discussed in this chapter and the previous one reflect two different approaches for researching domestic violence that have emerged in academia and spilled over into the social services: (1) the sociology of family violence and (2) a feminist approach to men's violence against women. These approaches serve as frames for defining, researching, and explaining the problem. They help shape research, including the theory and methods used for studying the problem. These approaches ask different questions about domestic violence and therefore come up with different explanations. In fact, the two approaches often are studying different types of abuse (Loseke 1992; Mann 2000). For example, the family violence approach includes elderly abuse in its scope of the problem, while feminist theory targets a wide range of men's violence against women—

from domestic abuse to prostitution. As a photographer adjusts the scope of a picture by changing the camera lens used, so does a researcher influence the image of a problem depending on the frame through which it is viewed.[3]

The social justice frame draws from concepts and research reflective of the feminist approach, while the antifeminist frame draws from research from the sociology of family violence. The frames in the political media are not identical to the academic research frames, but these media frames are often rooted in these different academic approaches. It is important to realize that the social justice and the antifeminist frames draw selectively from research that fits their approach.

The antifeminist frame found primarily in the more conservative political media draws from research conducted by "family violence researchers." A family violence perspective tends to conceptualize the problem as violence in the family and not just violence against women, which is the main focus of feminist theories. Core assumptions of this perspective are that social structures affect people's behavior and that all family members can be both offenders and victims of violence. Researchers using this perspective study all types of violence, including abuse at the hands of husbands, wives, siblings, children, and elderly caregivers. A central question in this research is How does society, and specifically the institution of the family, foster and promote violence? This perspective has its roots in sociology and is also prevalent in the social services (Yllö 1993; Mann 2000). As explained in Chapter 6, the most widely cited research used in the antifeminist frame draws from Richard Gelles and Murray Straus's research. The antifeminist frame ignores other research that indicates women are much more likely to be victims than men, and it disregards Gelles and Straus' own warnings about taking their data out of context. Even though Straus and Gelles say that women may be violent in the home, they agree that women sustain more physical injury, lose more time from work, and require more medical care (Straus and Gelles 1995).

The social justice frame on domestic violence reflects the battered women movement's construction of the problem. This frame focuses primarily on men's violence against women and emphasizes the cultural and structural context of the violence—two general assumptions shared with the battered women movement, which is part of the larger feminist movement.

What does "feminist" mean? I have students who tell me that feminism is just about hating men. An advocate in a shelter told me that anyone who cares about women is a feminist. Both of these definitions are sweeping generalizations that fail to articulate the roots of feminism. It is difficult to define "feminism" because it has developed many divergent directions and theories. Feminist theory has many camps, including liberal, radical, socialist, constructionist, and postmodern. I will not discuss the differences among feminist theories relating to domestic violence here, but rather give a general description of feminist theory as it frames research and provides a foundation for the social justice frame in political media.

Feminist theories on violence were first shaped during the battered women movement of the 1970s, which ignited public discussion, academic research, and media attention given to domestic violence. Theorists from a violence against women perspective argue that violence cannot be understood without looking at gender and power. More specifically, the research questions focus on men's violence against women rather than on all types of family violence. Many feminist scholars criticize the family violence perspective because it promotes a gender-neutral view of power in the family (Kurz 1997). Feminist theories claim that violence against women is a result of patriarchal attitudes held by individuals and institutions as opposed to some psychopathic sickness on the part of the abuser. Rather than being a "sickness," battering women is a normalized outcome of the male socialization process, in which domination over women is expected and taught (Dobash and Dobash 1992).

The political frames in media borrow from academic research, which is already shaped in part by politics. Those claims get translated, selected, and distorted as they go through the filtering system of the particular magazine, television show, or newspaper that is shaping the story. It is true that politics influences research and remains a part of academia. The questions that guide academic research influence media stories that describe the problem either as men's violence against women as portrayed in the social justice frame or as "human violence" as presented in the antifeminist frame. Media stories usually do not take into consideration the variety of viewpoints and research on domestic violence, but rather use the research that best supports the politics of the people and institutions responsible for them.

CONCLUSION

Though the political reasons why *The Nation* and *The Progressive* use a social justice frame differ from why *Penthouse* does, these scenarios illustrate how a magazine's politics shapes social problems such as domestic violence. Those who produce media stories transform social problems to fit their own needs, including the promotion of political viewpoints. The issue of domestic violence is filtered through the particular political lens of any given magazine. It is impossible to take the politics out of media or research, but it is important to recognize the implications politics has on our understanding and response to social problems.

The social justice frame gives us an alternative view of the domestic violence landscape that challenges us to consider the cultural and structural issues that foster violence. The emphasis on cultural and structural problems offers a perspective that goes beyond the victim. This view of social problems rarely gets heard in the mainstream media, which focus more on entertainment. Still missing in all of the frames is an in-depth analysis of the abusers. One of the reasons the media do not focus on abusers as much as victims lies in how the "public discovery" of domestic violence in the 1970s emerged *not* as a portrayal of abusers, but rather of battered women as victims who needed help to end their abuse. Because of the political and cultural context of the time, domestic violence emerged as a victim's problem. Why and how this happened are the topics of the next chapter.

NOTES

1. All of the quotes from editors are from interviews I conducted with top editors at these magazines. For each quote, I indicate for which magazine the editor works, but I am not including names to protect their identity.

2. The figure for *Good Housekeeping* is based on reports ending June 30, 2002, as reported by the Audit Bureau of Circulations. Figures for the political magazines and *Playboy* are for 2003 and are based on phone interviews with editors at the magazines.

3. It would be simplistic to divide all domestic violence into these two camps. However, there has been real antagonism between advocates of these two approaches. Some feminist advocates and researchers have labeled "family violence research" an adversary of feminism, and some family violence researchers and nonfeminist professionals have labeled feminists as radical dogmatists who deliberately distort the problem. Ruth Mann, who has studied the politics of domestic violence in a community, describes the rhetoric of this debate as "examples of inflammatory rhetoric, a practice aimed not at resolving issues but at polarizing, de-legitimizing, and discrediting" (2000:13).

8

Framing the Victim

The roots of the dominant focus on victims are in the initial "discovery" of domestic violence in the 1970s and how the problem was framed by the activists who brought it to the public's attention. These activists framed the problem in a way that emphasized the needs of battered women to end abuse, not the need to hold abusers accountable. Media looked to activists for information about this new problem and so it is not surprising that their coverage also focused on victims. The media's focus has remained primarily on victims for the past three decades except for attention directed toward female abusers, which began in the 1990s. To be fair, the battered women movement did attempt to draw attention to the cultural and structural factors that contributed to domestic violence. However, the cultural and political context of the time intensified the media's narrow focus on victims. Unfortunately, the problem has become increasingly personalized, further obscuring how our cultural and social structures foster domestic violence.

Battered women movement activists did not intend for victims to be held responsible for domestic violence. They wanted to exonerate victims from blame, identify abusers, locate abuse within the social and cultural context, and specify community responses and help for the victim. Advocates who are working to help victims of social problems use the idea of "victimization" to show others that the "victims" of a given problem are worthy of help. Research on victimization and victim empowerment suggests that these are useful approaches for responding to social problems. Why did the early framing of the problem by activists contribute to the framing of the victim rather than focusing on the root causes of the violence? What happened when their claims were disseminated through the media to the public? What are the implications for how we respond to domestic violence? I address these questions in this chapter. First, I discuss why early activists in the battered women movement framed domestic violence as the victim's problem and what consequences this has on policy and public understanding. Second, I explain the cultural and political context within which the battered women movement emerged, which contributed to the shaping of domestic violence as a victim's personal problem. And, finally, I explain what it means "to be a victim" and discuss the policy implications that come from framing the victim for domestic violence.

THE BATTERED WOMEN MOVEMENT

In this book, I have been discussing how the media have covered domestic violence in the past thirty years. Unfortunately, people have been involved in abusive relationships much longer than that. We know of documented cases of family violence in the United States as far back as the 1700s and in other cultures far earlier than that.[1] According to the Bible, the first brothers were involved in fatal family violence. What I have been discussing in this book is the "public discovery" of domestic violence. It is not that people did not know that there was violence in families before the 1970s, but it was just not talked about in the same way it is today. The battered women movement of the 1970s helped to increase public discussion, academic research, and media attention given to domestic violence.

Domestic violence has been debated and highlighted by several social movements throughout American history, including those that fought for child-protection, divorce rights, and temperance (Gordon 1988). These movements, largely organized by women, provided opportunities to discuss the problem of domestic violence indirectly through other issues. For example, one of the concerns in the temperance movement was that men who drank too much alcohol beat up their wives and children. So in this movement, family violence was discussed, but the main focus was on the prohibition of alcohol. Too much alcohol was the social problem being fought, not family violence.

It was not until the feminist movement of the 1960s and 1970s that the fight against domestic violence became a social movement on its own. Prior to domestic violence becoming a central issue, rape had emerged as a dominant theme within the women's movement. The antirape movement's goals, including fighting for stricter punishment for rapists and offering crisis line services and counseling to victims, set the stage for the battered women movement (Pleck 1987). Women with personal experience with abuse decided that wife-beating, the common term used at the time, was not getting enough attention. Early founders of the movement, such as Betty Friedan, Betsy Warrior, Andrea Dworkin, and Sally Kempton, shared their personal experiences of wife beating and rape with other women and then sought to understand those experiences in a larger political and structural context. The advocates in this movement sought to define wife-beating as a social problem, not just a problem within individual relationships (Gordon 1988).

Although it has not come near the goal of eliminating domestic violence, the battered women movement has made progress in getting some change in society's response to the problem. It has challenged sexist laws that contributed to violence against women and has constructed new terms and redefined issues to disclose violence occurring in the private realm that until recently was not acknowledged by the law.[2] Before this movement, the abuse of women in their homes was a private issue. There were no terms to describe a "battered woman," nothing called the "battered woman syndrome," and no shelters for abused women and children.[3] Significant results have come from the legal system, including orders of protection and the use of the battered woman syndrome to aid self-defense cases for women who kill their abusers. In addition, a vast amount of research has been conducted on domestic violence, and the plight of battered women is now the subject of media and public discussion.

The movement emerged most visibly in its provision of shelters and crisis services for battered women. With the opening of these shelters, women came together locally and nationally in an effort to end male violence against women. Erin Pizzey, who is credited with setting up the first battered women refuge, also publicized the violent treatment of women and the need for shelters in England. Following England's example, battered women advocates began setting up shelters in the United States. The number of shelters in the United States grew rapidly, from approximately twenty in 1976 to over three hundred by 1982 (Pleck 1987). By the year 2000 there were over two thousand domestic violence programs across the United States, most of which included shelters (Sullivan and Gillum 2001). Battered women shelters provide an array of services for battered women and their children, including counseling, legal and medical advocacy, parenting classes, help with securing housing, jobs, education, and immediate food and clothing needs.

Eventually, shelter founders from the feminist movement lost much of their control of many shelters, which drew more support from churches, community groups, and social services. Clinical language, psychotherapeutic intervention, and professional social workers took over many of the shelters. Many funding sources did not accept the feminist politics that accompanied the movement.[4] As I mentioned earlier, the battered women movement makes three major assumptions. First, victims should not be blamed for the abuse they receive. Second, domestic violence is primarily a problem of men abusing women. Third, domestic violence is one component of a patriarchal system that includes other forms of discrimination against women. Local communities and the government were not comfortable with the argument that wife-beating was a result of a cultural and structural system of gender discrimination. In order to secure funding and support, many feminists had to censure their own politics.

Due to this political context and to the movement's initial focus on the needs of victims, the recognition of domestic violence as a social problem emerged as an issue about the victims. Though part of the movement's goals included reducing the violence, many advocates wanted to avoid focusing on abusers because they feared scarce resources would be diverted from victims (Dobash and Dobash 1992). The dominant focus on victims as opposed to the abusers contrasted to the earlier child abuse movement. In 1978, Congress and the U.S. Civil Rights Commission held hearings to discuss battered women. Witnesses claimed that wife-beating had become a serious national problem and that intervention was needed to protect battered women and their children. Although the statements were similar to those on the hearings regarding child abuse, they differed significantly in their dominant focus on victims. For the hearing about child abuse, witnesses explained why parents abuse their children. When it came time to discuss wife abuse, abusers were not discussed, but rather, experts explained why women were willing to be beaten (Pleck 1987).

The battered women movement emerged during a cultural and political context that was focusing more intensely on victims. The 1960s and 1970s brought significant changes in how we think about victims. Domestic violence emerged as a social problem in the midst of this broader victim movement. I will briefly describe some of those changes to give a broader picture of the political and cultural context that helped shape the emergence of domestic violence as a social problem.

 POLITICALLY AND CULTURALLY: A VICTIM'S MOVEMENT

Most of my students were born after 1980. They grew up using e-mail and cell phones, browsing the web, and listening to CDs. These advances in technology did not seem like revolutionary changes in communication for them because they were "always there." In the same way, they grew up with many categories of victims in our society. It can be easy to forget that we have not always acknowledged that people can be victims of such problems as racism, sexual harassment, date rape, discrimination, or domestic violence. But just as e-mail and cell phones have changed the way we communicate, the victim movements have affected the way we understand social problems. Now, what that label of "victim" *means* to people is a whole other question, which I explore later in this chapter. But we need to review how the political and cultural context of the 1960s and

1970s helped to shape how we understand and respond to social problems such as domestic violence. This context will also give insight into how we started recognizing new groups as victims.

Victim's Rights

In his book *Random Violence,* Joel Best explains that during the 1960s and 1970s numerous emerging social movements changed the way we think about victims and victimization.[5] Some of these included the civil rights, women's rights, children's rights, and crime victim's rights movements. These movements and others helped set a new political and cultural context for calling attention to victims. In particular, the civil rights and women's rights movements provided a model for arguing that large groups of people were not being treated fairly and showing how these groups were being victimized (Best 1999). The focus of the civil rights movement was more focused on rights of "victims" (African-Americans) than on punishing the offenders. Though certainly there was (and continues to be) rhetoric about people who are guilty of discrimination and some laws have been developed that focus on the perpetrators (such as hate crime laws), the emergence of the civil rights movement focused on victims. These larger movements paved the way for other groups that began framing their issues in terms of victim's rights. Some of those groups/movements include animal rights, children's rights, prisoner's rights, crime victim's rights, unborn children's rights, and gay/lesbian rights movements.

Victimology: The Study of the Victim's Role in Crime

Not all victim talk during this time focused on the "rights" of victims. There was also an increased focus on holding victims responsible for provoking or not preventing their own victimization. During the 1960s there was an increasing awareness that the government could do little to reduce crime (Mawby and Walklate 1994; Karmen 1990). The 1967 President's Commission on Law Enforcement and Administration of Justice encouraged criminologists to pay more attention to victims: "One of the most neglected subjects in the study of crime is its victims. . . . Both the part the victim can play in the criminal act and the part he could have played in preventing it are often overlooked" (Task Force on Assessment 1967:80).

It is impossible to know when people first started discussing the role of victims in crime and violence. But we can trace the academic roots of victimology, which is the study of victims and their role in crime. Von Hentig's 1948 study on the resistance of rape victims introduced the idea of studying victims. Von Hentig was interested in the presumed vulnerabilities of some people as compared to the presumed culpability of others.

He argued that in a large percentage of criminal cases, the victim shares responsibility for his or her victimization. This idea of victim responsibility was reinforced by Mendelsohn, who is credited for coining the term "victimology." He wrote about victim culpability—or to what extent the victim made a guilty contribution to a crime (Karmen 1990). Mendelsohn classified victims into types based on culpability ranging from "complete innocence" to "full responsibility" (Roberts 1990). Since then a number of victimologists have devised various typologies to explain shared responsibility on the part of victims. Few of these typologies have been viewed as useful or credible, although the idea of victim culpability remains strong (Karmen 1990).

Placing responsibility on victims or potential victims draws attention away from other institutions or individuals that could be involved in preventing or intervening in the problem. People are warned to keep their doors locked, install security systems, not go out alone at night, avoid the "wrong" people and places, and behave responsibly in order to prevent crime and assaults. If this frame of responsibility is accepted, when an assault does happen, people are more likely to hold the victim accountable for his or her actions, as opposed to questioning why the perpetrator committed the crime, or how police could better prevent crime, or what laws could be passed to lower crime rates. Policing and prosecuting domestic violence and other crimes require resources. It is more economical—though not necessarily more efficient—to ask the victims to do more to prevent crime (and it is hard to argue against teaching personal safety). Thus, a focus on victimology can be politically advantageous because it promises a reduction in crime with little or no cost.

The Self-Help Movement

At the same time as the rise of victimology and the victim movements, a new "pop psychology" emerged that helped set guidelines for the new woman of the sixties and seventies. This movement was invigorating for millions of women who learned about these new life guidelines in therapy groups, self-help books, and magazine articles. This self-help culture taught individual improvement as a "cure-all" solution and ignored needed programs of social change.[6] Along with this new marketplace psychology came an increased demand for "psychological counseling." Although this demand led to a growth in the psychology industry, the new pop psychology was never contained by any academic discipline. People of all backgrounds could get in on the mass production of self-help books that started in the 1970s and continues to be popular today (Ehrenreich and English 1978; Simonds 1992). The self-help movement has also exploded into the world of television talk shows. Oprah's "change your life TV" leads the way in showing women in particular how to "regain their power" and change their own lives.[7] Dr. Phil is another popular television counselor who focuses on "self-help."

The rise of victimology and self-help culture in the 1960s and 1970s was the cultural background for the second wave of feminism, which led the campaign against domestic violence. Beginning in the early 1970s, the battered women movement focused heavily on lobbying and fighting for the needs of the victims. Its goals included providing shelters and crisis services for battered women and their children, lobbying for legislation to aid victims of domestic violence, and modifying court and police practices to be more responsive to battered women. Through their actions, women activists drew attention to the reluctance of the court and law enforcement systems to classify victims of domestic violence as "true victims" who were worthy of social and legal protection (Sebba 1996).

While the women's movement uncovered the "hidden problem" of domestic violence, it also contributed to the framing of women as victims.[8] Thanks to victories by the feminist movement, women were better able to voice their claims of victimhood. However, it appears that the more independence women gain, the less willing people are to grant them the label of legitimate and innocent victim (Christie 1986). For example, the other night while I lay awake at 3:00 A.M. I watched a congressional subcommittee hearing related to violence against women. One of the congresswomen said that with all the resources and services for abuse victims that are now available, there is no excuse for a woman not leaving an abusive relationship. What does it mean, then, to be labeled a victim?

TO BE A VICTIM

Victims are central characters in most stories about crime, violence, and other social problems. Many times victims are blamed for their own victimization. Questions about victims—particularly in cases of rape and domestic violence—are often asked in attempts to challenge the victim's innocence. Who was the victim? What was the victim wearing? What is the relationship between the victim and offender? Had the victim been doing drugs or drinking alcohol? Did the victim provoke the violence? Had she had prior sexual relationships? Some victims are portrayed in the media as more "worthy" of our sympathy than others.[9] Some victims are depicted as completely innocent, while others are depicted as partially or fully responsible for or deserving of the crime committed against them. Typically, young children are seen as fully innocent victims. Just recently I saw many media reports about a five-year-old girl who was abducted, sexually abused, and murdered. She was depicted as completely innocent and undeserving of that crime. However, media stories running at the same time about a woman allegedly assaulted by a professional basketball player questioned her credibility as a victim. People's desire to erode the credibility of a victim intensifies when the offender is a beloved celebrity, politician, sports hero, coach, or other popular figure.

Not all social problem frames that focus on victims are meant to blame them. Advocates often use dramatic, emotional stories of victims to raise public concern about a social problem and to generate resources to help its victims. Prosecutors and death penalty advocates often use victims' stories as evidence that the offenders need to be punished. And many activists, support groups, scholars, and victims' groups see "empowerment" as a very important aspect for helping victims. From this point of view, framing the victim is often seen as a good thing. So what has happened to the efforts to frame victims as a way to help them get support from the community—as opposed to being held responsible for the problem?

Advocates—people who are working to help victims of social problems—use victimization as a way to show others that these people are worthy of help. Some research suggests that this can be a useful approach for responding to social problems. However, there is a difference between the ideal goal of empowering victims and the popularized use of "victim empowerment" in mass media. In the media and in everyday conversations, people who are abused are usually labeled "victims," but what this label means for the victim is not always clear. I have attempted to show throughout this book that although recipients of domestic violence are labeled "victims," they are not absolved from responsibility; rather, they are actually the individuals held most responsible for the problem. In this section, I explore how the "victim" label in the case of domestic violence has not worked as advocates have intended. First, I describe academic theories behind the victim label and the idea of victim empowerment. Then I explain how the popularization of these ideas strips the political and social context that is meant to protect and help the victims.

Ideal Victims and Ideal Implications of Being Labeled a Victim

Labeling someone a victim is intended to guide other people's reaction to that individual. People also use the label of victim as an interpretive framework for shaping our understanding of a social problem. In "Rethinking Victimization: An Interactional Approach to Victimology," Jim Holstein and Gale Miller looked at the process of labeling and constructing victims (Holstein and Miller 1990). They argued that "victim status" is assigned to people through social interactions and through the ways stories are told about social problems. This was an important development beyond the tendency to just assume that some people are victims. As I mentioned before, people often forget that we have not always talked about victims of domestic violence like we do now. Joel Best claims that the victim movements drew attention to victimization and created a new way of talking about victims—what he describes as an ideology of victimization.[10] He argues that the ideology of victimization

> defines victimization as common, consequential, and clear-cut, yet unrecognized; it justifies helping individuals identify themselves as victims; it delegitimizes doubts about victims' claims; and it provides new, nonstigmatizing labels for those who have suffered. It is, in short, a set of beliefs that makes it easy to label victims, and very difficult to dispute those labels. (1999:117)

Advocates use this ideology of victimization to further their claims about a particular problem.

People who work hard to attach the label "victim" to particular groups and individuals do so because they want to tell others what to think about them. "We might view the production of 'victims' as the public articulation and dramatization of injury and innocence" (Holstein and Miller 1990:105). According to Holstein and Miller, one of the consequences of being labeled a victim is "exoneration from responsibility." Labeling one a victim absolves her from "fault for her troubles, and renders her worthy of others' concern" (ibid.:106). They claim that a victim designation serves practical purposes for the people or groups labeled victims. Three of these purposes are identified as deflecting responsibility, assigning causes, and specifying responses and remedies.

1. *Absolve victims from responsibility for the harm.* The first purpose of victimization is to absolve victims from responsibility for the harm. By deflecting responsibility, the victim is identified as the innocent party (Holstein and Miller 1990; and Best 1999). This argument relates to what other victimology scholars describe as "ideal victims." The ideal victim is a cultural conception of someone who is completely innocent of wrongdoing and plays no active role in his or her own victimization (Kennedy and Sacco 1998; Madriz 1997; Walklate 1989; Christie 1986). Ideal victims are those who not only unfairly suffer a loss but were helpless to prevent the loss (Bayley 1991).
2. *Assign causes and identify sources of harm.* A second purpose of the "victim" label is to assign causes—to identify the sources of harm—that implicitly designate a perpetrator of harm. Holstein and Miller claim that a victim cannot exist without a perpetrator. The dramatization of innocence and of evil are simultaneously accomplished. If one party (the victim) is identified as innocent of wrongdoing, then another party needs to be held accountable.
3. *Specify responses to the harm.* Specifying response and remedies is a third purpose of victimization. Labeling someone a victim "suggests

that the person deserves help or compensation, while indicating that others should be sanctioned" (Holstein and Miller 1990:110). Furthermore, Holstein and Miller indicate that failure to sanction the harm-doers can be portrayed as a "second victimization" of the innocent person. A central feature of being a victim is entitlement to social concern (Bayley 1991).

Victim Empowerment

Once someone has been labeled a victim, advocates, social service workers, and others aim to help the victim. As just described, a main purpose for labeling someone a victim is to get the person help from the community and to "right the wrong." One of the concepts used when working with people is "victim empowerment." I use this term to refer to the frame that saturates mass media, such as women's magazines and talk shows. However, the idea of empowerment did not originate with these media, and many scholars argue that the theory of empowerment goes way beyond the personal story. Here I briefly describe the roots of victim empowerment. Then I explain how in practice the original goals of empowerment are lost.

A common understanding in both social work and feminist literature is that empowerment requires an understanding that powerlessness is a result of structural and institutional forces that allow for inequality in power and control over resources. Therefore, empowerment should be a process that aims to identify and change the distribution of power within a culture to achieve social justice (Morgen and Bookman 1988; Collins 1991; Gutiérrez and Lewis 1999). Empowerment is a concept that has been used in the social work profession for several decades. There are three levels of empowerment as described in the social work literature: personal, interpersonal, and political (Gutiérrez and Lewis 1999). Trying to empower people on the personal level is supposed to set the stage for the other levels of empowerment. "Achieving personal empowerment involves recognizing and identifying the power one already has" (ibid.:11). On the interpersonal level, people increase their skills at influencing others. Political empowerment involves social action and a process of transferring power between groups.

This concept of empowerment includes an understanding that different groups in our society possess different levels of power and control over social resources (Simon 1994; Gutiérrez and Lewis 1999). Empowerment theory should then be applied to help individuals overcome the effects of powerlessness. Theoretically, the overall goal of empowerment should include social justice and a reduction of social inequality. However, the victim empowerment frame used in the popular media does not explain the different levels of power and control nor does it call for a reduction of this inequality. Instead, only the personal level of empowerment is discussed.

Indeed the victim movement of the 1960s and 1970s made it easier for people to claim victim status. And advocates, such as those involved in the battered women movement, wanted to achieve the purposes outlined above, including the ideal goal of victim empowerment. They wanted to exonerate victims from blame, identify the abusers, locate the abuse within the social and cultural context, and specify community responses and help for the victim. Their framing of the problem includes many of the points in the ideology of victimization that Best describes. However, the dominant framing of domestic violence in the media and by many individuals does not accept these same purposes and understandings of the victim status. The popular use of the victim label does not have the political and activist goals behind it. Although the abused person is usually granted the label of victim, the meaning behind that label is often contested and does not have the consequences described above. Why is this and what consequences does it have for social policy?

The Popularization of Victims and Victim Empowerment

The media use advocates' claims about victims and the concept of empowerment, but do so in a way that fits their own needs.[11] The media translate the concepts of victimization and empowerment into their own style of storytelling because they have different reasons for using domestic violence in their stories. While advocates are framing a social problem in a way that they think will help them achieve the desired responses to the problem, media are framing the problem in a way that will please their audience, be compatible with entertainment, and help ratings.

It is important to analyze how the media frame victims because people use the media to understand social problems. The media are the gate-keepers for advocates who are trying to get their claims to the public. Therefore, we are bound, at least in part, by how the media choose to frame social problems. Media portrayals of social problems affect common understandings of the problem, which spill over into individual responses by police officers, judges, jurors, lawyers, clergy, friends, family, and counselors. These individual understandings are also used in making laws, developing policy, and creating prevention programs.

The principles and guidelines that shape mass media stories tend to emphasize the personal and dramatic. They also often emphasize inspiring and uplifting stories. In this translation, the purposes for labeling someone a victim are lost. The battered women movement and other advocates fighting against domestic violence intend to use the label of victim as a way to also define who the perpetrator is, and what the community should do about the situation. However, the media use the frame of victim in a style of storytelling that leaves out the abuser and the cultural and structural context.

I discuss three main points concerning how the purposes and ideal implications of victim labels and victim empowerment fail to transfer to the mass media and public understandings. First, victims are held responsible for solving the problem. Second, male abusers are obscured. And finally, power is defined as a personal choice while ignoring the political and social dimensions of power.

Holding Victims Responsible and Promoting Victim-Based Solutions.   As I discussed above, the purposes behind labeling people victims include exonerating them from blame, deflecting responsibility away from them, and specifying help for the victim. However, in the popularized use of victimization, none of these purposes are realized. Instead, the victim's innocence is challenged and the victim is the person held most responsible for solving the problem.

In media accounts of domestic violence, the innocence and motives of victims are challenged. They are not exempted from blame, but rather portrayed as at least partially responsible. In Chapter 4 I noted that the victim empowerment perspective may include questions about what victims do to tell their abusers they can hit them. Victims may also be told to accept their responsibility for provoking the abuse. This challenging of victims is more explicit in the antifeminist frame. One of the main themes in the antifeminist frame is that domestic violence is the responsibility of both men and women and that women are not as "innocent" as they are usually portrayed. These articles challenge women's "innocence" in two ways. First, they argue that women are at least as violent as men and need to be held accountable for this abuse. Second, many of the articles hold women accountable when they are the victims in the relationship.

Victims of domestic violence are also not exonerated from responsibility in the mass media. Instead, the dominant topic continues to be why victims stay in abusive relationships and what they can do to solve the problem. Even when the legal system is discussed, it is done most often in the context of how to help the victim rather than how to punish the harmdoer. Far from being absolved from responsibility for their own victimization, victims of domestic violence are questioned and blamed for their role in their abuse. Victims and others often talk about what the victim should have done to stop or prevent the abuse. At times this perspective is quite hostile, as in stories that use an antifeminist frame. Victims are explicitly blamed for staying in the relationship. The victims are criticized for not leaving because they may actually enjoy the relationship too much, and, for denying their own role in the "dance of mutual destructiveness." In other media that use a victim empowerment frame, the discourse is kinder but still holds the victim partially responsible. The message is that the victims are responsible for ending the abuse. Authors give advice on how to leave and encourage victims to take control of their lives and get out. Victims are told explicitly that it is up to them to accept responsibility for their own lives.

Because victims are held responsible for solving their problems in the media frame of victimization, the solutions remain victim-based. The most common solutions offered in this perspective are for the victim to leave the abuser and for the victim to get counseling. Furthermore, stories that tell victims they need to "just get out" usually ignore research that shows one of the most dangerous times for a victim is when she tries to leave her abuser. Also, "potential victims" are held responsible for solving the problem by being aware of warning signs and not getting into abusive relationships in the first place. It is assumed that people can prevent abuse from happening, and thus they are also partially to blame when they do find themselves in abusive relationships.

Obscuring the (Male) Abuser.   Victimology scholars argue that when victims are labeled, perpetrators are simultaneously identified. However, in the media frame of victimization there is little focus on the perpetrators of domestic violence. In the antifeminist frame, female abusers are held responsible, but there is no discussion of male abusers. It is difficult to find media stories about where batterers can get help, how to recognize if you are a batterer, or how to avoid using violence in conflict resolution. Furthermore, public opinion research shows that people have little to say regarding why men abuse. When individuals do talk about abusers and what causes them to abuse, they focus on alcohol abuse and childhood abuse. People's lack of information regarding abusers reflects the absence of media attention to abusers.

Media that do focus on the legal system argue that either the system failed to intervene and protect victims of domestic violence, that more laws and training are needed for effective intervention, or that men's rights are being abused. Few articles give attention to tougher punishment for the batterer or even getting help for the batterer. Most of the media focus entirely or in part on the immediate needs of the victim. This, of course, is crucial. However, the system's failure to arrest, punish, counsel, prevent, or condemn abusers remains largely ignored.

The perpetrators of domestic violence do not fit the image of the "ideal offender." As I mentioned earlier, victimology researchers have argued that ideally when one labels someone a victim, he or she is also labeling a perpetrator. Just as there are "ideal victims" there are "ideal offenders" (Christie 1986). These researchers claim that cultural assumptions about victims recognize a clear moral division between the "innocent victims" and the "guilty offenders" (Lamb 1996; Kennedy and Sacco 1998). There is a polarization of the offender and the victim. It is emotionally appealing to represent crime as an epic battle between the forces of darkness and light, "with victims as the lambs and criminals the wolves, with victims as innocent and criminals guilty" (Madriz 1997:79). Ideal criminals are often depicted as animals, strangers, and extremely violent. Certainly perpetrators of other crimes are publicly dramatized as criminals and often as evil. Perhaps, though, abusers are too familiar to us, which makes this dramatization of evil uncomfortable. Abusers are typically our neighbors, fathers, sons, husbands, and brothers. The rhetoric traditionally reserved for offenders of most crimes often falls back onto domestic violence victims in warped ways. Rather than focusing on punishing the offender, media focus on victims' failure to leave the relationship, how they might have actually participated in the abuse, or how victims can end the abuse.

Power Is Defined As a Personal Choice.   In the victim empowerment perspective, power is defined as a personal choice. Particularly on talk shows and in women's magazine articles, victims are told that they need to "take back the power" to "take charge of their life." The popular use of "empowerment" is to give power to someone. In the case of domestic violence, to empower the victims is to give the victim power. This idea of empowerment depoliticizes power. In other words, it strips away the structural, cultural, historical, and gendered context of power. Perspectives that refer only to "individual self-assertion, upward mobility, or the psychological experience of 'feeling powerful'" are merely fashionable uses of the concept of empowerment and fail to take into account the political level of empowerment (Morgen and Bookman 1988:4). Power must be understood in social, economic, political, psychological, structural, and cultural contexts and include such issues as gender socialization, patriarchy, the structure of family and society, and cultural tolerance of violence.

Many articles in political media do address the political level of empowerment. The antifeminist frame in political media critiques the cultural context that tolerates female violence but does not provide a similar analysis for male violence. Articles in *The Progressive* and *The Nation* focus on the cultural and structural context of men's violence. However, audiences for these political magazines are much smaller than those of magazines such as *Penthouse* and *Ladies' Home Journal* and for talk shows such as *Oprah*, which all primarily focus on the personal level of victim empowerment.

THE PERSONAL SELLS (AND IS POLITICALLY SAFER)

Although academic theories have advanced our understanding of domestic violence to include structural and cultural factors, mass media continue to portray it as the victim's personal problem. The personal story is most often an "unfolding drama" with a beginning and an end—complete with dramatic images and descriptions of bruises, injuries, trauma, personal histories and characteristics, and acts of violence, including self-defense. The personal perspective explains what an individual can and should do to solve the problem. Though this personal framing could focus on the abuser, the dominant media stories target the victim. The battered women movement began as a transformation of abuse from a personal problem to a larger social problem.[12] But perceptions of battering as a social and political problem in the United States quickly were displaced by frames emphasizing the personal problems of victims. In 1982, Kathleen Tierney predicted that domestic violence would become increasingly medicalized and individualized. Her prediction has been realized. The personal analysis of social problems is politically safer. It is easier to gather public support for helping victims of domestic violence than to fight the social and cultural factors fostering violence.

The media continue to frame social problems as personal, dramatic stories about individuals with inspiring, victim-based solutions. The culture of individualism in the United States, coupled with the popularity of the self-help movement, has effectively transformed the social, cultural, and political issues of domestic violence into personal stories and personal problems (Dobash and Dobash 1992). Public responses to the problem are loaded with psychological language and solutions. Syndromes, profiles, low self-esteem, pathologies, and individual characteristics now describe the "social" problem. Counseling and advising the victim to leave the relationship are the most common solutions in the media.

Marketing fears play a role in the marginalization of perspectives that emphasize the social and cultural context of domestic violence. Editors maintain that personal dramatic stories sell more magazines than stories about the more complex social and political dynamics of a problem. Many magazines have article formats and guidelines that encourage writers to reproduce the individual frame. Editors, those of women's magazines in particular, seek articles that focus on intimate relationships and inspiring personal experiences. The emphasis is on how the individual overcomes the problem. The personal story evokes sympathy, inspiration, interest, and drama.

The political story is more likely to elicit controversy, flak, and unrest. It is easier to have a "happy ending" in a story about a victim who solved her problem as opposed to the unsettling ending of a culture in need of change. Keeping social problems on an individual level is more comfortable and less intrusive to the public. The personal only affects the individuals involved in the stories for the most part, while political/social frames of domestic violence potentially affect "everyone." For example, by discussing how victims can leave an abusive partner, only victims and their

abusers are targeted. However, efforts to change legal and economic institutions draw more resistance from powerful groups and individuals. A
call to change media images of men and women, or to end corporal punishment, or to challenge subtle and normalized male aggression is politically more volatile.

CONCLUSION

Framing the victim for the responsibility of solving domestic violence does
not work very well if our goal is to effectively work toward intervention
and prevention of the problem. In part this may be because the purposes
behind advocates' use of the victim label do not transfer to the popular
media's use of victimization and empowerment. Other scholars have noted
that the response to domestic violence victims shows that people do not see
them as "ideal victims." Victims of domestic violence are seen as at least
partially responsible for their victimization (Madriz 1997; Christie 1986).
Therefore, if people do not see domestic violence victims as "ideal victims"
then it becomes harder to free them from blame and responsibility.

The dominant perspective in the media normalizes the idea that the victim should be held responsible for solving her problem. It assumes that
social supports are readily available to help her leave—shelters housing
her, police protecting her, judges enforcing protection orders, employers
willing to hire her, family supporting her (Jones 1994). With the current
media primarily framing the victim for domestic violence, the source of
harm is generally ignored, resulting in very little public debate on why
abusers abuse. The solutions to the problem are victim-based and do not
further the effort to prevent domestic violence. With the rise of victimology, many crime reduction policies have focused on the victim's role.
Victim-blaming crime prevention strategies place responsibility for reducing crime on the victim, and the source of harm is ignored.[13] Holding
domestic violence victims responsible for their abuse reflects an individualistic approach to analyzing social problems. A victim-focused movement
diverts attention and resources from effective crime control and prevention programs. The root causes of violence and the social issues that foster
abuse are overshadowed by the attention given to victims. Prevention
needs to be focused on just as much as intervention. If we only focus on
helping victims *after* the violence has occurred, we will never make
progress in *reducing* the amount of violence occurring.

Since popular media have great influence on public understandings,
alternative perspectives that focus on abusers and the cultural context are
needed. A concentrated effort is necessary to break away from the dominant individual perspective on domestic violence. More stories need to

focus on the violence itself, the perpetrators of violence, including men, and the cultural and structural context. We need stories that inspire people to question the cultural attitudes that tolerate violence in the family and the larger society. A more proactive approach to discussing violence would include stories that discuss abusers, the roots of violence, and complex social, political, and economic dynamics. In the next chapter, I offer some recommendations for how we might accomplish these goals.

NOTES

1. To read more about domestic violence throughout history see Gordon (1987). To read short stories about domestic violence from the 1800s through the early 1990s see Koppelman (1996).

2. For more information on the results of the battered women movement see, for example, Renzetti and Edelson (2001), Freeman (1995), and Tierney (1982).

3. To read more about the social construction of shelters and the battered woman see Loseke (1992).

4. See Pleck (1987), Gordon (1988), Dobash and Dobash (1992), and Mann (2000) to read more about politics and the battered women movement.

5. For a more detailed discussion on the social construction of victims and the emergence of a victim's industry see Best (1999).

6. To read more about the self-help culture see Simonds (1992) and Ehrenreich and English (1978).

7. See Kathleen Lowney's *Baring Our Souls* (1999) for an extended look at how television talk shows connect to the self-help movement.

8. The research and literature on male violence against women had the effect of constructing women as lacking human agency. "Women were no longer so thoroughly objectified as male property, but they were reobjectified as victim" (Faith 1993:107). See also Madriz (1997).

9. See Loseke (2003) for more information on how claims-makers use victims in constructing their frames of the problem.

10. Best discusses in detail seven parts of the victimization ideology: (1) Victimization is widespread; (2) victimization is consequential; (3) victimization is relatively straightforward and unambiguous; (4) victimization often goes unrecognized; (5) individuals must be taught to recognize others' and their own victimization; (6) claims of victimization must be respected; and (7) the term "victim" has undesirable connotations. See Best (1999) for more information on these ideas.

11. To learn more about the connections among media, advocates, and other groups see Best's concept of the "iron quadrangle" of institutionalization in *Random Violence* (1999).

12. To read more about the history of the battered women movement see Gordon (1987) and Dobash and Dobash (1992).

13. See Walklate (1989) for more on victim-blaming crime prevention.

9

In Search of a *New* Social Problem about Violence

One day while I was sitting in a coffee shop writing this book, one of the workers, Jarrad, stopped by my table to see how my work was going.[1] We had talked before and he knew that I was writing about domestic violence. That day Jarrad approached me saying he wanted to tell me a story that might help my research.

Jarrad said that he had a friend who was a calm, gentle, and easygoing guy. Nothing would set him off except seeing someone hit a girl. About a month ago this guy saw a friend get hit by her boyfriend. This young man got angry and beat up the boyfriend, breaking his ankle and arm. The police came and arrested the injured guy for hitting the girl. The police officer told Jarrad's friend, who had assaulted the boyfriend, to just walk away. I asked Jarrad if he was surprised that this person got away with beating up the young man who assaulted the girl. He said he was surprised, but kind of liked the way it turned out.

After a brief moment, Jarrad admitted that he was actually the one in the story who beat up the other guy. I paused, wondering what to say next. I asked him how the girl who was hit felt about what happened. Jarrad said, "She was mad as hell at me. She wondered why I had to hurt him." But then he smiled and said that she has since thanked him for it. Jarrad has not seen the other guy since that night, which he thought was a good thing. Then he also told me that he knew the police officer involved and thought that helped him get away with his beating up the other guy. "So," he said before leaving, "I just wanted to tell you that story in case it helps."

When Jarrad told me that he was the one who beat up the abusive boyfriend, I was surprised and disappointed. He did not seem like he would be violent. How interesting that I would have this initial reaction when I know so well that "abusers" usually have both a public and private side. It would not be different for anyone who is violent, whether that vio-

162

lence is directed toward children, parents, friends, strangers, girlfriends, or boyfriends. People who abuse others do not usually look violent. We cannot pick them out in a crowd. They are everyday people who live and work with us. However, we expect some people to be violent because we have images in our heads about "violent people." We see media images about violence; the abusers, rapists, and murderers are rarely portrayed as the guy next door. They are usually portrayed as evil and dramatized as the "bad guy." It is rare to get a complex picture of someone who can be charming, respectable, helpful, and loving, and yet have a violent side. It is hard to recognize violence in people when we so often see the nonviolent side to them. I know all this, yet it was still surprising to discover that Jarrad had been so violent.

I thought a lot about Jarrad's story. How should we feel about it? Is there any "good" in what he did? Is it admirable that he stood up for his friend who was being assaulted? Are we not wanting people to take dating violence more seriously? And yet, what he did was also violence. Is one type of violence worse than the other? For many people, some assaults are justified. It seemed clear that Jarrad thought his violence was justified. Or did he? He did seem perplexed by the outcome, even if he was thankful not to have been arrested. He was happy the guy was not around anymore and thought that his friend was better off without her abusive boyfriend. Many of our most popular movies and television shows are designed to have us cheering for the "good guys" to beat the "bad guys." How do we know where to draw the line about what violence is good and what violence is bad?

It is no wonder that we are so confused about violence. One could argue that Jarrad's type of "justice" is not so different from "official justice." People often respond to violence with more violence. We are a culture of violent solutions. We use violent terms to depict our responses to social problems: a war on drugs, a war on poverty, a war on drunk driving (Best 1999). We tolerate hitting children (spanking) to tell them not to do wrong. We kill people (capital punishment) to tell them it was wrong to kill someone. We go to war with countries and kill thousands because those countries are killing people and threatening us with violence.[2] The issue of "just violence" and "unjust violence" is very complicated. Often it depends on the particular issue and one's political orientation. It might also depend on your standpoint concerning victimization—was "the victim" innocent or did he or she deserve the violence? One of the reasons it may be so difficult to focus on "violence" as the problem is that it is so hard to agree on how and when and by whom violence is a problem. As I explained in Chapter 2, people say that domestic violence is a problem. But when given particular scenarios, they say that sometimes violence in a family is necessary, justified, or provoked.

As I have argued in this book, domestic violence has emerged as a problem about the victims. It is not viewed as a problem about the violence. The battered women movement attempted to include the social and cultural context of violence and the accountability of abusers. However, these aspects of the problem have not successfully transferred to mainstream entertainment media or the general public. I have discussed various reasons that victims have been framed for this problem. In some cases, politics has made it difficult to discuss abusers, particularly male abusers. In other media, particularly mass entertainment media, victims are viewed as more dramatic, inspiring, and heroic than abusers, and therefore more marketable. And for many advocates, it is important to keep the focus on victims to help ensure continued attention and resources for them. Though focusing on the victim may contribute to useful outcomes for intervention and providing resources for victims, there remain serious barriers to achieving a public understanding of the context of this violence, which is important for prevention. The dominant focus on victims of domestic violence may actually impede social change that could lead to more effective prevention efforts. The root of the problem is the abusers—not the victims.

In this chapter, I argue that we need to construct a "new" social problem about domestic violence that focuses more on violence and abusers than the victims. We also need a cultural change in how we think about social problems. This change should include expanding our sources of information, challenging the entertainment and individualistic focus of social problems, and raising standards for how media cover these issues.

A NEW SOCIAL PROBLEM ABOUT VIOLENCE

We need a new social problem about violence. Probably most people would think that the last thing we need is a new social problem. Why would I favor another "violence" problem? How do we create a social problem and what would it look like? Hopefully by now you realize that I am not suggesting that we need more violence in our culture, but rather we need a new way of framing that violence, a new way of talking about the problem of violence. A social constructionist perspective explains that conditions are defined and framed as social problems when claims-makers have been successful at convincing people that the conditions are troublesome wrong, and that something can and should be done about them.[3] It is not that the claims-makers "make up" those conditions, such as poverty or drug abuse, but rather they are successful in framing the problem in a way that convinces others it is a problem.

I am not recommending that we necessarily try to transform how the media and public currently view "domestic violence." I think it would be too difficult to make the transformation from domestic violence as a story about the victims to a story about the abusers and the roots of violence. We have examples of frames that do portray the problem in this way. The social justice frame attempts to take the focus off victims and an occasional story in other media zooms in on the abuser (though more typically a female abuser) or on the social context of the violence. However, the mass entertainment media continue to focus on the victim for marketing reasons that have proved successful for them. I believe that it may be easier to construct a "new" social problem in the media. In addition, there can be some good reasons to focus on victims and illustrate what they go through in an abusive situation. There will continue to be a need for advocates and resources for victims, and in order to keep those services going it is helpful to have an active "social problem" that focuses on their situation. If domestic violence continues to be debated, even as a victim's problem, perhaps we will continue to see growth in people's understanding of that aspect of it. A final reason for attempting to construct a new social problem is that in order to understand domestic violence, we need to see the connections between it and other types of violence. The roots of our violence problem are best defined in frames that extend beyond "domestic violence."

In Chapter 2, I described the complex landscape of domestic violence. Included in that landscape are many issues about the roots of violence, the abusers, and the social tolerance of violence. I am recommending that we draw a box around those issues in an attempt to frame a new problem of violence and zoom in on why, how, and to what end violence is used as a means of conflict resolution and of maintaining control in relationships. We need to frame all use of violence as a social problem. Certainly this is not a new idea because many advocates, professionals, and others already hold this view. However, we need a public discovery of this problem similar to the discovery of domestic violence in the 1970s—except that we should shift the focus from victims to abusers and violence. It is time to pay attention to why people use violence and other abusive strategies, what can be done to help them, and how we can prevent others from abusing their partners and families. We have research and social programs that address these questions, but we have seen little of this knowledge get transferred through the media to the public. Though this chapter does not attempt to lay out all the details of this new social problem, I offer recommendations for shaping this perspective.

Glimpses of a New Social Problem

We need a social problem that condemns any use of violence as a means of conflict resolution. In media stories constructed using this frame, any use of violence in any type of relationship would be presented as abnormal and unacceptable. You might wonder why I argue this would be a new idea. Indeed many people do believe that any use of violence is wrong. However, violence is too often portrayed as a natural part of life, and when it happens in relationships, people are not surprised. Many people do not seem shocked that others are abusive or violent toward their loved ones. They are surprised that victims will "take it" or that victims do not leave. Because the problem of domestic violence frames the victim, people focus their questions and answers on what the victim could and should do. And now that there are more resources available for victims compared to thirty years ago, victims are under even more pressure to "just leave." People have to start asking, "Why do people abuse others?" "Why can they get away with that?" We need people to be disapproving of the abusers rather than shaming the victims. Mothers and fathers should start telling their children not just to leave a relationship if they get hit, but that it is not acceptable to hit people or to use other abusive tactics.

A new social problem about abuse and violence should clearly frame the use of control, abuse, and intimidation as wrong. Though many abusers know full well what they are doing is wrong, there are some people who see their behavior as acceptable or normal. There are also people who use these strategies without realizing they are wrong. Occasionally, I will have students in my violence class who begin to realize that they use abusive behavior in their relationships. One of my students told me that after spending a semester reading about domestic violence, he was concerned about some of his actions. He recounted a time that he punched a hole in the wall right next to his girlfriend's head as she stood paralyzed and pinned against the wall. Until we had sustained discussions in class about intimidation, control, violence, and abuse, he had not considered his behavior as "abusive." He did not know that what he was doing was a problem. I hope that he has indeed sought help. I believe that it was a positive first step for him to realize that those "outbursts" were part of a larger pattern of control and abuse.

This new social problem should expose the faces and strategies of abusers. Currently, victims and offenders are often depicted as part of an epic battle between darkness and light, "with victims as the lambs and criminals the wolves," with victims completely innocent and criminals completely evil (Madriz 1997:79). But the problem is that in real life (as opposed to the movies) abusers and rapists are rarely "evil." They are more likely those people who are familiar to us. They are our fathers, sons, husbands, brothers, uncles, best friends, coworkers, and neighbors. And sometimes they are also mothers, daughters, and sisters. It is not only difficult to dramatize as evil those people we are close to, but it is also unrealistic. I am not saying that abuse and rape are "good things." But people who abuse and use violence against others are not easily described as "bad people." However, these are the dominant media images of abusive and

violent people—at least those labeled as *unacceptably* violent. Frequently, when someone is accused of a violent act, many people comment that the accused could not do such a thing because he or she is such a nice person. A new social problem about violence should inform people that the faces of abusers are often those "nice people" who live and work with us. There is no one "look" or profile of someone who uses violence and intimidation to control others.

There should also be more discussion and more stories about the everyday use of violence and abuse. This would lead to a heightened awareness of these abusive strategies. Stories should disclose the way abusers think and operate and show how well they manipulate situations, deny the harm, and minimize the problems. The following is a quote from an abuser that illustrates how he rationalizes and minimizes the problem:

> I slapped her and I did toss the table at her, but then all I was trying to do was get her out of the room. . . . It was just a slap. I didn't say, "Right, I'm going to hit you." She scratched me and it was almost instantaneous. She had a gash on her head where the table had bashed her head, that was all, and a bit of a sore face, but there was no black eye or anything. I had slapped her but nothing—not really badly. (Dobash, Dobash, Cavanah, and Lewis 2000:15)

A new social problem could lead to more newspaper and magazine articles that look in depth at how people first started using abuse, why they use violence and control strategies, and how they continue to get away with it.

This new problem needs to explain that abusers choose when and toward whom the abuse will happen. People are abusive and violent because these strategies help them get what they want—not because a victim "made them do it." In the majority of cases, the abuser is in control of the violence. It is a distortion to think that people are abusive because they "lose control." Most abusers are not violent toward everyone in their life. This is part of the reason it is confusing to people who know an abuser but have never seen his or her abusive side. Power is a central part of this control. It is not as effective to attempt to control someone who has more power, such as your boss. Attitudes about relationships and boundaries also influence this controlled use of violence. It does not seem as acceptable for abusers to dominate relationships with friends as it does with their girlfriends or wives, which may reflect social attitudes about men's authority over women.

Though I am calling for a new problem about "violence," the scope of the problem should also include nonviolent abuse. Public opinion research shows that a majority of people agree that abuse that results in physical injury is a problem that warrants help. However, people often label other types of abuse as private family matters that would be better dealt with in counseling. What needs to be understood is that nonviolent or nonphysical abuse strategies are effective ways to control and intimidate others and that these nonphysical strategies devastate victims. We need a clearer understanding of abusive strategies used to maintain control in relationships that are not necessarily physically violent. Throughout the book, I have been using the term "domestic violence" to discuss a range of behaviors that I assume not only include physical abuse but also emotional, verbal, and psychological abuse. Furthermore, threats to harm children and family members, and strategies of isolation and economic control over one's partner also contribute to the control an abuser has over his or her victim.

So far I have focused primarily on the need to better understand individual abusers. However, there should also be more public awareness about the social and cultural factors that teach, tolerate, and contribute to the use of violence. For too long there has been ambivalence and a lack of discussion about the role of violence in our culture. Violence has also become an inseparable part of entertainment, including children's video games and cartoons. Cultural attitudes such as "boys will be boys" continue to guide some parents. High school, college, and professional athletes frequently use off-the-field violence that is overlooked because of the high status of sports.

Violence is also accepted as a form of discipline. We need a renewed debate about the effects of spanking.[4] Research studies indicate that spanking teaches aggressive and controlling strategies for solving the problems of living together and hinders the development of important problem-solving skills (Cast, Schweingruber, and Berns 2004). Corporal punishment in childhood is not only problematic because of the types of problem-solving strategies that children are taught (verbal and physical aggression and controlling behaviors) but also because of what it *fails* to teach them. Children who are spanked are less likely to learn effective nonviolent strategies for resolving conflict and living peacefully with other people. Physical punishment teaches children that aggression is normal, acceptable, and effective, and it leads to a greater tolerance of violence in other relationships (Gershoff 2002). Children are not learning the principle that conflict can and should be managed without violence (Straus 2001). There needs to be a public discussion of these effects of spanking and more education on alternative methods of discipline and ways to teach children nonviolent conflict resolution strategies.

A new social problem about control and violence should evaluate cultural messages that define masculinity and femininity too narrowly. Mas-

culinity is stereotypically defined by characteristics such as power, dominance, control, independence, aggression, strength, sexual prowess, and
athletic ability. Conversely, femininity is traditionally defined by qualities
such as passivity, dependence, weakness, submissiveness, caretaking, and
emotional volatility. I am not suggesting that all men and women believe
that these are the qualities that define their gender role, but these are
scripts that are still prominent in our culture. It is not that each of these
qualities is necessarily "bad," but taken together they depict gender roles
that, even slightly misinterpreted, encourage the need for men's aggression and control over women. Too many people still believe that masculinity includes being dominant over women, sexually promiscuous (and
aggressive if need be), and always in control. Masculinity is often defined
in opposition to women. Research studies show that men's talk—occurring in locker rooms, offices, homes, schools—includes competitive talk
about sexual conquests, bragging about physical domination over women,
and advice on how to keep women "in line."[5]

We also need more discussion about individual and cultural attitudes
that support violence. Examples of these attitudes are found in our sports
culture. According to a *Sports Illustrated* feature article on how the
sports culture cultivates attitudes that demean women,

> The subworld of the American athlete is one in which the ancient virtues of
> manhood—of the brave, cool, tough, dominating and aggressive male—are
> celebrated. It is one in which sexist machospeak and the demeaning of
> women have been the means by which men express their maleness. . . . Par-
> ticularly in the contact sports, things feminine have served as symbols of
> things to be avoided. (Nack and Munson 1995:68)

The article lists specific examples of these attitudes and practices,
including a high school football coach painting a picture of a vagina on a
tackling dummy, coaches accusing men of being women if they did not
perform well enough, and "jokes" about going home and beating up
wives after losing games.

Violence as Learned Behavior Gives Us Hope

An important aspect of this new problem—which ties together many of
the issues discussed already—is that abuse is a learned behavior. People
learn to be abusive; they are not born that way. Understanding this not only
helps target the roots of the problem, but it gives us hope. If people can learn
to be abusive, there is hope they can unlearn those strategies. People can
learn nonabusive strategies for conflict resolution. Many batterer programs
focus on teaching abusers new ways of thinking about relationships and

the use of violence. This type of change is long and difficult, and does not work for everyone, but teaching people alternative means of conflict resolution provides our best hope for future prevention of violence.

One of the limitations of programs that attempt to reeducate abusers is that the abusers leave their support group—an environment that tells them abuse is wrong—and enter a world that sends contradictory messages about violence and abuse. Abusers need to be held accountable by every individual and institution in their lives. This is why we need changes in institutional responses and cultural attitudes about the use of violence. For example, an abuser may be seeking help through a program that challenges him to learn that he does not have the right to control and slap his wife around. Then he hangs out with friends who tell him that it is necessary to slap around a woman once in a while when she is out of control. Or a police officer only gives him a warning after being called to the house after the abuser beat up his wife once again. Or these messages of tolerance may come in the form of silence. Perhaps the abuser has colleagues, church members, family, and friends who know what is going on, but say nothing about it. This silence sends the message that he can continue.

Children learn the value of violence while watching movies that glorify violence, playing video games that reward the killing of others, witnessing people's excitement about hard hits in football or fights in hockey games, and listening to praise for being tough and aggressive. We need more opportunities for children to learn about the value of nonviolent principles and practices. Children need models for resolving conflict through nonviolent means. And when people fail to learn these nonviolent strategies and principles as children, we need opportunities for them to learn them as adults.

Understanding how people learn to be abusive, why they continue to get away with this behavior, and how they can unlearn the use of violence will never happen if our dominant focus is on the victim. I have introduced a few ideas that could shape new media coverage of violence. Individuals need alternative perspectives in order to effectively resist and critique the dominant "victim's personal problem" perspective. Adding articles that question the cultural attitudes that tolerate violence in the family and the larger society will help balance the stories that question why victims stay. A more proactive approach to portraying violence would include articles that discuss abusers, the roots of violence, and complex social, political, and economic dynamics. Perhaps some of those stories would have titles such as "Leading Two Lives: The Public and Private Face of an Abuser," "How to Start a Violence Prevention Program in Your School or Community," "Why We Tolerate Violence in the Family," "Teach Your Children Nonabusive Conflict Strategies," "'Jokes' That Foster Violence," "Unequal Power Relationships in the Home, at Work, and in the Community," "Is Your Child at Risk of Being an Abuser?" and "How to Help a Friend Who Is Abusing His Wife."

The landscape of the social problem of violence expands far beyond what I have described here. These recommendations for framing a new perspective on violence are aimed at inspiring media coverage and public inquiry that focuses on the individuals who use violence and the social and cultural context of that violence. Not everyone will agree with the specific points I have raised, and that is alright. It is more important that we shift the types of questions that we are asking about violence. We need a space in public debate to question why people use violence, how they learn those strategies, and why we continue to tolerate attitudes and practices that contribute to the problem.

We do not need to wait for additional research and programs to begin before gathering information to shape this new social problem about violence. There are currently programs and organizations that are working with abusers. EMERGE, the first program for physically abusive men, began in Boston in 1977. Since then similar programs have expanded throughout the country, including programs for female abusers. These programs can serve as a source of information for learning more about why people use violence and how we should respond. Furthermore, there is already extensive research that can provide information for understanding the violence.

Would a New Social Problem Help?

If all the media attention on domestic violence has not already generated more stories and attention about the abusers and the use of violence and abusive tactics, why might a newly constructed problem work? The answer is that media producers are looking for "news," which includes either new problems or new ways of reporting old problems. Of course, any claims, stories, and research on abusers and violence will continue to go through the filtering process that I have discussed in this book. Politics will continue to be involved in shaping any new social problems. However, we cannot afford to wait until we figure out how to avoid politics before we start having more public discussion about the use of violence. It will continue to be difficult to get the mainstream media to focus on structural and cultural factors related to the violence. We do have political media that help to bring social issues into the discussion, but these stories may inform thousands of people while the mainstream media reach millions of people. However, even if media stories raise more awareness about individual abusers—how they get into an abusive relationship, when and how they realize that they are abusive, and what solutions help them change their ways—this attention would increase public understanding about violence in the family and other relationships.

There is a catch. People need to come on board and say that using violence is wrong. Will that happen? I do not know for sure. But I have to hope that we will see a cultural change in attitudes about abuse and violence. It is more likely that people will say these behaviors are unacceptable if they know more about them. In the 1970s, people thought victims stayed in abusive relationships because they enjoyed the abuse, that they were masochists. Though some people still have these attitudes today, the general public is more likely to say that victims stay because they love the abuser, they worry about their children, or they do not have the resources to leave, as opposed to accusing them of being masochistic. Even though I critique the dominant focus on the victims, I do acknowledge that media attention on domestic violence has educated the public on battered women. There is hope that a similar education could happen with a new social problem about abusers and violence.

A CULTURAL SHIFT IN HOW WE THINK ABOUT SOCIAL PROBLEMS

It is possible that my recommendation for a new social problem about violence could result in mostly a framing of the abusers and still not expose the social and cultural context of violence. This could happen if the public and mass media continue to value personal stories and individualism more than social and cultural analyses of problems. Though a focus on individual abusers might improve how we think about violence, a dominant focus on the individual level of the problem would still ignore the larger political, social, and cultural context. Avoiding the constraints of individualism and entertainment when portraying social problems remains a difficult problem. There need to be changes in how we think about social problems—not only about violence, but other issues as well. I will discuss three ways that the change could begin in how we think about social problems: diversifying our sources of information, reevaluating journalistic standards, and cultivating an interest that goes beyond the individual.

Diversifying Our Sources of Information
One way to change how we think about social problems is to diversify the sources of information we use to help understand their complex landscapes. There are diverse frames on social problems in non–mass media, such as political media. If you wanted to broaden your understanding of social problems, you could take steps to increase your exposure to diverse frames. For example, my husband reads twenty different magazines that run the gamut of political orientations. He learns about conservative frames from the *Weekly Standard* and liberal frames from *The Nation* and

The Progressive, more moderate views from *The New Republic,* Christian frames from *Christianity Today* and *Sojourners,* and mainstream news frames from *Newsweek.*

Another way to learn more about social problems is through formal education. One could take a class on domestic violence, such as the one I teach, which uses books and research articles and personal narratives that tell the stories from the viewpoints of victims, batterers, advocates, police, children, and others involved in the problem. And the readings also give an introduction to the differences in experiencing violence depending on one's race, class, gender, sexual orientation, religion, and age. If a class was not available, individuals could go to a library and find a range of books on most topics. Furthermore, the Internet provides space for many more perspectives. Anyone with access to the resources and knowledge about designing a website can post their views on social problems. Likewise, those with Internet access can surf the web to find out about a social problem. People can also expand their perspectives by spending time talking to advocates and other professionals whose work involves social problems. Or people could talk to individuals directly involved, such as the victims.

I am not arguing that magazines, the Internet, or any one class is always the best source of information. My point is that we can work at broadening our view of any social problem landscape. Diverse perspectives on social problems exist. Realistically, though, most people are not going to read twenty different magazines or have the opportunity to take classes on many social problems. Unless pressed with an immediate need to research a problem, most people do not take the time to research a problem or talk to people who are more directly involved. A majority of people continue to rely on the mass media to make sense of social problems. So it is important to be aware of how mass media are portraying social problems, and of the effects of these images on how we understand and respond to them. We also need to call for a movement to raise the standards for how journalists report social problems.

Raising Journalistic Standards for Media Coverage of Social Problems

We are firmly entrenched in an era of journalism that competes for ratings and is less concerned about gathering information. In mass media, investigative journalism has lost out to infotainment, reality crime shows, and the catchy theme music and slogans that announce the most recent social problem crisis. Though subsidized political media do more investigative journalism—albeit shaped by their politics—the mass media focus on entertainment, emotion, and drama. Millions of people tune into *Oprah* and *Dr. Phil,* go to the movies, watch made-for-TV movies, and read popular magazines. We become concerned, and at times obsessed, with social problems—though only those that are successfully disseminated through the media. And the public relies on the frames used in media to make sense of social problems. What is the ethical responsibility of journalists for covering social problems? Is it an acceptable standard to focus on entertainment, emotion, and drama? How much does it cost our society to have a media culture that sees "news" as the stories that are the most violent, dramatic, emotional, controversial, or sensational?

When journalists happen to be at the site of a tragedy and are able to capture the drama and violence on camera, these stories are much more likely to dominate news shows. For example, news cameras were lined up outside a California court house where a hearing for Robert Blake, a celebrity charged with murder, was being held. In an unrelated situation, a man took out a gun and started to shoot his lawyer, who was trying to dodge the bullets while hiding behind a narrow tree. The video of this horrific scene was played over and over on national news shows for the next few days. The victim was injured, but not fatally. It was a sad and unfortunate crime, but was it worthy of national news attention compared to other stories around the nation and the world? Furthermore, the story presented an opportunity to discuss the use of violence in our society, but that framing of the event was ignored. The news station had the violent and sensational video footage, so there was no need for a "story" beyond that image. The reason this story got so much attention is directly related to the raw footage. This is the "money shot" for journalists.

Evaluating how media cover stories and how this coverage affects public opinion is not a new topic. Academic researchers continue to investigate this topic, especially in the area of social problems. However, we have also seen some public discussion and media attention about journalistic standards, especially on the topic of how journalists cover politicians. A recent article in *The New Republic* illustrates a current debate about the standards for political journalism. The author, Jonathan Chait, argues that journalists fail to inform the public about what is really going on with politicians and public policy because of the faulty "basic conventions of political journalism itself" (Chait 2003:23). He says that not only do journalists express their own opinions when they should try to be objective, but conversely they too often fail to be critical enough when presenting "facts":

> Yet, when it comes to real matters of fact—that is, things that involve figures, dates, actual events—reporters frequently take the opposite approach. They are evenhanded to a fault, presenting every side of an argument as equally valid, even if one side uses demonstrably false information and the other doesn't. (ibid.:22)

Decisions about what stories are most important are too often influenced by the drama of the images. The drive for ratings, sensationalism, and entertainment is a poor standard for reporting the news. There are many entangled and complicated issues fueling the push for "infotainment," including the increasing corporate ownership of mass media and news shows being managed by business owners rather than journalists. Nonetheless, the possibility of raising standards should not be dismissed. We need a shift in our journalistic approach to covering social problems. A change in this cultural climate requires not only changes within the media institutions, but also pressure from the public. In order for this pressure to build, our public interest in social problems needs to go beyond entertainment and beyond the individual.

Cultivating an Interest That Goes Beyond the Individual

The United States is a society in which most social problems are viewed as personal issues requiring therapy, self-help, hard work, or other individualistic solutions. Media and public interest in social problems focus more on the psychology of victims, and for some social problems, the offenders. We do not lack media attention to social problems, but we are missing the *social* part of the problems. Individual opinions and public policy responses are loaded with psychological language and solutions. Syndromes, profiles, low self-esteem, pathologies, and individual characteristics now describe a majority of social problems.

A couple of years ago people would tell me how great Dr. Laura is and how I should listen to her. Currently, Dr. Phil is the most popular television pop psychologist or, as he refers to himself, a "life strategist." Both Dr. Phil and Dr. Laura use a general formula for most individuals and their problems. Generally, their advice is "Don't be a victim" and "Take control of your life." Though this indeed may be helpful advice for some, as a national philosophy it becomes too easy to lean on "self-help" and individual responsibility to solve our society's problems. This quickly carries over to complex problems such as welfare, homelessness, unemployment, poverty, and domestic violence. It is convenient and comforting to place much, if not all, of the responsibility on individuals. And it is also more uplifting to focus on how people overcome great obstacles rather than facing the bigger picture. I, too, enjoy the occasional inspirational story of people overcoming problems. It is not that I want to get rid of all the individual, self-help, inspirational, take care of yourself stories. However, it is problematic when that is the dominant view in our society and little is said in the mass media about the structural and cultural problems that underlie major problems. Editors feel it would be too overwhelming and depressing for readers to know about all the social, cultural, and structural factors related to social problems. They may be right. As my students find out all the time, it can be overwhelming and a "downer" to learn about the larger context of social problems. However, it is still important to know about these issues if we want to better understand social problems. We need to challenge the focus on entertainment as the reason we pay attention to social problems.

CONCLUSION

Social problems, such as violence and crime, are common stories in our world of entertainment. When people go to the theaters to be entertained by watching stories about drugs, war, rape, domestic violence, murder, organized crime, gang violence, homelessness, mental illness, poverty, or prostitution, they are also learning about the causes of and solutions for these social problems as represented in these entertainment frames. It is unfortunate that our entertainment industry has become a main source of information about social problems. The entertainment media transform and personalize these stories in ways that will help attract a large audience. Stories about social problems that are shaped to be inspiring and entertaining are usually simplistic and focus on just the individuals involved. Complex social problems are reduced to emotion, drama, and heroic tales.

For domestic violence, this process has resulted in the victim being framed. The dominant perspective in public opinion and mass media frames the victim for solving the problem of domestic violence. The victim is celebrated for having the courage to leave the abusive relationship or, conversely, blamed for staying and letting the abuse continue. The victim is told to take back his or her power and refuse to tolerate the abuse anymore. Framing domestic violence as a problem about the victims fails to expose the role of the abuser and society. Though focusing on the victim may have contributed to useful outcomes for intervention and providing resources for victims, there remain serious barriers to achieving a public understanding of the context of this violence, which is important for prevention.

There is a time to focus on the victims and try to help them regain control and find strength. Sadly, I had a recent opportunity to listen to a young woman who is currently in an abusive relationship. I cried with Lauren as she sat in my office and told me one example after another of how her boyfriend controls what she does and where she goes, who she can talk to, and what clothes and make-up she wears.[6] He yells at her, calls her names, and manipulates her emotions and identity. I talked to Lauren about what she could do to protect herself physically and mentally. We discussed options for how she might get out of the relationship. It was important for me to focus on Lauren and what she might do to help herself. It was appropriate and necessary for me to focus on the victim at this time. We will continue to need domestic violence advocates who provide services, advice, and counseling for victims. However, we should not stop with the victims. This is not the whole story.

The rest of the story is about the abusers and the culture that fosters and teaches—and at times ignores—the abuse and violence that people use to control others. How did Lauren's boyfriend, and countless numbers of other people, learn to use violence and other abusive strategies? What do we do to stop this abuse, and how do we prevent future generations from using violence? This is the direction in which we need to shift our public inquiry. The root of the problem is not the victim, but rather the people using the violence, as well as those individuals, structural factors, and cultural attitudes that allow the violence to continue. There is hope. We can construct new ways of thinking about violence that challenge the attitudes and practices that teach and tolerate abuse.

We can shift the way we think about other social problems as well. We need to create the desire and the opportunities for expanding our understanding of any social problem landscape. This process begins with analyzing the politics and processes that shape how we understand and respond to social problems. Social problems are complicated, and media stories do not give us the whole picture. Understanding the processes and motivations that lead the media, and other claims-makers, to create stories that shape our images of social problems is a start for developing a more comprehensive view of the problems that plague our society. As with any landscape, the frame makes all the difference in who or what we see as the problem and how we should respond. Hopefully, through this process of diversifying our sources of information, cultivating an interest in the social and cultural contexts, and challenging the dominant entertainment approach to shaping the stories, we can better evaluate who or what should be framed for our social problems.

NOTES

1. His name has been changed to protect his identity.
2. See Elias (1997) to learn more about a culture of violent solutions.
3. See Loseke (2003) for more detail on the definition and social acceptance of social problems.
4. In Gershoff's (2002) meta-analysis, several effects of corporal punishment are identified: aggression (McCranie and Simpson 1986; Muller 1996), criminal and antisocial behavior (Baer and Corrado 1974; McCord 1988), mental health problems (Lester 1991; Straus and Kantor 1994), and abuse of own child or spouse (Straus 1990; Straus 2001). Other studies have indicated that childhood physical punishment is also correlated with alienation and reduced earnings (Straus 2001).

5. See the following studies for more information on men's attitudes, conversations, and socialization: Lefkowitz (1998), Kivel (1992), Dobash et al. (2000), Gilmore (1994), Boswell and Spade (1996), Bancroft (2002), and Toch (1998).

6. Her name has been changed to protect her identity.

References

Abraham, Ken. 1998. "Exposing Domestic Violence." *New Man,* May, p. 34.

Aldrich, Liberty. 2000. "Sneak Attack on VAWA." *The Nation,* 2 October, p. 6.

Alexander, Brian. 1998. "A Murder among Friends." *Glamour,* October, pp. 302–8.

Altheide, David L. 2002. *Creating Fear: News and the Construction of Crisis.* Hawthorne, NY: Aldine de Gruyter.

Altheide, David L. and Robert P. Snow. 1991. *Media Worlds in the Postjournalism Era.* Hawthorne, NY: Aldine de Gruyter.

Anderson, Elijah. 1999. *Code of the Street: Decency, Violence, and the Moral Life of the Inner City.* New York: W.W. Norton & Co.

Ang, Ien. 1985. *Watching Dallas.* London: Methuen.

Aris, Brenda. 1994. "Battered Women Who Kill." *Glamour,* April, p. 160.

Baber, Asa. 1986. "The Iron Fist in the Iron Glove." *Playboy,* March, p. 29.

Baber, Asa. 1994. "A Campaign of Shame." *Playboy,* October, p. 36.

Baber, Asa. 1996. "Two to Tango." *Playboy*, March, p. 33.

Baer, Daniel and James Corrado. 1974. "Heroin Addict Relationships with Parents during Childhood and Early Adolescent Years." *Journal of Genetic Psychology* 124:99–103.

Baker, Nancy. 1983. "Why Women Stay with Men Who Beat Them." *Glamour,* August, p. 312.

Bancroft, Lundy 2002. *Why Does He Do That? Inside the Minds of Angry and Controlling Men.* New York: Putman.

Bayley, James E. 1991. "The Concept of Victimhood." Pp. 53–62 in *To Be a Victim,* edited by Diane Sank and David Caplan. New York: Plenum.

Beasley, Michele E. and Dorothy Q. Thomas. 1994. "Domestic Violence as a Human Rights Issue." Pp. 323–46 in *The Public Nature of Private Violence,* edited by Martha Albertson Fineman and Roxanne Mykitiuk. New York: Routledge.

Beckett, Katherine. 1996. "Culture and the Politics of Signification: The Case of Child Sexual Abuse." *Social Problems* 43:57–76.

Beckett, Katherine and Theodore Sasson. 2000. *The Politics of Injustice: Crime and Punishment in America.* Thousand Oaks, CA: Pine Forge.

Bedard, Virginia S. 1978. "Wife-Beating." *Glamour,* August, pp. 85–86.

Bennett, Larry W. and Oliver J. Williams. 2001. "Intervention Programs for Men Who Batter." Pp. 261–78 in *Sourcebook on Violence Against Women*, edited by Claire M. Renzetti, Jeffrey L. Edelson, and Raquel Kennedy Bergen. Thousand Oaks, CA: Sage.

Berger, Arthur Asa. 1991. *Media U.S.A.*, 2d ed. New York: Longman.

Berger, Ronald L., Marvin D. Free, and Patricia Searles. 2001. *Crime, Justice, and Society*. New York: McGraw-Hill.

Berk, Richard A., Sarah F. Berk, Donileen R. Loseke, and D. Rauma. 1983. "Mutual Combat and Other Family Violence Myths." Pp. 197–212 in *The Dark Side of Families*, edited by David Finkelhor, Richard J. Gelles, Gerald T. Hotaling, and Murray A. Straus. Beverly Hills, CA: Sage.

Berns, Nancy. 1999. "'My Problem and How I Solved It': Domestic Violence in Women's Magazines." *Sociological Quarterly*, 40:85–108.

Berns, Nancy. 2001. "Degendering the Problem and Gendering the Blame: Political Discourse on Women's Violence." *Gender & Society* 15:262–81.

Best, Joel. 1995. *Images of Issues*. Hawthorne, NY: Aldine de Gruyter.

Best, Joel. 1999. *Random Violence: How We Talk about New Crimes and New Victims*. Berkeley: University of California Press.

Best, Joel. 2001. *Damned Lies and Statistics*. Berkeley: University of California Press.

Bird, George. 1967. *Modern Article Writing*. Dubuque, IA: Wm. C. Brown.

Bond, Johanna and Robin Phillips. 2001. "Violence against Women as a Human Rights Violation: International Institutional Responses." Pp. 481–99 in *Sourcebook on Violence against Women*, edited by Claire M. Renzetti, Jeffrey L. Edelson, and Raquel Kennedy Bergen. Thousand Oaks, CA: Sage.

Boswell, A. Ayres and Joan Z. Spade. 1996 "Fraternities and Collegiate Rape Culture: Why Are Some Fraternities More Dangerous Places for Women?" *Gender & Society* 10:133–47.

Bowman, Elizabeth Atkins. 1998. "Wheel Power." *Essence*, September, p. 144.

"Boy, 4, Dies from Alleged Beating." 2002. *Des Moines Register*, 5 May.

"Boyfriend Abuse: Troubled Love." 1995. *'Teen*, May, pp. 52–53.

"Boyfriend Gets Life for Murder of Child." 2003. *Des Moines Register*, 4 April.

Branan, Karen. 1991. "Killer or Victim?" *Ladies' Home Journal*, October, p. 128.

Breiter, Toni. 1979. "Battered Women." *Essence*, June, p. 74.

Brennecke, Ernest, Jr. 1942. *Magazine Article Writing*. New York: Macmillan.

Brott, Armin. 1993. "We Are the Target." *Penthouse*, August, p. 31.

Brownstein, Henry H. 2000. *The Social Reality of Violence and Violent Crime*. Boston: Allyn & Bacon.

Brush, L. D. 1990. "Violent Acts and Injurious Outcomes in Married Couples: Methodological Issues in the National Survey of Families and Households." *Gender & Society* 4:56–67.

Buchanan, Lisa K. 2001. "When Your Best Friend Is Abused." *Redbook*, June, p. 98.

Burgdorff, Lauri and Jean Block. 1996. "Invisible Bruises." *Good Housekeeping*, May, p. 84.

Campbell, Jean Pierre. 1996. "Like Father, Like Son?" *Essence*, October, p. 48.

Campbell, Walter S. 1944. *Writing Non-Fiction*. Boston: The Writer, Inc.

Capellaro, Catherine. 1997. "Help for Battered Immigrant Women." *The Progressive*, July, p. 15.

Caplan, Gerald. 1991. "Battered Wives, Battered Justice." *National Review,* 25 February, p. 39.

Caputi, Jane. 1987. *The Age of Sex Crime.* Bowling Green, OH: Bowling Green University Press.

Caringella-MacDonald, Susan. 1998. "The Relative Visibility of Rape Cases in National Popular Magazines." *Violence Against Women* 4:62–80.

Carstens, Christopher. 1996. "Guy Alert: What You Need to Know." *'Teen,* June, p. 54.

Cast, Alicia D., David Schweingruber, and Nancy Berns. 2004. "Childhood Physical Punishment and Problem-Solving Strategies and Skills In Marriage." Paper presented at the Annual Meeting of the Midwest Sociological Society, Kansas City.

Chait, Jonathan. 2003. "Bad Press." *The New Republic,* 10 November, pp. 20–23.

Chesney-Lind, Meda. 1999. "Media Misogyny: Demonizing 'Violent' Girls and Women." Pp. 115–40 in *Making Trouble: Cultural Constructions of Crime, Deviance, and Control,* edited by Jeff Ferrell and Neil Websdale. Hawthorne, NY: Aldine de Gruyter.

Chittum, Samme, Mark Bauman, and Irene Nyborg-Andersen. 1990. "No Way Out." *Ladies' Home Journal,* April, p. 126.

Christie, Nils. 1986. "The Ideal Victim." Pp. 17–30 in *From Crime Policy to Victim Policy,* edited by Ezzat Fattah. London: Macmillan.

Cicourel, Aaron V. 1968. *The Social Organization of Juvenile Justice.* New York: Wiley.

Cole, Lewis. 1994. "Court TV." *The Nation,* 21 February, p. 24–25.

Collins, Patricia Hill. 1991. *Black Feminist Thought.* New York: Routledge.

Cool, Lisa Collier. 1995. "Unholy Matrimony." *Penthouse,* March, p. 27.

"Could You Imagine Killing an Abusive Mate?" 1991. *Glamour,* September, p. 193.

Crenshaw, Kimberlé Williams. 1994. "Mapping the Margins: Intersectionality, Identity Politics, and Violence against Women of Color." Pp. 93–118 in *The Public Nature of Private Violence,* edited by Martha Albertson Fineman and Roxanne Mykitiuk. New York: Routledge.

Croteau, David and William Hoynes. 2000. *Media Society: Industries, Images, and Audiences,* 2nd ed. Thousand Oaks, CA: Pine Forge.

Cunningham, Laura. 1982. "Love and Rage." *Vogue,* July, p. 60.

Davis, Patti. 1998. "Dangerous Liaison." *Ladies' Home Journal,* April, p. 70.

Decarlo, Tessa. 2000. "The Secret of Violence of Women." *Redbook,* October, p. 174.

Deimling, Paula. 1984. *1985 Writer's Market.* Cincinnati, OH: Writer's Digest Books.

Denzin, Norman K. 1984. "Toward a Phenomenology of Domestic, Family Violence." *American Journal of Sociology* 90:483–513.

Dobash, R. Emerson and Russell P. Dobash. 1979. *Violence against Wives: A Case against Patriarchy.* New York: Free Press.

Dobash, R. Emerson and Russell P. Dobash. 1992. *Women, Violence and Social Change.* New York: Routledge.

Dobash, R. Emerson and Russell P. Dobash. 1998. "Domestic Violence: Who Reports Best, Women or Victims." Paper presented at the American Society of Criminology Annual Conference. Washington D.C.

Dobash, R. Emerson, Russell P. Dobash, Kate Cavanah, and Ruth Lewis. 2000. *Changing Violent Men.* Thousand Oaks, CA: Sage.

Dobash, Russell P., R. Emerson Dobash, Margo Wilson, and Martin Daly. 1992. "The Myth of Sexual Symmetry in Marital Violence." *Social Problems* 39:71–91.

Dodge, Mary and Edith Greene. 1991. "Juror and Expert Conceptions of Battered Women." *Violence and Victims* 6:271–82.

Douglas, Susan. 1993. "Some Violence Is Not 'News.'" *The Progressive,* May, p. 21.

Douglas, Susan. 1994. "Blame It on Battered Women." *The Progressive,* August, p. 15.

Dunn, Katherine. 1994. "Truth Abuse." *The New Republic,* 1 August, p. 16.

Durbin, Karen. 1976. "Battered Women." *Mademoiselle,* December, p. 60.

Eckman, Fern Marja. 1987. "Battered Women." *McCall's,* November, p. 157.

Ehrenreich, Barbara and Deirdre English. 1978. *For Her Own Good.* New York: Doubleday.

Eisler, Riane. 1997. "Human Rights and Violence: Integrating the Private and Public Spheres." Pp. 161–85 in *The Web of Violence: From Interpersonal to Global,* edited by Jennifer Turpin and Lester R. Kurtz. Urbana: University of Illinois Press.

Elias, Robert. 1997. "A Culture of Violent Solutions." Pp. 117–47 in *The Web of Violence: From Interpersonal to Global,* edited by Jennifer Turpin and Lester R. Kurtz. Urbana: University of Illinois Press.

Elshtain, Jean. 1992. "Battered Reason." *The New Republic,* 5 October, p. 25.

Endres, Kathleen L. and Therese L. Lueck (Eds.). 1995. *Women's Periodicals in the United States: Consumer Magazines.* Westport, CT: Greenwood.

Faith, Karlene. 1993. *Unruly Women. The Politics of Confinement and Resistance.* Vancouver: Press Gang.

Faludi, Susan. 1991. *Backlash: The Undeclared War against Women.* New York: Doubleday.

Feeney, Sheila. 1989. "Hedda's Secret: What No One Understands about Abused Women." *Mademoiselle,* March, pp. 242–45.

Ferrell, Jeff and Neil Websdale. 1999. *Making Trouble: Cultural Constructions of Crime, Deviance, and Control.* Hawthorne, NY: Aldine de Gruyter.

Finkelstein, Katherine Eban. 1997. "Dating Violence: The Hidden Danger College Women Face." *Glamour,* October, p. 320.

Fishman, Mark and Gray Cavender. 1998. *Entertaining Crime: Television Reality Programs.* Hawthorne, NY: Aldine de Gruyter.

Fiske, John. 1987. *Television Culture.* London: Methuen.

"Florida's Perspective on Domestic Violence." 1999. *Survey of Public Opinion by the Florida Department of Corrections.* On-line: www.dc.state.fl.us.

Foucault, Michel. 1979. *Discipline and Punish: The Birth of the Prison.* New York: Vintage.

Foucault, Michel. 1991. "Politics and the Study of Discourse." Pp. 53–72 in *The Foucault Effect: Studies in Governmentality,* edited by G. Burchell, C. Gordon, and P. Miller. Hemel Hempstead: Harvester Wheatsheaf.

France, David. 1995. "Life after Death." *Good Housekeeping,* July, pp. 110–13.

Freeman, Jo (Ed.). 1995. *Women,* 5th ed. Mountain View, CA: Mayfield.

Frieze, I. H. and Angela Browne. 1989. "Violence in Marriage." Pp. 163–218 in *Family Violence,* edited by L. Ohlin and M. Tonry. Chicago: University of Chicago Press.

Gage, Diane and Marcia Coppess. 1994. *Get Published: 100 Top Magazine Editors Tell You How.* New York: Henry Holt.

Gamson, William A. 1992. *Talking Politics.* Cambridge: Cambridge University Press.

Gamson, William A. and Andre Modigliani. 1989. "Media Discourse and Public Opinion on Nuclear Power." *American Journal of Sociology* 95:1–37.

Gaquin, Deirdre A. 1977–78. "Spouse Abuse: Data From the National Crime Survey." *Victimology* 2:632–43.

Gelles, Richard J. 1993. "Through a Sociological Lens: Social Structure and Family Violence." Pp. 31–46 in *Current Controversies on Family Violence,* edited by Richard J. Gelles and Donileen R. Loseke. Newbury Park, CA: Sage.

Gelles, Richard J. 1997. *Intimate Violence in Families,* 3d ed. Thousand Oaks, CA: Sage.

Gelles, Richard J. 1999. "Family Violence." Pp. 1–32 in *Family Violence,* 2d ed., edited by Robert L. Hampton. Thousand Oaks, CA: Sage.

Gelles, Richard J. and Murray Straus. 1988. *Intimate Violence: The Causes and Consequences of Abuse in the American Family.* New York: Simon & Schuster.

Gershoff, Elizabeth Thompson. 2002. "Corporal Punishment by Parents and Associated Child Behaviors and Experiences: A Meta-Analytic and Theoretical Review." *Psychological Bulletin* 128:539–79.

Gilmore, Sean Michael. 1994. "Sport Sex: Toward a Theory of Sexual Aggression." Pp. 129–35 in *Differences That Make a Difference: Examining the Assumptions in Gender Research,* edited by Lynn H. Turner and Helen M. Sterk. Westport, CT: Bergin & Garvey.

Glatzer, Randi. 2002. "Should Women Be Punished for Returning to the Men Who Abuse Them?" *Glamour,* July, p. 134.

Goffman, Erving. 1974. *Frame Analysis.* New York: Harper & Row.

Golding, Eugenia and Ronny Frishman. 1996. "My Ex-husband Harassed Me from Prison." *McCall's,* February, p. 58.

Golline, Albert E. 1988. "Media Power: On Closer Inspection, It's Not That Threatening." Pp. 41–44 in *Impacts of Mass Media,* 2d ed., edited by Ray Eldon Hiebert and Carol Reuss. New York: Longman.

Gonnerman, Jennifer. 1997. "Welfare's Domestic Violence." *The Nation,* 10 March, pp. 21–23.

Gordon, Linda. 1988. *Heroes of Their Own Lives: The Politics and History of Family Violence.* New York: Viking.

Grindstaff, Laura. 2002. *The Money Shot.* Chicago: University of Chicago Press.

Gross, Andrea. 1993. "A Question of Rape." *Ladies' Home Journal,* November, p. 170.

Gutiérrez, Lorraine M. and Edith A. Lewis. 1999. *Empowering Women of Color.* New York: Columbia University Press.

Guttman, M. 1993. "Are All Men Rapists?" *National Review,* 23 August, pp. 44–47.

Hagen, Margaret A. 1998. "Bad Attitude." *National Review,* 20 July, pp. 38–39.

Hamlin, Julia. 1993. "Relationship Abuse: Love Gone Wrong." *'Teen,* June, p. 44.

Harris, Ellen. 2000. "My Husband Poisoned Me." *McCall's,* March, p. 68.

Harrison, Scherryl Jefferson. 1999. "Her Toughest Case." *Essence,* August, p. 94

Hilton, N. Zoe. 1993. "Police Intervention and Public Opinion." Pp. 37–61 in *Legal Responses to Wife Assault.* Newbury Park, CA: Sage.

Holm, Kirsten (Ed.). 1997. *1998 Writer's Market.* Cincinnati, OH: Writer's Digest Books.

Holstein, James A. and Jaber F. Gubrium. 1995. *The Active Interview.* Thousand Oaks, CA: Sage.

Holstein, James A. and Gale Miller. 1990. "Rethinking Victimization: An Interactional Approach to Victimology." *Symbolic Interaction* 13:103–22.

Holstein, James A. and Gale Miller. 1993. "Social Constructionism and Social Problems Work." Pp. 151–72 in *Reconsidering Social Constructionism,* edited by J. Holstein and G. Miller. Hawthorne, NY: Aldine de Gruyter.

hooks, bell. 1994. "When Brothers Are Batterers." *Essence,* September, p. 148.

Howe, Adrian. 1999. "'The War against Women': Media Representations of Men's Violence against Women in Australia." Pp. 141–56 in *Making Trouble: Cultural Constructions of Crime, Deviance, and Control,* edited by Jeff Ferrell and Neil Websdale. Hawthorne, NY: Aldine de Gruyter.

Hunter, Jean E. 1990. "A Daring New Concept: The *Ladies' Home Journal* and Modern Feminism." *NWSA Journal* 2:583–602.

"I Just Didn't Think It Was Any of My Business." 1988. *Glamour,* May, p. 82.

Iovanni, LeeAnn and Susan L. Miller. 2001. "Criminal Justice System Responses to Domestic Violence: Law Enforcement and the Courts." Pp. 303–28 in *Sourcebook on Violence against Women,* edited by Claire M. Renzetti, Jeffrey L. Edelson, and Raquel Kennedy Bergen. Thousand Oaks, CA: Sage.

Itzin, Catherine. 1992. "Pornography and the Social Construction of Sexual Inequality." Pp. 57–75 in *Pornography,* edited by Catherine Itzin. Oxford: Oxford University Press.

Jasinski, Jana L. 2001. "Theoretical Explanations for Violence against Women." Pp. 5–22 in *Sourcebook on Violence against Women,* edited by Claire M. Renzetti, Jeffrey L. Edelson, and Raquel Kennedy Bergen. Thousand Oaks, CA: Sage.

Jenkins, Philip. 1994. *Using Murder: The Social Construction of Serial Murder.* Hawthorne, NY: Aldine de Gruyter.

Jetter, Alexis. 1994. "How Battered Wives Can Learn to Leave." *McCall's,* September, p. 98.

Jones, Ann. 1994. *Next Time, She'll Be Dead: Battering and How to Stop It.* Boston: Beacon.

Kappeler, Victor E., Mark Blumberg, and Gary W. Potter. 2000. *The Mythology of Crime and Criminal Justice,* 3d ed. Prospect Heights, IL: Waveland.

Karmen, Andrew. 1990. *Crime Victims: An Introduction to Victimology,* 2d ed. Pacific Grove, CA: Brooks/Cole.

Katz, Elihu and Paul F. Lazarsfeld. 1955. *Personal Influence.* New York: Free Press.

Kays, Alice. 1997. "The Four Words That Saved My Life." *Redbook,* April, p. 75.

Kelley, Jerone E. 1978. *Magazine Writing Today.* Cincinnati, OH: Writer's Digest Books.

Kellner, Douglas. 1995. *Media Culture.* London: Routledge.

Kennedy, Leslie W. and Vincent F. Sacco. 1998. *Crime Victims in Context.* Los Angeles: Roxbury.

"Killing the Enemy." 1991. *National Review,* 29 April, pp. 13–15.

Kivel, Paul. 1992. *Men's Work: How to Stop the Violence That Tears Our Lives Apart.* Center City, MN: Hazelden.

Klein, Ethel, Jacquelyn Campbell, Esta Soler, and Marissa Ghez. 1997. *Ending Domestic Violence.* Thousand Oaks, CA: Sage.

Koppelman, Susan (Ed.). 1996. *Women in the Trees: U.S. Women's Short Stories about Battering & Resistance, 1839–1994*. Boston: Beacon.

Krauthammer, Charles. 1993. "Defining Deviancy Up." *The New Republic*, 22 November, pp. 20–25.

Kurz, Demie. 1997. "Violence against Women or Family Violence?" Pp. 443–53 in *Gender Violence: Interdisciplinary Perspectives*, edited by Laura L. O'Toole and Jessica R. Schiffman. New York: New York University Press.

Lamb, Sharon. 1996. *The Trouble with Blame: Victims, Perpetrators, and Responsibility*. Cambridge, MA: Harvard University Press.

Lardner, George. 1997. "No Place to Hide." *Good Housekeeping*, October, p. 104.

Lazarsfeld, Paul F., Bernard Berelson, and Hazel Gaudet. 1944. *The People's Choice: How the Voter Makes Up His Mind in a Presidential Election*. New York: Duell, Sloan and Pearce.

Lefkowitz, Bernard. 1998. *Our Guys: The Glen Ridge Rape and the Secret Life of the Perfect Suburb*. New York: Vintage.

Lester, David. 1991. "Physical Abuse and Physical Punishment as Precursors of Suicidal Behavior." *Stress Medicine* 7:255–56.

Lewis, Debra. 1990. "When Love Turns Violent." *Glamour*, August, pp. 234–35.

"Lisa Steinberg's Torturers." 1988. *National Review*, 30 December, p. 19.

Locke, Lisa M. and Charles Richman 1999. "Attitudes toward Domestic Violence: Race and Gender Issues." *Sex Roles* 40(February):227–47.

Lockwood, Annette. 1995 "The Murder Next Door." *Mademoiselle*, May, p. 171.

Loseke, Donileen R. 1992. *The Battered Woman and Shelters: The Social Construction of Wife Abuse*. Albany: State University of New York Press.

Loseke, Donileen R. 1998. "The Two Realities of Wife Abuse." Pp. 291–300 in *Inside Social Life*, edited by Spencer E. Cahill. Los Angeles: Roxbury.

Loseke, Donileen R. 2003. *Thinking about Social Problems*, 2d ed. Hawthorne, NY: Aldine de Gruyter.

Loseke, Donileen R. and Joel Best (Eds.). 2003. *Social Problems: Constructionist Readings*. Hawthorne, NY: Aldine de Gruyter.

Loseke, Donileen R. and Spencer E. Cahill. 1984. "The Social Construction of Deviance: Experts on Battered Women." *Social Problems* 31:296–310.

Lowney, Kathleen. 1999. *Baring Our Souls: TV Talk Shows and the Religion of Recovery*. Hawthorne, NY: Aldine de Gruyter.

Lutz, Catherine and Jon Elliston. 2002. "Domestic Terror: When Several Soldiers Killed Their Wives, An Old Problem Was Suddenly News." *The Nation*, 14 October, p. 18.

MacKinnon, Catherine 1993. "Feminism, Marxism, Method, and the State." Pp. 201–27 in *Violence against Women: The Bloody Footprints*, edited by Pauline Bart and Eileen Moran. Newbury Park, CA: Sage.

Madriz, Esther. 1997. *Nothing Bad Happens to Good Girls: Fear of Crime in Women's Lives*. Berkeley: University of California Press.

Mann, Ruth M. 2000. *Who Owns Domestic Abuse? The Local Politics of a Social Problem*. Toronto: University of Toronto Press.

Marcus, Isabel. 1994. "Reframing 'Domestic Violence': Terrorism in the Home." Pp. 11–35 in *The Public Nature of Private Violence*, edited by Martha Albertson Fineman and Roxanne Mykitiuk. New York: Routledge.

Marks, Jane. 1999. "He Can't Control His Anger." *Ladies' Home Journal*, January, p. 16.

Mawby, R. I. and S. Walklate. 1994. *Critical Victimology: International Perspectives.* London: Sage.

McCord, Joan. 1988. "Parental Behavior in the Cycle of Aggression." *Psychiatry* 51:14–23.

McCracken, Ellen. 1993. *Decoding Women's Magazines.* New York: St. Martin's.

McCranie, Edward W. and Miles E. Simpson. 1986. "Parental Child-Rearing Antecedents of Type A Behavior." *Personality and Social Psychology Bulletin* 12:493–501.

McElroy, Wendy. 1995. "The Unfair Sex? The Politics of Violence against Women." *National Review,* 1 May, p. 74

Mednick, Martha. 1989. "On the Politics of Psychological Constructs: Stop the Bandwagon, I Want to Get Off." *American Psychologist* 44:1118–23.

Melendez, Andrea. 2003. "Macksburg's Skillets Aren't Used for Cooking." *Des Moines Register,* 16 June, sec. B1.

Meyers, Marian. 1997. *News Coverage of Violence against Women: Engendering Blame.* Thousand Oaks, CA: Sage.

Morgen, Sandra and Ann Bookman. 1988. *Women and the Politics of Empowerment.* Philadelphia: Temple University Press.

Morley, David. 1986. *Family Television: Cultural Power and Domestic Leisure.* London: Comedia.

Muller, Robert T. 1996. "Family Aggressiveness Factors in the Prediction of Corporal Punishment: Reciprocal Effects and the Impact of Observer Perspective." *Journal of Family Psychology* 10:474–89.

Nabi, Robin L. and Jennifer R. Horner. 2001. "Victims with Voices: How Abused Women Conceptualize the Problem of Spousal Abuse and Implications for Intervention and Prevention." *Journal of Family Violence* 16:237–53.

Nack, William and Lester Munson. 1995. "Sports' Dirty Secret." *Sports Illustrated,* 31 July, pp. 63–74.

Neal, Harry Edward. 1949. *Writing and Selling Fact and Fiction.* New York: Wilfred Funk.

Nyberg, Amy Kiste. 1998. "Comic Books and Juvenile Delinquency: A Historical Perspective." Pp. 61–70 in *Popular Culture, Crime and Justice,* edited by Frankie Bailey and Donna Hale. Belmont, CA: Wadsworth.

Oprah Winfrey Show. 2002. "All-Time Best Dr. Phil Moments." 10 September.

Oprah Winfrey Show. 2003. "What Should We Do When Families Turn Violent?" 23 January.

"Our Home Was a Battlefield." 1972. *Good Housekeeping,* October, p. 79.

Pagelow, Mildred Daley. 1984. *Family Violence.* New York: Praeger.

Paglia, Camile. 1992. Letter to the editor. *The New Republic,* 13 April, p. 4–5.

Pascoe, Elizabeth Jean. 1976. "Shelters for Battered Wives." *McCall's,* October, p. 51.

Patterson, Helen. 1939. *Writing and Selling Special Feature Articles.* New York: Prentice-Hall.

Peele, Stanton. 1991. "Getting Away with Murder." *Reason,* August/September, p. 40–41.

Pleck, Elizabeth. 1987. *Domestic Tyranny: The Making of American Social Policy against Family Violence from Colonial Times to the Present.* New York: Oxford University Press.

Polaneczky, Ronnie. 1998. "Vanished: When a Loving Wife Just Disappears." *Redbook,* September, p. 148.

Pollitt, Katha. 1995. "Subject to Debate." *The Nation,* 23 October, p. 45–47.

Potter, Gary W. and Victor E. Kappeler. 1996. *Constructing Crime: Perspectives on Making News and Social Problems.* Prospect Heights, IL: Waveland.

Radway, Janice. 1984. *Reading the Romance: Women, Patriarchy, and Popular Literature.* Chapel Hill: University of North Carolina Press.

Rapping, Elayne. 1994. "What Evil Lurks in the Hearts of Men?" *The Progressive,* November, p. 34–36.

Renzetti, Claire M. 1992. *Violent Betrayal: Partner Abuse in Lesbian Relationships.* Newbury Park, CA: Sage.

Renzetti, Claire M. 1997. "Violence and Abuse among Same-Sex Couples." Pp. 70–89 in *Violence Between Intimate Partners: Patterns, Causes, and Effects,* edited by Albert P. Cardarelli. Boston: Allyn and Bacon.

Renzetti, Claire M. and Jefrey L. Edelson (Eds.). 2001. *Sourcebook on Violence against Women.* Thousand Oaks, CA: Sage.

Rhode Island Violence Prevention Program. 1997. "Public Education & Information Initiative: The Network to End Domestic Violence and Sexual Assault." On-line: www.health.ri.gov/disease/violence.

Roberts, Albert R. 1990. *Helping Crime Victims: Research, Policy, and Practice.* Newbury Park, CA: Sage.

Rock, Maxine. 1983. "How Could This Happen to My Friend?" *McCall's,* April, p. 54.

Roiphe, Katherine Anne. 1993. *The Morning After: Sex, Fear, and Feminism on Campus.* Boston: Little, Brown.

Ronai, Carol Rambo. 1997. "In the Line of Sight at *Public Eye*: In Search of a Victim." Pp. 139–57 in *New Versions of Victims,* edited by Sharon Lamb. New York: New York University Press.

Rosen, Margery D. 1994. "The Marriages That Shouldn't Be Saved." *Ladies' Home Journal,* October, p. 152.

Rosen, Margery D. 1996. "He Hit Me." *Ladies' Home Journal,* April, p. 16.

Rubin, Bonnie Miller. 1996. "From Battered Wife to Top Cop." *Good Housekeeping,* August, p. 20.

Russell, Diana E. H. (Ed.). 1993. *Making Violence Sexy: Feminist Views on Pornography.* New York: Teachers College Press.

Ryan, Joan. 1995. "Why Sports Heroes Abuse Their Wives." *Redbook,* September, p. 83.

Sales, Nancy. 1995. "When Boy Beats Girl." *Mademoiselle,* January, pp. 118–21.

Sasson, Theodore. 1995. *Crime Talk: How Citizens Construct a Social Problem.* Hawthorne, NY: Aldine de Gruyter.

Saunders, Daniel. 1988. Wife Abuse, Husband Abuse, or Mutual Combat? In *Feminist Perspectives on Wife Abuse,* edited by K. Ÿllö and M. Bograd. Newbury Park, CA: Sage.

"Scarred Lives of Battered Women." 1980. *Glamour,* October, p. 56.

Schlesinger, Philip, R. Emerson Dobash, Russell P. Dobash, and C. Kay Weaver. 1992. *Women Viewing Violence.* London: British Film Institute.

Schudson, Michael. 2003. *The Sociology of News.* New York: W.W. Norton.

Schuller Regina and Neil Vidmar. 1992. "Battered Woman Syndrome Evidence in the Courtroom." *Law and Human Behavior* 16:273–91.

Schwartz, Martin D. 1987. "Gender and Injury in Spousal Assault." *Sociological Focus* 20:61–75.

Schwartz, Martin D. and DeKeseredy, W. S. 1993. "The Return of the Battered Husband Syndrome through the Typification of Women as Violent." *Crime, Law and Social Change* 20:249–65.

Schwartz, Martin D. and DeKeseredy, W. S. 1997. *Sexual Assault on the College Campus: The Role of Male Peer Support.* Thousand Oaks, CA: Sage.

Sebba, Leslie. 1996. *Third Parties: Victims and the Criminal Justice System.* Columbus: Ohio State University Press.

Sheffield, Carole J. 1995. "Sexual Terrorism." Pp. 1–21, in *Women,* 5th ed., edited by Jo Freeman. Mountain View, CA: Mayfield.

Shelton, Anna. 1999. "Battered Women: A New Asylum Case." *The Progressive,* November, p. 25.

Sherven, Judith and James Sniechowski. 1994. "Women Are Responsible, Too." *Playboy,* November, p. 45.

Shimberg, Elaine Fantle. 1988. "Writing for the Women's Magazines." Pp. 170–77, in *Handbook of Magazine Article Writing,* edited by Jean M. Fredette. Cincinnati, OH: Writer's Digest Books.

Shupe, Anson, Lonnie R. Hazlewood, and William A. Stacey. 1987. *Violent Men, Violent Couples: The Dynamics of Domestic Violence.* Lexington, MA: Lexington Publishing.

Siller, Sidney. 1983. "Wife Rape—Who Really Gets Screwed." *Penthouse,* May, p. 104.

Siller, Sidney. 1986. "Men's Rights." *Penthouse,* November, p. 26.

Siller, Sidney. 1996. "Men's Rights." *Penthouse,* April, p. 22.

Simon, B. L. 1994. *The Empowerment Tradition in American Social Work: A History.* New York: Columbia University Press.

Simonds, Wendy. 1992. *Women and Self-Help Culture.* New Brunswick, NJ: Rutgers University Press.

Slaughter, Jane. 1987. "A Beaut of a Shiner." *The Progressive,* May, p. 50.

Smart, Carol. 1989. *Feminism and the Power of Law.* London: Routledge.

Smith, Marcia. 1997. "When Violence Strikes Home." *The Nation,* 30 June, pp. 23–24.

Sommers, Christiana Hoff. 1992. "Sister Soldiers." *The New Republic,* 5 October, pp. 29–33.

Soothill, K., and Walby S. 1991. *Sex Crime in the News.* New York: Routledge Kegan Paul.

Spector, Malcolm and John I. Kitsuse. 1987. *Constructing Social Problems.* Hawthorne, NY: Aldine de Gruyter.

Staggenborg, Suzanne. 1998. *Gender, Family, and Social Movements.* Thousand Oaks, CA: Pine Forge.

Stalans, Loretta. 1996. "Family Harmony or Individual Protection? Public Recommendations about How Policy Can Handle Domestic Violence Situations." *American Behavioral Scientist* 39:433–49.

Stalans, Loretta and Arthur J. Lurigio. 1995. "Public Preferences for the Court's Handling of Domestic Violence Situations." *Crime and Delinquency* 41:399–413

Steinmetz, Suzanne. 1977. *The Cycle of Violence: Assertive, Aggressive, and Abusive Family Interaction.* New York: Praeger.

Steinmetz, Suzanne. 1978. "The Battered Husband Syndrome." *Victimology* 2: 499–509.

Straton, Jack C. 1997. "The Myth of the Battered Husband Syndrome." Pp. 126–28 in *Gender through the Prism of Difference,* edited by Maxine Baca Zinn, Pierrette Hondagneu-Sotelo, and Michael A. Messner. Boston: Allyn and Bacon.

Straus, Murray A. 1976. "Sexual Inequality, Cultural Norms, and Wife-Beating." *Victimology* 1:54–70.

Straus, Murray A. 1990. "Ordinary Violence, Child Abuse, and Wife Beating: What Do They Have in Common?" Pp. 403–24 in *Physical Violence in American Families,* edited by Murray A. Straus and Richard J. Gelles. New Brunswick, NJ: Transaction.

Straus, Murray A. 1993. "Physical Assaults by Wives: A Major Social Problem." Pp. 67–87, in *Current Controversies on Family Violence,* edited by Richard J. Gelles and Donileen R. Loseke. Newbury Park, CA: Sage.

Straus, Murray A. 2001. *Beating the Devil Out of Them,* 2d ed. New Brunswick, NJ: Transaction.

Straus, Murray A. and Richard J. Gelles (Eds.). 1995. *Physical Violence in American Families: Risk Factors and Adaptations to Violence in 8,145 Families.* New Brunswick, NJ: Transaction.

Straus, Murray A. and Glenda Kaufman Kantor. 1994. "Corporal Punishment of Adolescents by Parents: "A Risk Factor in the Epidemiology of Depression, Suicide, Alcohol Abuse, Child Abuse, and Wife Beating." *Adolescence* 29: 543–61.

Stuller, Jay. 1988. "A Matter of Expertise." Pp. 34–39 in *Handbook of Magazine Article Writing,* edited by Jean M. Fredette. Cincinnati, OH: Writer's Digest Books.

Sullivan, Cris M. and Tameka Gillum. 2001. "Shelters and Other Community-Based Services for Battered Women and Their Children." Pp. 247–60 in *Sourcebook on Violence against Women,* edited by Claire M. Renzetti, Jeffrey L. Edelson, and Raquel Kennedy Bergen. Thousand Oaks, CA: Sage.

Surette, Ray. 1998. *Media, Crime, and Criminal Justice: Images and Realities,* 2d ed. Belmont, CA: Wadsworth.

Task Force on Assessment. 1967. "The Victims Of Crime." Pp. 80–84 in the President's Commission on Law Enforcement and Administration of Justice." *Task Force Report: Crime and Its Impact—An Assessment.* Washington, DC: U.S. Government Printing Office.

Taylor, Susan L. 1994. "Owning Your Life." *Essence,* September, p. 65.

Thomas, Gary. 1999. "The Husband Abusers." *New Man* March/April, pp. 56–60.

Tierney, Kathleen. 1982. "The Battered Women Movement and the Creation of the Wife Beating Problem." *Social Problems* 29:207–20.

Toch, Hans. 1998. "Hypermasculinity and Prison Violence." Pp. 168–78 in *Masculinities and Violence,* edited by Lee H. Bowker. Thousand Oaks, CA: Sage.

Ussher, Jane M. 1997. *Fantasies of Femininity: Reframing the Boundaries of Sex.* New Brunswick, NJ: Rutgers University Press.

Vachss, Alice. 1993. "Rape and Denial." *The New Republic,* November 22, pp. 14–15.

Valente, Roberta L., Barbara J. Hart, Seema Zeya, and Mary Malefyt. 2001. "The Violence against Women Act of 1994: The Federal Commitment to Ending Domestic Violence, Sexual Assault, Stalking, and Gender-Based Crimes of Violence." Pp. 279–302 in *Sourcebook on Violence against Women,* edited by Claire M. Renzetti, Jeffrey L. Edelson, and Raquel Kennedy Bergen. Thousand Oaks, CA: Sage.

Vander Pluym, Adrea R. 1999. "My Boyfriend Abused Me." *'Teen,* April, p. 74

Vanzant, Iyanla. 2002. "Ask Iyanla." *Essence,* December, p. 96.

Von Hentig, Hans. 1948. *The Criminal and His Victim.* New Haven: Yale University Press.

Walker, Lenore. 1989. *Terrifying Love: Why Battered Women Kill and How Society Responds.* New York: Harper Perennial.

Walklate, Sandra. 1989. *Victimology: The Victim and the Criminal Justice Process.* London: Unwin Hyman.

Webb, Lillean Frier. 1987. "Battered Wife's Dilemma." *Essence,* November, p. 14.

Websdale, Neil. 1999. "The Social Construction of 'Stranger-Danger' in Washington State as a Form of Patriarchal Ideology." Pp. 91–114 in *Making Trouble: Cultural Constructions of Crime, Deviance, and Control,* edited by Jeff Ferrell and Neil Websdale. Hawthorne, NY: Aldine de Gruyter.

Weems, Renita. 1988. "When Love Hurts." *Essence,* October, p. 81.

Weinstock, Nicholas. 1994. "How I Realized I Was Dangerous." *Glamour,* November, p. 91.

Weisbord, Marvin (Ed.). 1965. *A Treasury of Tips for Writers.* Cincinnati, OH: Writer's Digest Books.

Werner, Laurie. 1986. "My Husband Hit Me." *Ladies' Home Journal,* November, p. 14.

Williams, Oliver. 2002. "Breaking the Cycle." *Essence,* November, p. 252.

Wolf, Naomi. 1992. "Feminist Fatale." *The New Republic,* March 16, pp. 23–25.

Wolfgang, Marvin and Franco Ferracuti. 1982. *The Subculture of Violence: Toward an Integrated Theory of Criminology.* Beverly Hills, CA: Sage.

Wood, Julia T. 1999. *Gendered Lives: Communication, Gender, and Culture,* 3d ed. Belmont, CA: Wadsworth.

Woodward, Whitney. 1990. "Dating Violence: Troubled Love." *'Teen,* April, p. 12.

Wright, Robert. 1994. "Feminists, Meet Mr. Darwin." *The New Republic,* 28 November, pp. 34–46.

Yllö, Kersti. 1993. "Through a Feminist Lens: Gender, Power, and Violence." Pp. 47–62 in *Current Controversies on Family Violence,* edited by Richard J. Gelles and Donileen R. Loseke. Newbury Park, CA: Sage.

Young, Cathy. 1994. "Abused Statistics." *National Review,* 1 August, pp. 43–46.

Index